T0320806

Information Resolution and Subnational Capital Markets

Information Resolution and Subnational Capital Markets

Christine R. Martell, Tima T. Moldogaziev, and Salvador Espinosa

OXFORD
UNIVERSITY PRESS

OXFORD
UNIVERSITY PRESS

Oxford University Press is a department of the University of Oxford. It furthers
the University's objective of excellence in research, scholarship, and education
by publishing worldwide. Oxford is a registered trade mark of Oxford University
Press in the UK and certain other countries.

Published in the United States of America by Oxford University Press
198 Madison Avenue, New York, NY 10016, United States of America.

Library of Congress Cataloging-in-Publication Data
Names: Martell, Christine R., author. | Moldogaziev, Temirlan Tilekovich, author. |
Espinosa, Salvador, author.
Title: Information resolution and subnational capital markets /
Christine R. Martell, Tima T. Moldogaziev, Salvador Espinosa.
Description: New York, NY : Oxford University Press, 2021. |
Includes bibliographical references and index. Identifiers: LCCN 2021016427 |
ISBN 9780190089337 (hardback) | ISBN 9780190089351 (epub) | ISBN 9780190089368
Subjects: LCSH: Local finance. | Debts, Public. | Capital market. |
Government information—Access control. | Credit ratings—Access control. |
Financial disclosure. | Credit control. | Transparency in government. |
Decentralization in government. | Subnational governments.
Classification: LCC HJ9105 .M334 2021 | DDC 336/.014—dc23
LC record available at https://lccn.loc.gov/2021016427

DOI: 10.1093/oso/9780190089337.001.0001

1 3 5 7 9 8 6 4 2

Printed by Integrated Books International, United States of America

To my daughters, Annemarte and Tessa Fé
Christine R. Martell

To my sons, Erkejan and Kenjebai
Tima T. Moldogaziev

To my daughter, Lilia Esperanza
To my parents, Salvador and Elvia Lilia
Salvador Espinosa

Contents

Preface

This book examines the informational aspects of subnational government (SNG) borrowing. It posits that information resolution institutions and mechanisms are critical for the development of SNG capital markets. Despite the pressure on lower-level governments to finance infrastructure demands due to decentralized governance and growing urbanization pressures, most fail to utilize a full array of financing alternatives. The book builds on the existing research and practice, which largely focus on the institutions governing SNG finance and debt, to argue that improvements to transparency, disclosure, regulatory quality, and mechanisms for borrower information certification and monitoring are critical to advancing SNG capital markets.

The book departs from previous research, which focuses largely on institutional design decisions made by national governments, to stress that cities have a role in determining their own agency. SNG agency and competence in signaling creditworthiness, especially at the city level, are essential to leverage capital finance to carry out key governance tasks efficiently, effectively, and equitably.

Unlike previous research on the subject, this book employs two quantitative empirical analyses and two case studies. Both are based on data collected by the authors over multiple years. The quantitative studies allow identification of patterns, controlling for governance institutions advanced in existing research. The qualitative studies provide insight to the nuances of how information resolution impacts SNG borrowing and debt composition. Thus, the theoretical arguments are evaluated with both quantitative and qualitative data.

This book advances a new conceptual model of SNG debt. It holds that information resolution is just as important to SNG capital market development and financing options as the fundamental governance institutions previously identified.

Christine R. Martell
Professor
School of Public Affairs
University of Colorado Denver

Tima T. Moldogaziev
Associate Professor
School of Public Policy
The Pennsylvania State University

Salvador Espinosa
Associate Professor
School of Public Affairs
San Diego State University

Acknowledgments

We, authors Christine R. Martell, Tima T. Moldogaziev, and Salvador Espinosa, extend our deep gratitude to those who have supported our efforts. The valuable support of our colleagues, practitioner community, institutions, and family and friends has enhanced the quality of our collaboration and final product.

Our doctoral studies at Indiana University provided the formation of our public finance knowledge, and we especially attribute our insight into capital markets to Professor Craig L. Johnson. We appreciate the ongoing support for this project from our many Association of Budgeting and Financial Management colleagues, for feedback, discussion, and friendship, and give a special shout out to Yulianti Abbas, Bob Bland, Dwight Dennison, Todd Ely, Robert Greer, George Guess, Merl Hackbart, Bart Hildreth, Mikhail Ivonchyk, Phil Joyce, Sharon Kioko, Kenneth Kriz, Felipe Lozano, Martin Luby, Justin Marlowe, Michael Pagano, Jinsol Park, Ringa Raudla, Mark Robbins, James Savage, Bill Simonsen, Olu Sonola, Min Su, Heidi Smith, Ruth Winecoff, and Kate Yang.

We recognize with appreciation the many who have provided thought leadership for this project, most especially Jim Alm, Roy Bahl, Richard Bird, Naomi Caiden, Octaviano Canuto, Bob Ebel, Mila Freire, Jason Hackworth, Robert Inman, Lily Liu, Jorge Martinez-Vazquez, John Petersen, Raghuram G. Rajan, Dennis Rodden, Timothy Sinclair, Paul Smoke, and Luigi Zingales.

Many practitioners from over 50 countries made our laborious data collection possible, for which we are most appreciative. Our research would have been incomplete otherwise, and we thank you. The practitioner community provided data, directed us to the data, responded to freedom of information requests, and helped us interpret the data.

We appreciate our academic institutions for the time and support to research and write this book: San Diego State University, University of Colorado Denver, the University of Georgia, and The Pennsylvania State University. We thank Natasha Adler, Mikhail Ivonchyk, Youkyoung Jeong, and Jekyung Lee for research assistance.

Our guidance from editors David Pervin and James Cook at Oxford University Press, as well as the copyediting team, was instrumental to the success of this project. Thank you. We also deeply appreciate the feedback of three reviewers, who provided thoughtful and thorough suggestions that helped improve the manuscript.

Finally, we benefited dearly from family and friends, and send our deepest thanks for your ongoing patience and support.

Abbreviations and Acronyms

ARG	Argentina
AUC	Auckland (New Zealand)
AUS	Australia
AUT	Austria
BAR	Barcelona (Spain)
BEL	Belgium
BGR	Bulgaria
BOL	Bolivia
BRA	Brazil
CAN	Canada
CHE	Switzerland
CIP	capital improvement plan
COL	Colombia
CREPMF	Regional Council for Public Savings and Financial Markets
CRI	Costa Rica
CYP	Cyprus
CZE	Czechia
DEU	Germany
DNK	Denmark
ESP	Spain
EST	Estonia
EU	European Union
FIN	Finland
FRA	France
GBR	Great Britain (The United Kingdom)
GCP	gross city product
GDP	gross domestic product
GNE	gross national expense
GNU	gross national income
GRC	Greece
GS	gross savings
HRV	Croatia
HUN	Hungary
IND	India
IRL	Ireland
IST	Istanbul (Turkey)
ITA	Italy
JPN	Japan

KOR	South Korea
LTU	Lithuania
LVA	Latvia
LVI	Lviv (Ukraine)
MED	Medellin (Colombia)
MEX	Mexico
MIL	Milan (Italy)
MKD	North Macedonia
MON	Monterrey (Mexico)
NLD	The Netherlands
NOR	Norway
NZL	New Zealand
OECD	Organization for Economic Cooperation and Development
OSA	Osaka (Japan)
PAR	Paris (France)
PEFA	Public Expenditure and Financial Accountability
PER	Peru
PHL	The Philippines
POL	Poland
PPP	public-private partnership
PRT	Portugal
RIO	Rio de Janeiro (Brazil)
ROM	Romania
RUS	Russian Federation
SEO	Seoul (South Korea)
SIB	social impact bond
SLV	El Salvador
SNG	subnational government
SOF	Sofia (Bulgaria)
SRB	Serbia
SVK	Slovakia
SVN	Slovenia
SWE	Sweden
S&P	Standard and Poor's
THA	Thailand
TUR	Turkey
UKR	Ukraine
URY	Uruguay
US	United States
USD	United States dollar
WB	World Bank
WGI	World Governance Indicators
ZAF	South Africa

1
Subnational Capital Finance

Subnational governments (SNGs) across the globe bear increasing responsibilities for the provision of goods and services, including local infrastructure, resulting from decentralization efforts begun largely in the 1990s.
Simultaneously, rapid urbanization both in developed and developing
contexts means that cities are facing the brunt of service demands. Fiscal governance is a key task of SNGs, and critical to fiscal policy is the provision and
acquisition of financing for capital infrastructure. Infrastructure financing is
costly, has lumpy payments, and must account for inter-jurisdictional and intergenerational impacts, requiring the need to equitably match the costs and
benefits of finance. Recent research in public sector capital finance shows that
top-down decentralization policies and bottom-up service and competition
pressures have created significant gaps between the capital-financing needs of
SNGs and their funding capacity.

In the face of continued urbanization pressures, local governments, especially cities, require access to a variety of capital-financing resources to supple-
ment existing internal borrowing options. To address this fiscal governance
task, SNGs need to establish access to and adopt a full range of internal and
external financing alternatives. Traditionally, central governments have provided infrastructure financing, but both political and fiscal constraints, especially reforms to improve national fiscal balance, can limit resource flows to
localities. While the infrastructure needs of many SNGs remain unmet, numerous examples exist on how cities leverage the administrative and fiscal
authority that decentralized governance can offer. Among the set of external
financing options they utilize are those that private capital markets offer,
allowing for efficient, autonomous financing that can be tailored to local
contexts and preferences.

Despite the decades-long trends in decentralization and successful theoretical and practical applications of decentralization reforms in the field (e.g.,
Freire and Petersen 2004), only a minor share of countries has consistently
created options for SNGs to access external sources of capital finance. This
is understandable, as the issues of SNG capital market formation are complex. They embody a wide range of institutional considerations, including
credit contractibility in the financial system, fiscal institutions that define the

Information Resolution and Subnational Capital Markets. Christine R. Martell, Tima T. Moldogaziev, and Salvador Espinosa,
Oxford University Press. © Oxford University Press 2021. DOI: 10.1093/oso/9780190089337.003.0001

parameters for subnational fiscal and financial rights and responsibilities, financial and market institutions that foster or impede subnational capital markets, and government policies at the local level that may enhance or retard credit quality (e.g., Leigland 1997; Freire and Petersen 2004; Martell and Guess 2006).

Existing research and practice in SNG capital market development largely prescribe a top-down approach. One focus is on laws and fiscal rules, largely pertaining to measures and limits of fiscal responsibility and discipline, that reduce SNG opportunities for moral hazard behaviors that may negatively affect the central government, limit the central government's liability, or preclude expectations of a bailout. Another is on intergovernmental fiscal structures—the vertical and horizontal arrangements of revenue authority, expenditure responsibility, and resource-sharing conditions. Yet, a third and weakest focus has been on developing market infrastructure where SNGs would exercise authority and attend to their own capital-financing needs by utilizing all reasonable internal and external resources. Why then, in the face of current-day realities, has there been limited use of capital financing and an aversion to apply the benefits of external capital financing in executing key governance tasks at the local level?

In fact, the promises and significance of capital market efficiency have been unable to change the persistent distrust of and resistance to the use of capital markets. Aside from the commonly advanced argument that subnational debt threatens macroeconomic stability, concern abounds that local governments that move away from dependence on the central government simply trade masters in favor of market arrangements, resulting in a concern that SNGs become subjects of financial sector firms. *Glocalization*, the twin process of linking and engaging global finance to local governance tasks, has been assigned a negative reputation in existing research for commodifying public assets to largely fit the interests of the financial sector.

However, a key fiscal governance task at the local level is the facilitation of the use, exchange, and distribution of resources from both internal and external sources of financing in a jurisdiction. While a concerned view of the role of finance is that a "path is characterized by the reduction of public subsidies and regulations, the aggressive promotion of real estate development, . . . and the privatization of previously public services" (Hackworth 2007: 16), our view of finance in governance is rather optimistic. We maintain that financialization, a term initially developed with negative undertones, at the local level entails "a complex process of governing urban problems through finance" (Ashton et al. 2016: 1396). As decentralized governance and urban growth pressures are likely to remain, the benefits of *glocalization* and the role of finance in SNG infrastructure financing must be revisited. Given the myriad of institutional arrangements across nations, the pertinent issues of the day are as follows: How can national governments advance subnational capital market financing options? How can SNGs position themselves to leverage borrowing options instead of being portrayed as victims to them? And, how can local borrowers gain competence and agency at the table vis-à-vis financial sector firms?

The Key Is Information Resolution

The key to expanding SNG capital market financing options, in general, and enhancing local government alternatives, in particular, is to directly broach the role of information resolution, that is the reduction of information problems. Information, while an undercurrent of the institutional foci in existing top-down prescriptions to capital market building, has not been explicitly studied with respect to SNG financing. However, the ability to resolve information problems relates directly to the success of market exchanges between the public and private uses of financial resources. Information problems can persist at the national institutional level as well as at the local and financial instrument levels that may hinder access to capital market financing options.

Understanding the role that information plays, as well as designing policies and tools to enhance information resolution, is critical to building subnational capital market financing options. At the national level, policies may seek to encourage credit contractibility through the enhancement of transparency and depth of credit information, extent of disclosure, and regulatory quality. At the subnational level, understanding the information resolution mechanisms and the informational content that those mechanisms signal to market participants is paramount to SNGs' work and agency with financial sector intermediaries and investors. It is especially important to address both information institutions and information resolution mechanisms for subnational financing, as the sources of finance may be global while the location of capital infrastructure and credit risk often tend to be local.

Subnational Government Agency

It is important to note that SNGs, be they regions or cities or their dependent entities, must operate within the national context in which they reside. Largely, they are embedded within vertical and horizontal institutional arrangements and rules. At times, subnational interests may also differ from national interests, and gaining agency over external resources may become critical for local policymakers.

SNGs are not impotent or bystanders in capital-financing decisions. It is true that subnational actors need to live within their national institutional environments, but they are also players in their own right. Within these constraints, there is a wide range of policy options that SNGs can implement, which will contribute to broader access to internal and external capital-financing options. SNGs are in position to gain agency by knowing when and how to utilize the range of financing options, evaluating and intentionally engaging in financing alternatives and instruments commensurate with their creditworthiness, and ensuring that they do not find themselves at the whims of capricious markets. Certain subnational borrowers, regional and local governments alike, have mastered this, and many more can follow their example. Those that do will increase their agency and strengthen their autonomy with respect to both the national government and the capital market actors. In doing so, they also improve their chances for leveraging capital finance and meeting the infrastructure needs that citizens demand in an efficient, effective, and equitable manner. This positive view of the role of finance and utilization of both internal and external capital-financing alternatives already allows numerous SNGs to achieve their key governance tasks.

Information Terms

The theoretical underpinning of this book is that information resolution is the necessary and missing component of subnational capital market development. The following discussion of information resolution, institutions, and mechanisms permeates the book.

Information Problems

Information problems arise in SNG borrowing when parties in a transaction have asymmetric information about a debt issue, the borrower, repayment capacity, or the financial contract. Problems arise when information production, sharing, dissemination, and monitoring are lacking. Information asymmetries can lead to undesired outcomes, including adverse selection, where a party misrepresents its type to gain access to a favorable outcome, and moral hazard behavior, where a party behaves in a manner that undermines the interest of the other party. The absence of measures to resolve information problems can lead to market failure, that is, when markets become unable to reach their optimal potential and/or may shut down entirely.

Information problems most relevant to the subject of SNG capital finance are those among levels of government (i.e., between the national government and SNG), and those occurring between a subnational borrower (as current or potential participants in capital markets) and external investors or holders of public sector debt. For example, a SNG might not put forth full effort to collect local taxes, but the national government does not have the ability to measure that effort. Should the SNG not collect the own-source revenue it projected, it could default on its interest payments and put the national government into a situation of having to decide whether to bail out the SNG. Hard budget constraints (such as a law of financial responsibility and a no-bailout position of the national government) or monitoring and data-transparency mechanisms are important to mitigate this moral hazard behavior. In another example, borrowers and investors always have asymmetric levels of information about the government's creditworthiness. When an investor cannot verify the credit quality of a borrower, capital markets may require higher interest rates to compensate for unknown risks or choose not to lend at all, both of which are inefficient. Credit ratings, offered by third-party information intermediation and monitoring firms, are a key mechanism to mitigate these information asymmetries. Rules that require, pay for, and/or encourage the use of information evaluation are examples of public and private arrangements that contribute to resolving information problems.

Information Institutions

Information institutions refer to the formal rules, codified by constitution, statute, or law, and informal rules (norms and practices) that enable or inhibit the production, sharing, dissemination, and monitoring of information. In the context of SNGs, information institutions enable credit contractibility.

In the context of national governance institutions and capital markets, critical information institutions exist at the system level. These system-level information institutions govern the resolution of information problems by providing transparency and depth of credit information, extent of disclosure, and regulatory quality.

Information Resolution

Information resolution refers to the reduction of information problems among parties using public and private information evaluation, certification, and monitoring mechanisms. Information resolution mechanisms may include means to enhance information production, sharing, dissemination, and monitoring, as well as self-certification or third-party certification of credit quality via administrative or market processes. Third-party information resolution mechanisms have emerged as the most cost-effective way of credit quality assessment. Large credit-rating firms such as Fitch, Standard & Poor's, and Moody's are information intermediaries that operate globally, and their credit ratings and reports are the most widespread information certification and monitoring tools that enable SNGs access to capital market financing.

Contributions of This Book

This book takes the position that capital markets are a viable financing alternative for subnational borrowers and that SNGs can manage their fiscal and debt choices to leverage capital markets to finance efficient, effective, and equitable infrastructure provision. It builds on previous work in two fundamental ways. First, this study explores the role of information institutions, arguing that resolving information problems is critical to the success of subnational capital markets. Second, this study advances the options for SNG agency as active market participants. SNGs are one leg of a three-legged stool, where the national government and the markets are the other two legs. Subnational agency, developed through experience in navigating and utilizing information resolution tools, balances the interests of the three sets of players and reduces subnational dependence on either of the potential "masters of capital"—the other two legs of the stool. SNGs are not passive players; rather, with acquired competence they can accomplish their key governance tasks efficiently, effectively, and equitably.

Regardless of their nation's history or current capital-financing context, understanding how local choices affect information resolution allows SNGs to utilize a broader range of financing options, achieving both autonomy and fiscal governance objectives. In this regard, information resolution contexts and information resolution mechanisms are critical because, with competing incentive structures of suppliers of capital and borrowers in the web of institutional governance arrangements, information problems are inevitable. The core of this book is about what national and city actors can do to improve information resolution, not about them being paralyzed by information problems.

This study sets out to answer the following queries: How does information permeate the landscape and outcomes of SNG borrowing, broadly at the aggregate subnational level and narrowly at the city level? What measures and mechanisms can national governments and SNGs take to resolve information problems? What can cities do to enhance their agency vis-à-vis central governments and capital market actors, so that they can command a voice in managing internal and external sources of capital financing?

Organization of the Book

Information institutions are part of broader institutions governing subnational debt. This study borrows from the corporate finance literature to build an argument that information resolution contributes to SNG capital markets (Chapter 2). Other contributing factors pertain to the institutional arrangements set forth in decentralization laws and rules, financial market structures, as well as concerns that the use of capital markets will result in undesirable outcomes for both national governments and SNGs (Chapter 3).

To assess how information institutions relate to SNG capital markets, this study embarks on empirical analyses that focus on national and subnational information resolution. The first of these analyses establishes that information resolution institutions in the system affect SNG capital market borrowing, even controlling for fundamental dimensions of governance institutions (Chapter 4). This analysis addresses the questions: Does information resolution matter? Which component of information resolution matters the most? How does information resolution affect the aggregate size of SNG borrowing? *Providing empirical support of widely held accepted wisdom, the analysis at this level underscores the importance of information resolution institutions in the national context for aggregate levels of subnational borrowing, all else constant.*

SNGs broadly include both regional governments (states, provinces) and local governments (cities, towns, special districts, etc.). The book, however, narrowly focuses on cities as an important level of interest in the second empirical analysis (Chapter 5). We seek to understand how credit contractibility and the underlying informational content of city credit quality relate to city borrowing levels and city debt composition. The chapter asks: What debt levels do cities have, and what is the composition of that debt? How do information resolution institutions and mechanisms influence borrowing outcomes, both volume and debt type? *The analysis at this level supports the importance of information resolution institutions and the information content of city credit quality on city borrowing levels and composition, all else constant.*

Just knowing that information resolution affects SNG capital-financing choices is inadequate to guide local policymakers toward attaining their own agency and autonomy. We find it necessary to drill down to the city level of analysis and evaluate the fundamental informational components of city credit quality (Chapter 6). We ask: What elements of city credit quality information are contained in credit ratings? How can city policymakers evaluate their credit quality and benchmark risks to other cities? What can city policymakers do to improve their agency? *This analysis addresses economic, fiscal, debt and financial, and governance fundamentals that city policymakers may focus on to understand and assess their credit quality and gain agency by actively communicating their market readiness and competence.*

Without concerted efforts at the national level to resolve information problems and without choices at the city level to broaden their choices of external financing, SNG capital markets are likely to fall short of their potential. Understanding the successes and impediments to information resolution are important components underlying policy design recommendations. By examining cities from distinct historical contexts (Chapter 7), we ask: How did policies at the national level influence information resolution institutions and mechanisms for three cities? How do they relate to city borrowing? *The case study analysis in this chapter exemplifies how changes in national policy and city credit quality relate to city debt choices and borrowing options.*

With these research questions in mind, the point of departure of this book is that SNGs can and should have an active role in infrastructure-financing decisions, and that institutions and mechanisms that resolve information problems aid local policymakers in establishing agency to carry out their key governance tasks. Based on analyses from four chapters (Chapters 4–7), we present policy recommendations for national and subnational policymakers (Chapter 8).

2
A Theory of Subnational Government Capital Market Information

As introduced, a key fiscal governance task is to provide subnational governments (SNGs) with access to capital markets. Capital markets can improve risk sharing, allocative efficiency, and the availability of long-term financing through price signals and other information (Laeven 2014; Greenwood and Smith 1997). SNGs, in either a unitary or a federal system, refer to those jurisdictions whose authority falls below that of the national sovereign. Although types of SNGs vary by country, generally mid-level SNGs include provinces, governorates, regions, länder, or states; and local-level SNGs include cities, towns, metropolitan governments, counties, as well as special districts created and financed to meet specific purposes. Market-based capital typically refers to capital deriving from private external sources, including bank loans and capital underwriting firms via securities markets or direct placements. Borrowing from Freire and Petersen (2004: xxix), the term "*markets* implies a system with a variety of borrowers and lenders and with credit allocation based on pricing decisions that balance supply and demand. It also implies an array of alternatives for accessing capital funds."

The applied and academic approach taken to building SNG capital markets, while grounded in economics and finance, has focused on institutional dimensions and top-down technical arrangements. The institutional dimensions referenced, and developed in Chapter 3, relate to economic, financial and market, political, and legal institutions. The argument holds that institutional contexts and designs can facilitate, or retard, subnational capital markets by overcoming, or exacerbating, the problems of coordination, fiscal discipline, and macroeconomic stability, albeit with insufficient attention to information institutions that handle directly adverse selection and moral hazard problems. Emphasis in the literature thus far has been on non-informational preconditions and design alternatives, such as ex ante and ex post fiscal rules, for subnational capital markets (Rodden et al. 2003; Freire and Petersen 2004; Martell and Guess 2006; Canuto and Liu 2013). Stated directly, although the literature recognizes the need to overcome problems of information, none of the extant studies explicitly pursues the relationship

Information Resolution and Subnational Capital Markets. Christine R. Martell, Tima T. Moldogaziev, and Salvador Espinosa, Oxford University Press. © Oxford University Press 2021. DOI: 10.1093/oso/9780190089337.003.0002

between information resolution institutions and capital markets. The application of the theoretical underpinning remains understudied.

Notwithstanding the importance of institutional arrangements, this book takes the position that information resolution institutions and mechanisms are an overlooked but critical piece of developing successful SNG capital markets. Information resolution is the fundamental component connecting institutional arrangements in SNG capital market development. The premise of this book is that institutions of information resolution, that is, the ability to resolve information problems, are necessary for SNG capital market growth. Specifically, although countries must have a certain level of maturity along economic, financial and market, political, and legal institutions before successfully managing a well-functioning SNG capital market, the crowning factor behind an efficient SNG capital market, above and beyond the fundamental dimensions of institutional maturity, is credit contractibility in the system and tools of information certification and monitoring available to SNGs.

This chapter develops the theoretical base for why and how information resolution is expected to relate to and shape SNG capital market outcomes. The next section details how information problems manifest in credit contractibility. The attention then turns to a review of how information relates to capital finance and applies theories of capital markets to SNG borrowing, debt size, and debt composition. The chapter then discusses how information resolution institutions can enhance SNG capital markets and proposes testable hypotheses. This is followed with a discussion of how the informational content of credit quality is the most useful instrument for SNGs to certify and communicate underlying creditworthiness to credit markets. A conclusion wraps up the chapter.

Information Problems of Subnational Debt

As noted in Chapter 1, SNG borrowing is riddled with the twin conditions of limited access to capital markets and dominant lending from or through the central government via grants, loans, credit assistance, or donor funds (Freire and Petersen 2004). A competing and equally pernicious problem exists too: the over-indebtedness of SNGs and their unwillingness to repay debts (Martell 2016; Rodden et al. 2003). Information problems underlie these conditions.

An intergovernmental system is particularly prone to information problems of moral hazard and adverse selection, principal agent, and collective action. These problems may exist in multiple intergovernmental arrangements, including transfer designs and expenditure assignments, and these problems specifically affect SNG borrowing. Although beyond the primary concern of this project, not only do the information problems exist within the subnational-borrowing environment, other design features associated with revenue and expenditure assignments may exacerbate the information problems that ultimately also affect capital financing .

The fundamental issue concerns the asymmetry of information between two parties, which results in problems of moral hazard and adverse selection. The problem of *moral hazard* is "where one party to a transaction may undertake certain actions that (a) affect the other party's valuation of the transaction but that (b) the second party cannot monitor/enforce perfectly" (Kreps 1990: 577). In the case of SNG borrowing, moral hazard is where the borrower has incentive to undermine a contractual agreement. Even if a borrower's true type is discernable and markets can set prices according to risk, there remains the ongoing potential that a borrower may at a future date behave in a manner not in the best interests of the creditor. Namely, the borrower may fail to make full and timely debt service payments.

A special form of the moral hazard problem is *adverse selection*. It refers to when two parties have asymmetrical information, and the informed party misrepresents its type to reap benefits afforded to the other type. Applied to subnational borrowing, a subnational jurisdiction might have incentive to present as poor and to reduce revenue-generating effort to receive subsidized financing from the central government. Alternatively, a subnational jurisdiction might have incentive to present as a low-risk, high-quality borrower to attain favorable market rates. Without risk-evaluation and monitoring efforts, which are costly, an investor may not be able to assess a borrower's true type. Without credible information on quality and risk, as well as costly financial intermediation to overcome the information asymmetry, the market may close down (Akerloff 1970).

When the subnational government engages in moral hazard behavior, it may also impose the cost of its inability to manage within hard budget constraints on other subnational and central governments. In the case of subnational borrowing, moral hazard behavior resulting in over-indebtedness is encouraged by expectation of a bail out (Rodden et al. 2003; Inman 2003). When budget constraints are soft, the jurisdiction's gains of overspending create a negative externality whose costs are borne primarily by persons or entities outside the jurisdiction. Therefore, the total costs, absorbed by the system at large, include the costs to all taxpayers of refinancing or relieving the jurisdiction of its debt, the cost to the creditors in the form of lower or delayed return, and the cost of trust in the subnational-borrowing system. The impact of collective action or coordination problems leads to prohibition or limitation of subnational government debt by the central government; market contraction and lower credit supply; increased borrowing rates for SNGs due to contagion; and tighter control of SNG capital access, further exacerbating the twin problems of limited access to capital markets and government-dominated lending (Freire and Petersen 2004; Canuto and Liu 2013; Martell 2016). Information asymmetries are at the root of these behaviors and cyclical problems.

Theory: Information as It Relates to Capital Markets

The literature on capital finance, as it relates to information, grounds this book. Information resolution affects market development—existence, type, size, and structure—in general, and financial markets in particular, and identifies applications to the SNG capital market.

Type of Borrowing System and Credit Contractibility

The central theoretical argument is that information plays a critical role in markets (Akerlof 1970; Stiglitz and Weiss 1981; Diamond 1984; Ramakrishnan and Thakor 1984; Leland and Pyle 1977; Bertomeu and Marinovic 2016; Liberti and Petersen 2017; Rajan and Zingales 1998). The degree of information resolution bears directly on how capital markets develop and is the lynchpin between characterizing a borrowing system as market based or relationship based (Rajan 1992; Merton 1995; Rajan and Zingales 1998). Markets rely on the ability, through information, to differentiate credit quality so that borrowing rates can reflect default risk (Jaffee and Modigliani 1969; Jaffee 1972). Better institutions and mechanisms of information resolution are associated with a transparent information environment and greater market development (Libereti and Petersen 2017).

Conversely, the absence of perfect information has been recognized as a major impediment to market development (Akerlof 1970; Rajan and Zingales 1998). Akerlof (1970) demonstrates that when products of differing quality arrive on the market and no mechanism exists to distinguish high- from poor-quality products, the market will attract only the poorer quality products and drive the higher quality products out of the market. Eventually investors know that the poorer quality goods dominate the market and become unwilling to offer credit. Thus, the market may break down and fewer or no market transactions may occur. With imperfect information, credit is either not provided or is rationed by non-price means (Stiglitz and Weiss 1981). When credit is rationed by non-price means, as in a relationship-based system, the price of credit is divorced from risk and provides no sorting or incentive effects to counter moral hazard and adverse selection. The practice of non-price driven credit allocation is common in opaque contexts in both developed and developing economies (Williamson 1986; Rajan and Zingales 1998).

Consistent with the argument that information is the distinguishing factor between market-based and relationship-based borrowing systems, Rajan and Zingales (1998) juxtapose the credit "contractibility" characteristic of each type of financial system. Based on principles of information economics, contractibility refers to the financial system's degree of transparency or depth of credit information, extent of financial disclosure, and regulatory quality. Whereas a relationship-based system of credit allocation must exist due to the opacity of information, a market-based system of credit contractibility relies on information resolution.

To elaborate further, a relationship-based borrowing system exists with the opacity of information, where it allows the financier to negotiate lower profits in one period for the monopoly to extract higher profits in a future period, allowing for inter-temporal smoothing. Initially, borrowers may benefit from access to capital with greater monitoring, but potentially at higher interest costs until the borrower and bank have developed a relationship (Blackwell and Winters 1997). Entry barriers, from regulation or lack of information resolution, maintain the financier's lending power. Moreover, as relationships are self-governing, they can survive when the legal environment is too weak to enforce contracts. While a relationship-based credit allocation system can protect new borrowers by internally controlling the problems of adverse selection and moral hazard, "the absence of competition and disclosure . . . imply that there are really no price signals to guide decisions" (Rajan and Zingales 1998: 42). The continuous access to cash allows managers to ignore the price signals sent by poor financial management indicators. Another downside of a relationship-based arrangement is that firms financed by relationship-based financiers exert lower effort because the share of profits extracted by the financier is higher (Rajan 1992). In analogy to the subnational debt-financing contracts, a relationship-based credit system is likely to protect new and weaker borrowers and those in weak institutional environments, although at the expense of inefficient project selection, limited response to financial management indicators, and levers to private actors at the expense of public interest.

At the other end of the spectrum of borrowing systems, market-based systems rely on information resolution and are characterized by enforceable contracts between arm's length lenders and borrowers, whereby price is determined as a function of risk. The disclosure of information and the courts' ability to enforce contracts are necessary to protect the lender. Firms financed under market-based arrangements demonstrate higher effort (Rajan 1992), and mature borrowers face lower costs in a market-based system (Rajan and Zingales 1998). The price signals of a market-based system allow for more efficient allocation of capital. Yet, as arm's length lenders have little power over the borrower, in contrast to a relationship-based system, the borrowers can engage in principal-agent behavior that needs to be assessed and monitored. Institutions of information resolution are the antidote for such problems. In analogy to the subnational debt-financing contracts, a market-based credit system is likely to allocate capital more efficiently, allow lower prices for creditworthy borrowers, and stimulate the continued need to maintain credit contractibility.

Contractibility, therefore, is directly related to the type of capital market development. Credit systems with low contractibility will be defined by relationship-based credit allocation, and systems with high contractibility will be better served by arm's length transactions. Relationship-based and transaction-based competitive systems may coexist (Rajan 1992), but ultimately arm's length transactions will be more efficient, as they respect the risk-reward relationship. When lenders suffer from insufficient information, a relationship-based system allows for flexible negotiations, versus contract enforcement, but at the cost of the lender having a claim on the borrower's private information and surplus (Rajan 1992). As the degree of information, and thus contractibility, impacts the type of capital market system, it also impacts the type of debt that the borrowers hold (Sharma and Knight 2016; Liberti and Petersen 2017; Kwan and Carleton 2010; Rajan and Zingales 1998; Rajan 1992).

By extending the discussion of types of credit systems, it should hold that the role of information has significance not just for private sector capital markets but also for all market types that involve borrowers and lenders (Merton 1995; Moldogaziev et al. 2018), including SNG capital markets. Capital markets, be they for private or public sectors, are subject to supply and demand forces within their institutional contexts. Any type of lending involves an exchange between two parties, the flow of capital to productive uses, and a return on investment to the lender for that exchange. Assuming that the fundamental relationships of exchange are preserved regardless of the borrower, it is useful to apply private capital market credit-allocation frameworks to SNG capital markets. In fact, existing research shows a positive relationship between information resolution institutions and SNG capital market size (Moldogaziev et al. 2018), as well as information density and allocation of urban infrastructure capital (Sharma and Knight 2016).

Consequently, information is critical for two key elements of capital finance: access to capital and means of credit allocation. As such, a system's information bases of credit contractibility and mechanisms of information certification and monitoring between capital market participants will impact whether a SNG capital market system can evolve from a relationship-based to a market-based credit-allocation arrangement.

Debt Composition Choices

Theories of information and agency are fundamental to understanding not only SNG's use of capital markets but also their capital structure (or debt composition). Capital structure refers to how an entity finances its operations from different sources of internal and external resources. In the corporate world, capital structure includes the source of financing, such as debt or equity; the prioritization of repayment, such as senior versus subordinated debt or preferred versus common equity; the placement of debt securities, such as in a bank loan, a privately placed or a publicly sold debt; and credit enhancements, such as a degree of securitization or uses of covenants. In the public sector, debt composition similarly includes multiple sources of capital financing, such as from a grant, a loan, or a market security (including a variety of debt securities); source and prioritization of repayment, such as general obligation or specific revenues; placement of debt with either public or private creditors; and credit enhancements and guarantees, such as insurance or any collateral and risk-sharing schemes.

As shown in existing capital finance literature, there is a direct relationship between the degree of information resolution and the type of debt that borrowers select (Sharma and Knight 2016; Liberti and Petersen 2017; Kwan and Carleton 2010; Rajan and Zingales 1998; Rajan 1992). Research on corporate finance shows that a borrower's capital structure responds to the information environment and disclosure choices (Dhaliwal et al. 2011). Disclosure has a greater impact on debt placement when credit quality is low (Dhaliwal et al. 2011). Firms with greater need to certify, protect proprietary information, develop a reputation, and renegotiate contracts will prefer bank loans instead of public debt (Kale and Meneghetti 2011; Yosha 1995). Similarly, firms with greater contracting costs due to information asymmetries and the potential for moral hazard behavior seek private, or relationship-based, debt (Krishnaswami et al. 1999). Once chosen, capital structure impacts the incentives of both managers to develop creditworthy reputations and creditor commitments to monitor capital investments.

From early research on capital structure, it is clear that information resolution affects a firm's choice between equity and debt. In the presence of information asymmetries, the ratio of debt to equity signals firm value (Leland and Pyle 1977; Ross 1977; Heinkel 1982; Krishnaswami et al. 1999). Debt can also be a signal to investors about the quality of management (Harris and Raviv 1990). Subsequent research has found that, similar to equity and debt trade-offs, information and the ability to resolve information problems is associated with the firm's placement of debt between privately placed and publicly sold debt options (Diamond 1991; Krishnaswami et al. 1999; Cantillo and Wright 2000).

According to the theory of financial intermediation, monitoring functions mitigate information costs (Diamond 1991). Monitoring functions established by banks or investors of privately placed debt, thus, can be expected when there is reason to resolve information problems, such as when there are conflicts between bondholders and shareholders and when the potential for moral hazard exists (Krishnaswami et al. 1999). These privately placed bonds have more investor input in covenant design and monitoring structures, more restrictive covenants, and greater ease of renegotiation, similar to borrowing in a relationship-based arrangement (Kwan and Carleton 2010). Banks holding firm debt can liquidate the firm or renegotiate contracts with greater facility than can holders of public debt (Kale and Maneghetti 2011). Public debt, without affiliated monitoring functions, is more likely to be present when firms issue large quantities of debt and can leverage economies of scale, when there are increased cash and collateral levels, and when firms already have established reputations (Cantillo and Wright 2000; Diamond 1991).

However, debt structure is dynamic and responds to the information resolution environment. Different debt instruments have different properties regarding cash-flow risk, sensitivity to information, and managerial incentives (Rauh and Sufi 2010). In particular, corporate debt structure changes dynamically in response to information on credit quality. Firms in countries where one model dominates, either market oriented or relationship oriented, proportionately mimic the mix of public debt versus bank loans, respectively (Rajan and Zingales 1995). Finally, any borrower's composition of debt affects the levels of its risk exposure (Mehl and Reynaud 2010).

There is clear evidence that information affects capital structure and debt composition in the corporate sector. By extension to SNG capital financing, it is reasonable to expect a relationship between information and debt composition. Specifically, information resolution is likely to yield greater levels of market-based capital flows and better pricing (Marlowe 2010; Robbins and Simonsen 2010; Peng and Brucato 2004). Given that SNG borrowing in cases of poor information resolution is primarily relationship based, it follows from the corporate finance literature (Arena 2011; Kwan and Carleton 2010; Blackwell and Kidwell 1988; Carey et al. 1993) that an increase in information resolution would be necessary for a movement of SNG debt to market-based capital financing arrangements.

Information Resolution and the SNG Capital Market

Building on the argument that information problems undermine SNG capital markets, consider information resolution institutions and mechanisms to be the lynchpin of supporting SNG capital markets.

Guided by key fiscal governance concerns, the objective is for SNGs to have a number of options for borrowing, including the option to borrow from private investors in addition to public sources. The first item of interest in the book is the level of SNG debt. The share of SNG capital market debt reflects the extent of credit contractibility and the maturity of public sector capital-financing options. Greater access to capital financing means that the SNGs can fulfill this fiscal governance task on their own. Chapter 4 evaluates the key covariates of aggregate levels of SNG borrowing in 52 countries, while Chapter 5 seeks to evaluate borrowing at the city level.

Aggregate SNG or city-borrowing levels, however, mask the composition profiles of SNG debt. The composition of SNG debt refers to the distribution of debt by public and private sources and allows assessment of the extent of financing from different market-based sources, loans, or debt securities. Essentially, the composition of debt toward debt securities can also reveal whether the borrowing environment is closer to a market-based capital-financing system. The second item of interest in the book is the percent of debt securities in the composition of city debt, which Chapter 5 explores.

When city policymakers seek financing from external capital market sources, they need to communicate information to market participants about their own creditworthiness. This can be done by city policymakers themselves or with the help of financial sector firms. A key mechanism to do so is through credit-rating firms, which have become significant information intermediaries in financial markets both for private and public sector borrowers. Chapter 6 explores the key informational components of credit quality and discusses how city policymakers can strengthen their agency to expand borrowing options and access to market capital. This is the third item of interest in the book.

The last item of interest in the book is the profile of reforms seeking to enhance information resolution institutions in the system and to enhance mechanisms available for SNGs for information generation and monitoring. Chapter 7 evaluates key changes in public sector capital finance approaches in three select countries and discusses the depth of capital market borrowing, debt options, and changes in the varieties of borrowing instruments for a benchmark city from each of the three countries.

Applying Theory to Empirical Tests

In line with existing research (Bharath et al. 2009; Peng and Brucato 2004; Reck and Wilson 2006; Moldogaziev et al. 2018), our theoretical framework posits that information resolution plays a critical role in SNG capital market access and activity. While countries must acquire a certain level of institutional maturity—necessary alignments in economic, financial and market, political, and legal institutions—before adopting and successfully managing a well-functioning SNG capital market, information resolution institutions in the nation's system matter significantly. It follows that information resolution institutions—which relate directly to credit contractibility—will yield greater SNG capital market activity as measured by the level and composition of debt. For those countries weak on institutional maturity, information resolution institutions will yield a greater range of motion to cities within the constraints of their environment, increase the opportunities for financing predominantly from internal sources, but potentially from external sources too. Empirical testing of this expectation is outside the scope of this study.

At the national level, information resolution institutions are conceptualized along the dimensions of transparency and depth of credit information, extent of disclosure, and regulatory quality (Rajan and Zingales 1998; Moldogaziev et al. 2018). More precisely, the transparency, or depth of credit information, indicates the availability of credit information, writ large, within a country's financial system. The extent of disclosure evaluates country-level disclosure quality for private firms that obtain credit from investors. Finally, regulatory quality measures the central government's ability to advance policies and regulations that foment private enterprise. These dimensions of information resolution are the bases of credit contractibility. At the system level, our formal, testable hypothesis is that information resolution institutions will have a positive association with SNG capital market borrowing, controlling for economic, financial and market, political, and legal institutions. Chapter 4 tests this hypothesis empirically.

Debt composition and instrument options for SNGs also depend on mechanisms and tools of information certification and monitoring. Capital finance literature shows that the most effective mechanisms for information resolution involve contracting third-party information evaluation and credit-monitoring intermediaries. Information certification and credit-monitoring mechanisms by financial sector firms improve information resolution and influence access to financing (Berlin and Loeys 1988; Diamond 1991; Berlin and Mester 1992; Chemmanuer and Fulghieri 1994). Incentives—embedded in a financial contract design, debt structure, and risk-sharing arrangements— and monitoring the borrower can mitigate divergent behavior (Grossman and Hart 1983; Johnson et al. 2014). The costs associated with the financial contract design and monitoring are referred to as agency costs. Although costly, monitoring also adds value by developing a borrower's reputation (Diamond 1991). The ability to leverage incentives depends on the quality of financial contracting and legal enforcement. Weak property rights and concentrated ownership reduces the functional efficiency of capital markets (Eklund and Desai 2014). Information mechanisms utilized by capital market participants, above and beyond national information environments, contribute to lower financing costs (Dhaliwal et al. 2011; Botosan 1997; Sengupta 1998; Rajan and Zingales 1998; Peng and Brucato 2004; Johnson and Kriz 1999, 2005).

Financial intermediaries can provide financial contracting and monitoring services. Intermediaries improve the market for information before and after a transaction (Leland and Pyle 1977). Financial intermediation also serves to improve a borrower's reputation through monitoring mechanisms (Thakor 1991; Diamond 1984, 1991). Although intermediation can be costly for some, intermediaries possess both the economies of scale and scope in the capital market (Cantillo and Wright 2000). Rajan and Zingales (1998) suggest that financial intermediation, either by governments or private sector firms, can assist credit markets as they transition from relationship-based to arm's length capital finance. Merton (1995) argues that the functions that financial intermediaries serve are to facilitate the allocation and deployment of economic resources, to manage risk, and to issue guarantees. He further argues, "the most efficient institutional structure for fulfilling the functions of the financial system generally changes over time and differs across geopolitical subdivisions" (Merton 1995: 24). However, as financial intermediaries are dynamic, capital market efficiency is best achieved when national governments and SNGs gain managerial and regulatory competence as opposed to avoiding finance in governance tasks.

At the borrower level, information resolution refers to mechanisms available to SNGs that reveal and verify their information and credit quality. The tools we are interested in are assessments of underlying city credit quality either in-house or through third-party information intermediaries. Credit ratings are important for a number of reasons, as discussed in detail in Chapter 6. Suffice it to say here that credit-rating firms have emerged as key information intermediaries of SNG creditworthiness on a global scale. A testable hypothesis follows that city debt levels and debt composition are associated with city credit quality, controlling for information resolution institutions. Chapter 5 empirically tests this hypothesis.

Applying Theory to Practice

While theory guides the inquiry in Chapters 4 and 5, lessons from those results inform exploration of subnational capital finance policies in Chapters 6 and 7. Given the findings of these theory-driven models and that cities are an increasingly important level of SNGs, what practical implications emerge from the book for cities—an increasingly important level of subnational government? What can policymakers do in light of what they know about the qualities of the city's governance system and about the strength of credit quality the city possesses? How can policymakers participate in co-production of information and actively maintain agency when working with financial sector firms?

Whereas a city is nested in a given national context and must take the system-level information resolution institutions as given, it still has access to information certification and monitoring mechanisms at its disposal. National contexts become particularly important when countries engage in reforms that result in policy inputs with regards to system information resolution institutions on the one hand, and information certification and monitoring mechanisms that become available to SNGs on the other hand. Rather than be a passive respondent, city policymakers can improve their position vis-à-vis financial sector firms by understanding the fundamental informational components of city credit quality. At the same time, reforms may open access to new financial sector products and services that can bring opportunities hitherto unavailable to SNGs.

3
Review of Literature on Subnational Government Borrowing

Subnational governments (SNGs) continue to face pressures for infrastructure provision that exceed the financing means of operating budgets. Rapid decentralization and urbanization processes increase demand for infrastructure, ranging from transportation to housing to utilities. Simultaneously, there are intergenerational and inter-jurisdictional concerns that SNGs must balance when engaging in costly capital-financing projects. Despite demand, SNGs, cities in particular, fail to leverage a full range of financing and resource alternatives due to institutional constraints (some of which are outside their control), while they continue to neglect alternative tools within their reach. Most specifically, their access to and use of capital markets in a number of countries are limited and underutilized, even though external resources would expand SNGs' options to tackle key governance tasks (Sbragia 1996; Martell and Guess 2006; Freire 2014).

This chapter sets the context for why we care and what we know about SNG capital markets. It begins with a review of the fiscal governance task in the face of demands for SNG infrastructure provision and the institutional contexts of SNG borrowing. The chapter then discusses how SNG infrastructure provision and borrowing fit with a growing perspective of financial governance innovations. It continues with an introduction to capital-financing options, an overview of SNG borrowing, and potential problems with SNG debt. Then, the chapter explores fundamental dimensions of institutional contexts that affect SNG borrowing depth and breadth. It ends by explicitly recognizing the role of information and setting a research agenda on efforts to improve information resolution institutions and mechanisms for information certification and monitoring.

Fiscal Governance Task

In numerous countries, the dual trends of fiscally decentralized and compartmentalized governance and fast city growth continue. Under such trends,

Information Resolution and Subnational Capital Markets. Christine R. Martell, Tima T. Moldogaziev, and Salvador Espinosa, Oxford University Press. © Oxford University Press 2021. DOI: 10.1093/oso/9780190089337.003.0003

many SNGs find themselves underutilizing internal and external financing sources. The central governance tasks of SNGs are to provide goods and services desired by citizens of the jurisdiction in an efficient, effective, and equitable manner (Oates 2005). Some of those goods and services require investments in infrastructure, such as urban transportation networks, commercial and residential buildings, broadband technology, water and sanitation facilities, energy utilities, and healthcare and recreation facilities. These investments improve the quality of citizens' lives by decreasing travel times, housing educational facilities and civic events, increasing technological connectivity to banks and medical resources, providing clean water and removing waste material, and accessing electric power, among many other outcomes (Alm 2015). They also improve the quality of the jurisdiction's governance by improving opportunities for localized economic development, wealth accumulation, and revenue generation (Sbragia 1996).

The fiscal governance task, therefore, is one of the critical governance tasks; increasingly the responsibility of SNGs to manage fiscal affairs so that they are able to provide desired goods and services to citizens. Fiscal governance refers to the management of day-to-day operations, as well as long-term planning, borrowing, and investment of internal and external resources. Infrastructure financing is a long-term and, often, costly objective. When current revenues are insufficient to pay for capital investments, or the costs of capital financing require multigenerational smoothing, it is necessary for localities to complete their fiscal governance task through the acquisition of long-term financing. Thus, a particular focus of fiscal governance is the acquisition of financial resources to pay for projects, an area experiencing significant growth across many countries with varying degrees of success, especially for infrastructure provision at the city level (Hildreth and Zorn 2005; Pagano and Perry 2008; Bahl et al. 2013; Freire 2014; Moldogaziev et al. 2018). A specific fiscal objective is to improve SNGs' access to capital financing.

A problem in the past has been that there is not enough access to financing for those who need it, and too much access and debt for those SNGs that cannot control their debt (Martell 2016). Many SNGs rely on financing from the central government, either in the form of grants or loans, or from international finance institutions, but do not leverage a full range of capital market financing options. This book frames the study of access to capital financing as one of the key and rapidly growing governance tasks at the SNG level. Governance, as opposed to governments, refers to the leveraging of public and nonpublic sectors collaboratively working for the production of goods and services in such a manner that is both economically efficient and in concert with citizen's values, voices, and demands. Governance structures are made up of hierarchies and markets and refer to the open system of institutional arrangements for the provision of goods and services. Governance in a decentralized environment takes on a specific dimension, as the actions at the local level are embedded within a national context.

Existing urban research emphasizes the links between national institutional arrangements and city-level policy outcomes: "It is certainly essential that cities upgrade their institutional capacities but, perhaps even more critical, nation-states need to develop national urban policies that allow local governments to fulfill their crucial roles. Effective moves toward empowering city or metropolitan governments to establish a transition to a more sustainable society are rare" (da Cruz et al. 2019: 10). At the same time, fiscal governance, and the task of financing city infrastructure, has become and will continue to be increasingly relevant as countries trend toward fiscal decentralization, growth of the financial sector, *glocalization* of urban governance (Pagano and Perry 2008; Torrance 2008; 2009; Bahl et al. 2013; Bahl and Linn 2014; Freire 2014), and "growing demands for urban services as urbanization continues in major cities around the world" (Alm 2015: 239).

Infrastructure and Capital Financing: Why the City?

Subnational development, especially urban growth, and the need for local infrastructure are pressing. Since 2007, more than half the world's population resides in urban areas. Whereas 33.6 percent of the population was urban in 1960, 55.3 percent was in 2018 with projections of 60 percent by 2030 (United Nations 2018; World Bank 2018). Wealthier countries have greater rates of urbanization, with 2018 shares ranging from 33 percent in low-income countries up to 81 percent in high-income countries, but 27 of 33 megacities are located in less wealthy countries (United Nations 2018). While urbanization growth rates have decreased over recent decades to an average of 1.9 percent worldwide, they remain higher among lower income countries, especially in Africa and Asia. The urbanization growth rates range from 4 percent in low-income countries to 0.7 percent in high-income countries. As cities continue to grow, they also assume more of the responsibility of providing services such as primary education, public health, public safety, potable water, sanitation, and transit (Blanco et al. 2016; Pagano and Hoene 2018).

Investment in infrastructure is important for economic growth and productivity, most especially in poorer countries (Estache 2010). Infrastructure refers to physical assets with a long life that require ongoing maintenance and operations, and whose acquisition requires substantial upfront costs. As Bahl and Bird (2018: 124) point out, infrastructure development entails "the construction, operation and maintenance of long-lived physical assets required to deliver such specific public services as land transportation (highways, roads, streets, bridges and ancillary services such as street lighting, street cleaning, signage, etc.), potable water (supply, distribution), wastewater management (sewerage, disposal), and solid waste collection and disposal (including hazardous waste)."

Despite rapid urbanization, city infrastructure is often inadequate. Only 74.2 percent of cities had municipal solid waste collection coverage in 2017, and only 87.4 percent of the world's population had access to electricity in 2016. In 2015, 71.2 percent of the world's population used safely managed drinking water services, with only 39.3 percent using safely managed sanitation services (United Nations 2019). Transportation networks leave a billion people without access to all-weather roads (Estache 2010). Moreover, demand varies by income level with the greatest need in developing countries. In 2017, 48.6 percent of the population accessed the internet globally, with only 15 percent from low-income countries and up to 82 percent from high-income countries doing so (World Bank 2018). Similarly, residents of low-income countries had 57 mobile phones per 100 residents, compared to 125 mobile phones per 100 in high-income countries. In 2014, 23 percent of the population lived in urban slums (United Nations 2019). Even in localities that had some level of coverage for these services, quality can vary greatly between and within cities.

In addition to the demands of urbanization for infrastructure, policymakers must grapple with the crippling effects of natural disasters due to climate change, such as droughts and flooding, fires, and land shifts and landslides (Deshkar and Adane 2016). With most cities vulnerable to at least one type of natural disaster (United Nations 2018), the demands for resiliency and disaster relief increase. These demands call for the resilience of infrastructure and its ability to mitigate the impacts of natural disasters, as well as for the provision of infrastructure to facilitate recovery from natural disasters. The United Nations' adoption of the New Urban Agenda in 2016 promotes sustainable city growth. Based on a study of 40 medium-sized cities in Latin America and the Caribbean, investment needs in transportation; land use, planning, and zoning; sanitation and drainage; vulnerability to natural disasters and climate change; urban inequality; water; and solid waste management totaled US$21.4 billion (Bonilla and Zapparoli 2017). "Globally, the need for infrastructure investment is forecast to reach $94 trillion by 2040, and a further $3.5 trillion will be required to meet the United Nations' Sustainable Development Goals"

(Global Infrastructure Outlook 2017: 4). Ahmad et al. (2019) estimate the sustainable urban infrastructure financing gap to exceed US$1 trillion a year.

While central governments often carry the burden of scale investments such as water projects, electrical grids, and highways, increasingly they hold SNGs as co-participants in key projects or responsible for investments in their own projects. Expectations for SNG infrastructure provision, as well as the need for financing at that level, are greater when central governments impose on SNGs either an unfunded infrastructure mandate or a requirement to match central government funds. Delays or absence of financing at the subnational level can retard national efforts to stimulate economic development.

It is inefficient, and unlikely, that SNGs pay for these overwhelming investment needs with resources from their annual budgets. Despite nationalization efforts in some countries, empirical evidence supports that the use of private capital to finance infrastructure has positive efficiency, equity, and fiscal benefits (Estache 2010). One means for SNGs to finance capital is through borrowing from external sources. "The rationale for borrowing is not to obtain additional revenues, but rather to smooth out the difference between benefits/revenues coming in and expenditures going out" (Bahl and Bird 2018: 152). Subnational fiscal arrangements, local capacity, and creditworthiness may challenge SNGs' ability to manage capital finance (Bahl and Bird 2018; Bonilla and Zapparoli 2017). "The most essential element of a sound subnational borrowing program is thus a sound subnational fiscal structure in terms of adequate access to 'own revenues' backed by a well-designed and stable intergovernmental transfer system, with an institutional structure capable of dealing appropriately with any problems that might arise" (Bahl and Bird 2018: 152).

Contextual Framing of Subnational Borrowing

The development of financing opportunities for SNGs goes hand in hand with fiscal decentralization, and the approach to subnational debt needs to consider a country's existing arrangements and institutions of fiscal governance. The focus on fiscal decentralization and subnational borrowing fit within a broader debate of regional and local development, namely the inroads of financialized tools and solutions in delivering key governance tasks. There are opportunities and challenges to decentralized infrastructure provision and financing.

Fiscal Decentralization—Opportunities and Challenges

Fiscal decentralization refers to the allocation of powers to SNGs to make spending and financing decisions (Bahl and Bird 2018). According to the decentralization theorem advanced by Oates (1972), when the service provision area is commensurate with the geographic area—subject to externalities or production economy of scale issues—there are efficiency gains. As is true for other services, the theoretical justification for decentralizing infrastructure to SNGs is to match expenditures with local preferences and to leverage local knowledge of local conditions (Bahl and Bird 2018). Matching infrastructure users and payers and incorporating local knowledge may improve infrastructure provision through better project selection and implementation—selecting the appropriate scope and quality of product and better user support for operating and maintaining physical assets. When local government responds to local preferences, leverages local information, is accountable to local citizens, and is responsive to pressures of competing benchmark governments, local investment captures efficiency and democratic benefits. Aside from promising improvements in allocative efficiency, decentralized and thoughtfully designed infrastructure provision can reduce poverty, providing an equity benefit as well (Jalan and Vavallion 2002; Majuder 2012).

Similar to general service provision, there are challenges to achieving this theoretical ideal for subnational infrastructure provision and financing, as there are a number of threats to the optimality of infrastructure decentralization, including lack of responsiveness to local preferences, scale economies, coordination costs, externalities, limited local revenue generation, and local capacity to manage projects (Bahl and Bird 2018). A key to capturing efficiency benefits is that citizens can vote or otherwise voice their preferences, not subject to interest group capture or higher level political will. Another is that the project scale fits the jurisdiction's size and will, and that the local government can manage the coordination costs of standards and regulations imposed by higher level governments. Externalities of project benefits or costs to extra-jurisdictional neighbors reduce the allocative efficiency through either underspending or overspending. Policies of unbundling the components of infrastructure to multiple parts and providing proper management of externalities is an option to internalize the benefits and costs of capital financing.

The threats of revenue adequacy and local government capacity pertain more directly to the fiscal decentralization framework and the local government's ability and willingness to raise revenue. Just as the decentralization theorem supports the assignment of spending to the lowest level without externalities or economy of scale issues, it supports correspondence between those who bear the costs of paying revenues and those who decide revenues (Schroeder 2003), allowing for users to have full cost information to select quantity and quality of service or infrastructure. For infrastructure provision to be truly decentralized, local selection and implementation of projects needs the support of local revenue sources. Bahl and Bird (2018) stress the importance of local governments being able to raise revenues to meet their operating and capital-financing obligations.

Yet, in many countries, the lion's share of local revenues comes from transfers from higher level governments, and there is a vertical imbalance between SNGs' share of expenditures and revenues. For a sample of 18 countries, 2016 data show that the share of own-source revenues for local government and all SNGs are 11.5 percent and 17.8 percent respectively (IMF 2019). These own-source revenues are inadequate to cover subnational expenditure responsibilities. The mean vertical fiscal imbalance values, representing the ratio of own-source revenue to spending, are 44.6 percent and 4 percent for local and subnational governments, respectively. The property tax is the largest source of own-source taxes for SNGs; local governments raise 69.3 percent of the property tax and all SNGs raise 80.4 percent of the property tax. Despite its prominence, property tax revenues are underutilized in many countries (Blanco et al. 2016). Whereas they represent 2.2 percent of GDP in developed countries, they account for less than 0.7 percent of GDP in developing countries (Bahl and Martinez-Vazquez 2008). In a nutshell, poor regional and local government capacity—inability to raise revenue compounded by poor administrative capacity to plan, select, implement, monitor, and provide ongoing operations and maintenance of infrastructure—limits options for local infrastructure provision and financing.

Scant attention has been paid to the means of capital financing, with recent focus more on public-private partnerships (PPPs), privatization, concessions, and franchises and less on the underlying issues of local revenue mobilization (Bahl and Bird 2018). Furthermore, "nor has more than token attention been paid to ensuring that how projects are financed is consistent with reaching the presumed core objective of getting the right projects in the right places at the right time. Arguably, a key element in achieving this goal is to ensure that users should pay for what they get, to the extent that it is essential that they do so (that is, allowing for externalities) and feasible for them to do so (that is, allowing for distributional concerns)" (Bahl and Bird 2018: 143).

Whether the revenues come from user fees, local taxes, or intergovernmental transfers, local governments need the autonomy, incentive, and political will to raise revenue. As higher level governments continue adopting tax and expenditure restrictions; historical cultures of low tax effort and tax evasion at the national and local levels in a number of countries; political corruption; and inter-jurisdictional fiscal disparities that weaken local governments' revenues exist, it is critical to create incentives to improve SNG fiscal capacities. For efficient subnational infrastructure provision, local own-source revenue generation is a prerequisite. For the theoretical benefits of local infrastructure provision to hold, payments must derive directly from users through own-source revenues made up of taxes and fees. This requires that local governments have the autonomy to access tax bases and set tax rates, levy fees and charges, and have the capacity to administer the collection of these revenues.

Subnational Borrowing—A Means to Achieve the Fiscal Governance Task

Not only can certain infrastructure provision responsibilities be decentralized, so too can the options for financing infrastructure. It is worth differentiating the terms *revenue* and *finance*. Often they are confounded, as proceeds from debt transactions finance capital infrastructure. However, whereas revenues represent payments to the SNG from residents (own-source revenues) or from higher-level governments (transfer revenues) for the purpose of service and infrastructure provision, the proceeds from capital financing represent a debt and a repayment obligation of the jurisdiction. Capital financing is not a revenue-generation tool. It is merely a means to smooth payments over time to match beneficiaries and payers, consistent with the benefit and risk principles. *Capital financing* refers to raising capital to fund the upfront, lumpy, and expensive costs of capital and committing future cash flows, derived from current revenue, to the repayment of principal and interest.

Many borrowing options exist, ranging from loans from the central government to debt securities placed directly in capital markets, by an individual jurisdiction or via a pooled mechanism (Hildreth and Zorn 2005; Freire 2014). The latter offers the promise of efficiency enhancements over other borrowing arrangements for some SNGs. Before elaborating on subnational borrowing options, the advantages and disadvantages of them, and the institutional arrangements underlying them, consider first how urban governance literature frames SNG borrowing.

Urban Governance and Utilization of Financial Instruments

Reactions against a market orientation to the supply of financial resources for subnational borrowers can be strong and fraught with concern. How can cities be trusted to not become over-indebted? Do cities have the adequate fiscal autonomy to raise, as well as the capacity to manage, own-source revenue? Do city policymakers have adequate capacity to plan for infrastructure, know how to access the market, and manage debt repayment? What if the cities derive more financial autonomy vis-à-vis higher level governments? And, what if the idea of accessing markets and carrying long-term planning seems a daunting task? What if the issuance of debt via capital markets results in inequitable distribution of resources and undermines redistributive policies? What about concerns over who controls capital, who benefits and who loses?

The ability of local government to assist, collaborate with, and function like a competent participant alongside higher level governments and civil society came to define good local governance (Tendler 1997; Kersting et al. 2009). One of the key roles of governments is to facilitate the use, exchange, and distribution of resources within their jurisdictions: Markets offer a set of additional means to accomplish these roles. A concerned view of financialized governance framework states that a "path is characterized by the reduction of public subsidies and regulations, the aggressive promotion of real estate development, . . . and the privatization of previously public services" (Hackworth 2007: 16). A positive view of a financialized governance framework will argue that financialization at the local level entails "a complex process of governing urban problems through finance" (Ashton et al. 2016: 1396). While numerous studies have shown that under unregulated and unrestrained arrangements, the outcomes of financialized governance can be inequitable (Ashton et al. 2016; Anguelov et al. 2018), a more careful crafting of incentives and distributions of access to subnational services differentiate successful governments from the laggards. To be successful, therefore, city policymakers and residents must plan, obtain autonomy to participate and navigate options in the capital market, and have competence at the table when dealing with financial sector instruments and firms. Anguelov et al. (2018) refer to this as *governmentality*. Although criticized for undermining democratic urban governance and contributing to spatial and social inequities, a supportive perspective of financialized governance is that urban governance shapes local capital finance by selecting investments and assets for collateral, protecting income streams derived from those assets, and preserving public value in their services.

Citing the United States' experience as a harbinger of changes globally, Hackworth notes two fundamental shifts in the political economy of urban governance—an increase in the rights and responsibilities of local governments, and a retraction of federal finance for subnational social and infrastructure investments—that have resulted in the subsequent increased dependence of local governments on capital market debt finance (Hackworth

2007). Given similar patterns elsewhere, SNGs' reliance on capital markets for infrastructure financing continues to extend globally. This is consistent with the process known as *glocalization*, the simultaneous linkage of global resources to local infrastructure projects with the help of financial sector actors (Torrance 2008, 2009).

Local governance is not an entirely local affair, however, and access to financial markets means that arrangements engineered by external institutions and actors with no formal governing authority over local governments may create challenges for local government capacity to balance the provision of goods and services with collective consumption. Even with constitutions and laws that permit fiscal and financial autonomy to local governments, management of city autonomy can increasingly become constrained by institutions of capital finance through financial contracts (Hackworth 2007). "Though less frequently cited in this regard, bond-rating firms, such as Moody's Investors Service and Standard and Poor's (S&P), are perhaps the single most influential institutional force in determining the quantity, quality, and geography of local investment in the developed world" (Hackworth 2007: 19; see also Gill 1995; Sassen 1996; Hewson and Sinclair 1999; Sinclair 1994a, 1994b, 1999). The increase in fiscal decentralization and devolution of responsibilities has increased the co-production between local governments and private capital. Several studies note an uneven development within and across cities as a consequence of capital's bipolar tension between expansion and exclusion (Plotkin 1987; Smith 1990; Hackworth 2007).

Credit-rating firms have had a growing influence in the allocation of capital since the Great Depression of the 1930s. In the US, this is due to limited federal maintenance of local governments, institutional constraints that public funds be invested at investment grade, the late 20th-century disintermediation shift from investment banking to direct investment (i.e., a shift from relationship-based to market-based credit), changes in tax laws, and the lack of federal guarantee of subnational debt (Sbragia 1996; Hackworth 2007). The US case demonstrates that market powers derive from public policy (Sbragia 1996). Credit-rating agencies are thought to have become the default providers of information to investors, as well as the unofficial gatekeepers of the allocation of capital. With credit-rating agencies providing information to investors, cities' connection with capital markets is increasingly determined by market-oriented standards (Hackworth 2007). Arguably, the standards are onerous and limit the city's choice set; the standards steer local governments toward entrepreneurial activity that is economically efficient, business-friendly, and anti-deficit (Hackworth 2007), and markets exercise discipline on those that stray from standards.

The key role of the credit-rating agencies, however, is to bridge the information asymmetry gap between borrowers and investors and transcend country boundaries. Given the influence that credit-rating agencies have on SNGs' access to capital, and the potentially damaging effects to efficiency and equity of not heeding that power, it is critical for local policymakers to increase their competence to make deliberate choices about financing options. While the view in Hackworth (2007) may certainly be true for some cities, other research shows that cities can and do gain benefits in the capital market (Ashton et al. 2016). Freire (2014) argues that management of external resources, of which capital financing is a component, is rapidly improving in a number of countries, with fiscal institutions ensuring discipline among both local governments and financial sector firms.

Capital-Financing Options

Ensuring SNGs' access to capital markets broadens their range of financing options and increases the overall efficiency in the distribution of capital. Ideally, capital-financing options match SNG borrowers with the debt instrument that offers affordable rates and maturities whose terms match the life of the capital project (Leigland 1997; Bahl and Bird 2018). A variety of public and private sector borrowing arrangements and debt instruments exist, each with their own benefits and costs. On one end of the spectrum, SNGs may be able to access non-market financing (Noel 2000). This includes direct capital expenditures, loans, and grants arranged through a higher level government, typically the central government or a state-owned capital-financing authority. On another end of the spectrum, SNGs may be able to access competitive market-based financing instruments, arm's-length debt by private actors through markets, including loans from commercial banks and bonds or securities from individual or institutional investors. Between these two options rests relations-based financing, such as that provided by financial firms, including development banks and revolving funds.

As Freire and Petersen (2004: xxxiv) explain:

> There are strong twin traditions of curtailing SNG access to private credit markets and of meeting capital needs through national government grants and concessionary lending programs. The long-term loan capital available for these programs typically is provided by multilateral and bilateral donor organizations through on-lending programs administered by central government agencies and guaranteed by the sovereign. While such competition makes private market development

more costly and difficult, SNGs will need to find a route if they are to meet large and growing needs for capital and to lessen obvious dependencies.

If capital markets offer the promise of increased access to capital at reasonable borrowing rates, then SNGs need to consider them as a potential capital-financing option. Doing so would be in line with the fiscal governance task at the local level and would help with meeting the demand for infrastructure, despite the growing pains associated with the need to keep track of innovations in financial instruments.

However, Noel (2000: 1) writes that "in many developing and transition countries, there is a pending development clash between the rapidly increasing investment financing needs of sub-national entities and the limited development of the domestic sub-national debt market." At that time, there were "practically no examples of competitive market structures among major developing and transition countries" (Noel 2000: 5). By 2018, a number of cities including Paris, Kyiv, Medellín, St. Petersburg, and Toronto had accessed capital markets; however despite sporadic growth in SNG capital markets since 2000, they remain underused. Many SNGs across the globe, particularly in developing countries, rely on subsidized financing from the central government (Public-Private Infrastructure Advisory Facility 2013). This fact may be puzzling given the theoretically expected benefits of capital markets that, beyond efficiency gains, promise broader access to capital at lower borrowing rates.

The cost advantages of different bond structures are well established. Competitive bids typically perform better than negotiated deals (Joehnk and Kidwell 1980; Braswell et al. 1983; Bland 1985; Reid 1990; Simonsen and Robbins 1996; Simonsen et al. 2001; Robbins and Simonsen 2007; Guzman and Moldogaziev 2012). Private placement, under certain conditions, can offer lower arbitrage yields and issuance costs relative to competitive and negotiated borrowing (Moldogaziev et al. 2019). General obligation debt has lower interest costs than revenue debt, all else equal (Granof 1984; Gamkhar and Koerner 2002). And, debt used for less risky purposes faces lower costs (Guzman and Moldogaziev 2012). Although smaller jurisdictions pay an interest cost and transaction cost premium when issuing debt (Simonsen et al. 2001; Robbins and Simonsen 2013), pooling arrangements can offer advantages by combining risk and reducing administrative and transaction costs (Zorn and Towfighi 1986; Robbins and Simonsen 2013). Bond banks and state revolving funds can have interest cost advantages for small, low-rated, inexperienced borrowers, and for those issuing revenue bonds (Cole and Millar 1982; Kidwell and Rogowski 1983; Reid 1990; Johnson 1995).

The use of SNG debt is uneven across countries, with more use in federal countries and in higher income countries. The debt is made up of predominantly bank loans (OECD/UCLG 2019). SNG debt, including debt at both the regional and local levels for both general-purpose government and for public and quasi-public entities, accounts for an average of 8 percent of GDP, representing almost 12 percent of total public debt. The distribution is uneven across countries, ranging from near 0 in many countries to about 67 percent of GDP in Canada. SNGs in federal countries incur more debt, about 18 percent of GDP, than those in unitary countries, with almost 5 percent of GDP. In general, SNGs in OECD countries incur more debt, roughly 29 percent of GDP, than non-OECD countries, which is a little over 7 percent of GDP.

Eleven countries for which United Cities and Local Governments reports disaggregated data indicate variation in subnational debt issuance by level of government (OECD/UCLG 2016). South Africa, for example, only allows subnational debt at the local level; and for some countries, like Australia, Belgium, Spain, and Germany, regional governments or authorities issue almost all the subnational debt. Debt levels are low among SNGs that are subject to fiscal and debt rules. In general, local governments hold lower outstanding debt levels than regional governments; 27 local governments have debt less than 1.5 percent of GDP. Some prominent exceptions stand out, with Japan's local government outstanding debt at almost 4 percent of GDP.

Levels of SNG debt relate to GDP, indicating that wealth or the institutions underlying wealth support the conditions for debt issuance. Subnational debt is made up of, on average, 57 percent loans, 12 percent debt securities, and 31 percent other types of obligations; although SNGs in federal countries incur more debt securities, 27 percent, than those in unitary countries, 8 percent (OECD/UCLG 2016). As with SNG debt levels, debt composition varies greatly within and between localities in many countries.

Potential Problems with SNG Borrowing

There is just cause for concern about SNG borrowing as inefficient debt levels, soft budget constraints, and poor fiscal controls and administrative capacity can undermine not only the subnational jurisdiction's efforts to provide services and infrastructure but also have detrimental outcomes for the country's macroeconomic stability. These concerns dampen support for capital market borrowing, as risk spillovers could result in financial contagion. On the one hand, over-indebtedness, or political gaming, can result in moral hazard behavior, with the SNG not making full and timely debt payments. An SNG that borrows more than its revenue base allows, as well as political will that affects the risk of repayment, impose negative externalities on the central government by straining macroeconomic balance and by imposing an implicit (if not explicit) contingent liability on the central government (Prud'homme 1995; Tanzi 1995, 1996). Additionally, SNG default penalizes other jurisdictions when the central government diverts its resources to bailout the defaulting jurisdiction. Under-indebtedness, on the other hand, can result in the opportunity costs of foregone infrastructure investments; missed opportunity for economic development; and increased reliance of the local government on the central government for service and infrastructure provision, leading to poor incentives for own-source revenue collection effort.

Problems of poor SNG capacity exacerbate the problems of information resolution, especially when SNGs take adverse actions to undermine, or fail to develop, their own credit quality. However, this problem also poses an opportunity for local governments. Local government officials cannot control the constraints imposed by the external environment, but they can decide how to manage their governance tasks within those constraints. The market emphasis on credit quality provides a map for local government capital-financing choices.

Fundamental Governance Institutions of SNG Borrowing

Both broad institutional structures and local market features influence the depth of capital financing at the subnational level (Halbert and Attuyer 2016; Weingast 2014). Successful SNG capital markets require investor demand to meet borrower supply (Leigland 1997). Investors want certainty in processes and rules, familiarity and confidence in legal norms, and the ability and freedom to trade and invest with acceptable return. Investors also require credit-quality information, information regarding risks, and assistance in interpreting information. Deeper markets have many investors and allow ease of investor entry and exit. Borrowers want acceptable borrowing costs, longer term maturities spanning the useful life of infrastructure, and formal assistance schemes when access to capital financing becomes costly. Institutional arrangements shape the opportunities and constraints for SNGs to meet the demands of capital markets (Leigland and Thomas 1999; Noel 2000; Attinasi and Brugnoli 2001; Freire and Petersen 2004; Martell and Guess 2006; Canuto and Liu 2013; Bahl and Bird 2018). SNG capital markets depend on institutional arrangements (Noel 2000; Freire and Petersen 2004; Moldogaziev et al.

2018), the most studied aspects of which pertain to the economic, financial and market, political, and legal institutional contexts.

> Countries differ . . . in the role that SNGs have in financial markets and in the nature of their financial markets. Whatever the goals of greater autonomy and capacity at the subnational level, SNGs vary greatly in political power and decision-making authority, in part reflecting differences among unitary states, hierarchical federal states, and governance systems that recognize separate spheres for each level. These differences are embedded in constitutions and legal systems that condition the degree to which SNGs are free to act and to control the resources with which to act. (Freire and Petersen 2004: 2)

An important factor is the economic context, which refers to the ability of the SNG environment to support prudent economic policies to maintain macroeconomic stability and the economic base (Freire and Petersen 2004). The stability of a country's economy is the bedrock of SNGs for capital markets to develop (Laeven 2014). At the country level, institutional context also refers to policies, fiscal management, and fiscal controls that keep inflation, interest rates, and unemployment low; direct a healthy economy through the careful balance of spending with revenue generation; fuel private sector investment; and control sovereign borrowing (Laeven 2014). Not only do economic institutions affect SNG borrowing by providing environments with sufficient economic activity, but the converse also holds, and subnational credit risks may impact economic stability (Canuto and Liu 2010, 2013). While, in theory, decentralized fiscal arrangements should bring about subnational behavior to maintain macroeconomic stability, if poorly designed, decentralization can undermine it (Freire and Petersen 2004). "Decentralization of a large share of public expenditures, even when SNGs are constrained by taxation and borrowing limits, can adversely affect [a country's] aggregate demand and international competitiveness, undermining national stabilization policy" (Freire and Petersen 2004: 17). In short, stronger economic contexts allow greater access to external capital finance and with that increased market scrutiny and discipline (de Mello 2005).

The financial and market context refers to the parameters that support and constrain market actors. The financial component of this dimension captures the intergovernmental fiscal design; structure for SNG autonomy to raise revenue, spend, and borrow; and policies governing the fiscal health of local governments. Included are fiscal regulations, such as ex ante constraints on borrowing and sanctions for noncompliance or ex post administrative or judicial sanctioning processes, that limit subnational fiscal or debt activities in an effort to maintain fiscal discipline. Fiscal rules include limits on revenue generation, expenditures, or debt indicators and activities. For example, a SNG may be restricted from spending more than a certain share of all expenditures on personnel, may not alter a centrally decided tax rate, or may not issue more than a certain amount of debt per revenue. Policies and laws, which came into vogue starting in the early 2000s, such as a law of fiscal responsibility or law of fiscal discipline, express these rules (Webb 2004). One commonly adopted rule, known as the golden rule, limits long-term debt issuance to long-term investment purposes. The financial dimension includes allowances and prohibitions on SNG use of revenue streams for repayment. Fiscal rules contribute to the environment of hard budget constraints (Rodden et al. 2003; Inman 2003; Oates 2005) and are seen as the antidote to moral hazard behavior. Ultimately, the financial dimension captures how SNGs perform, given the fiscal framework, with measures of local government fiscal health and debt management.

The financial and market context also refers to the arrangements that govern access to and pricing of capital, including practices that encourage or discourage the development and use of capital markets by private sector firms. In the narrower public sector sense, it pertains to subnational borrowing arrangements. It includes the rights and restrictions on investor entry to and exit from SNG capital markets; the existence and quality of buying and selling platforms; processes for risk evaluation and monitoring; processes for acquiring debt; range of allowable debt instruments; frameworks for debt issuance and conduct, clearing and settlement processes; and parameters of trading platforms (Leigland 1997; Kehew et al. 2005; Leaven 2014). Additionally, this component refers to policies on investor protection and information management, including reporting and disclosure protocols (Canuto and Liu 2010), as well as the extent that investment professionals (i.e., risk evaluators, municipal advisors, and in-house experts in capital market debt finance) support SNG borrowing.

The political context refers to the strength of government and its ability to respond in a fair and impartial manner to the diverse needs of the citizenry. Based in good governance and management, this dimension captures the stability, accountability, and effectiveness of the governance system. Political ideology and political cycles impact fiscal conditions and debt issuance decisions (Roubini and Sachs 1989; Borrelli and Royed 1995; Blais et al. 1993; Seitz 2000; Alesina et al. 1993; Schneider 2006; Benton and Smith 2017), as well as investor's perception of risk and return. The political dimension also captures willingness to support SNGs via established channels of capital financing or willingness to bailout SNGs in cases of financial distress.

The legal context refers to the rules and regulations that govern public and private concerns with an emphasis on the degree that law facilitates or retards market transactions (Awadzi 2015). Legal institutions, grounded in legal origin, set the parameters for borrowing (Canuto and Liu 2010; La Porta et al. 1997). The rules govern and adjudicate who may borrow or lend. This dimension also addresses whether there are laws to govern default proceedings and whether they are thorough, clear, and consistent. Importantly, it captures the degree of enforcement. Lack of enforcement undermines investor confidence and incentives for credit provision. The disregard of rules or inconsistent application of them, the extreme case being public sector corruption, creates uncertainty for markets and negatively impacts SNG borrowing (Butler et al. 2009; Depken and LaFountain 2006; Moldogaziev et al. 2017; Liu et al. 2017).

Role of Information and Research Agenda

Previous research offers considerable evidence that the institutions of fiscal governance are required for economic development, public investment, and administrative and fiscal performance of governments (Ter-Minassian 1997; de Mello and Barenstein 2001; Ahmad et al. 2005; Sellers and Lindstrom 2007; North et al. 2008; Faguet 2008; Morrissey and Udomkerdmongkol 2012; Bertelli 2012; Harbers 2015; Grindle 2004). Institutional arrangements, such as hard budget constraints, revenue floors and ceilings, or mismatches between administrative and fiscal responsibilities, bear on the success of decentralized governance (Rodden et al. 2003). Capital markets recognize the benefits and costs of fiscal institutions and reflect them in prices, rewarding discipline and penalizing inflexibility. However, the literature does not explicitly consider how the system's information resolution institutions impact capital market formation and maturation.

Thus, despite the known institutional dimensions affecting SNG access to capital markets, there remains the concern that they overlook an important, underdeveloped, institutional element: information resolution. Pulsing though discussions of institutional context, but not explicitly brought to light, is the ability of the system to resolve information problems. Conditional on institutional contexts articulated in this chapter and borrowing from the literature on capital markets in the private sector (Akerlof 1970; Stiglitz and Weiss 1981; Diamond 1984, 1991; Ramakrishnan and Thakor 1984; Leland and Pyle 1977; Bertomeu and Marinovic 2016; Liberti and Petersen 2017), the information resolution institutions are critical for market development and infrastructure finance. It serves to reduce the costs associated with information asymmetries, thereby providing investors with better opportunities to assess risk accurately and SNGs with a wider range of capital-financing options, often at a lower rate.

The SNG borrowing literature is then incomplete, but a turn in emphasis toward information broadens the scope of theoretical and policy import. Whereas the institutional contexts refer to the SNG borrower's external environment, the emphasis on information expands the focus to include the mechanisms that subnational borrowers may utilize. By placing SNGs in the middle of the dual processes of *glocalization* and fiscal decentralization, it is clear that they must navigate a two-pronged set of constraints: those imposed by national institutional contexts and those imposed by global financial players. Furthermore, as credit ratings, issued by credit-rating firms, have become the key channel of access to, or exclusion from, SNG capital markets, it serves to understand better their role in information certification and monitoring.

The relevant question at the national level is: How do informational institutions, made up of transparency and depth of information, extent of disclosure, and regulatory quality, influence SNG borrowing? The relevant questions at the local level, with a focus on cities, are: What can city policymakers do within institutional contexts to gain access to capital finance? How can city policymakers capitalize on or navigate within their institutional constraints to secure capital financing? How can city policymakers utilize the resources of the capital market to their advantage? The following chapters explore these issues.

4
System-Level Information Resolution and Contractibility

This chapter advances the book's argument that information resolution is critical for SNG capital markets by focusing on system-level, or nationwide, information resolution institutions and how they bear upon the activity and size of SNG capital markets. Based on this argument, and the theoretical underpinnings developed in Chapter 2, this chapter presents and tests hypotheses about how contractibility impacts SNG debt.

We posit that conditional on economic, financial and market, political, and legal institutions, the institutions of information resolution—transparency and depth of credit information, extent of disclosure, and regulatory quality—which ensure contractibility, must be an explicit focus of SNG capital market research. Institutions of information resolution are important for capital markets, including SNG access to capital markets, and affect directly whether and how credit is allocated in the system.

The next section reviews the literature as it pertains to economic studies of information on borrowing outcomes. The chapter then formalizes research questions and introduces the empirical data. It is followed by descriptive data about SNG debt and information capacity. We then summarize the methodological approach and analyze the relationships between information resolution institutions and SNG borrowing. The final section translates our empirical findings into policy relevant recommendations.

Economic Studies of Information Resolution and Debt Financing

The literature identifies a number of institutional covariates of SNG debt, including economic, financial and market, political, and legal institutions that are critical for understanding SNG capital market development; however, in and of themselves, they are inadequate as they fail to explain fully the growth of SNG debt and its composition among different sources of capital. Despite robust theoretical reasoning and empirical evidence to account for

Information Resolution and Subnational Capital Markets. Christine R. Martell, Tima T. Moldogaziev, and Salvador Espinosa, Oxford University Press. © Oxford University Press 2021. DOI: 10.1093/oso/9780190089337.003.0004

the impacts of information on private sector capital markets, research on SNG capital markets is deficient of this element. As the underlying principles of information economics are equally present in any capital market, evaluating the impact of information resolution institutions on SNG debt is useful for both theory building and practice. This section expands the argument established in economic studies from one that information affects debt outcomes in corporate capital markets to one where information affects debt outcomes in SNG capital markets. It is reasonable to expect that national credit systems determine the environment of market participants with comparable institutions for information resolution, whether the investments are stocks, corporate bonds, or SNG debt instruments. Thus, while economic, financial and market, political, and legal institutions are necessary, information resolution in the system matters significantly for adopting, implementing, and managing a well-functioning SNG capital market.

Information institutions enable the financial system's ability to resolve information problems. It is consistent with contractibility, as introduced by Rajan and Zingales (1998), which refers to a system's ability to resolve information problems through transparency, disclosure, and regulatory accountability or quality. System- or national-level information resolution pertains to the transparency, disclosure, and regulatory quality in the broad financial environment. Transparency captures the concept that positive and negative information on credit-market participants are visible to not just internal actors but also to actors external to the firm, through the distribution of information to individuals and firms. Disclosure represents the timely and accurate provision of information, as well as its verifiability. Disclosure captures reporting requirements and mechanisms for information production and dissemination. It includes the disclosure of activities, including conflict of interest, between firms and investors and other relevant parties. Regulatory quality refers to the government's ability to advance policies and regulations that promote market accountability and predictability. Regulatory mechanisms include bankruptcy and contract laws, accounting standards, auditing standards, and property rights enforcement. Regulations guide the degree to which the financial system is open to competition by influencing the costs of entry and processes for violations and recourse. The regulatory quality determines the degree to which contracts are enforceable.

As explained in Chapter 2, information resolution institutions are intimately connected with types of borrowing systems (Rajan and Zingales 1998). Market-based borrowing relies on information transparency and disclosure and on regulations that ensure enforceable contracts between lenders and borrowers, as illustrated in the case of Bangladesh in Box 4.1. The presence of information institutions, represented by transparency, disclosure, and regulatory quality, in the financial system allows lenders to accurately assess the risk of an investment or the probability of return. Moreover, information resolution affects the type of debt, placement of debt, and capital structure, especially when the borrower's credit quality is low (Sharma and Knight 2016; Liberti and Petersen 2017; Kwan and Carleton 2010; Rajan and Zingales 1998; Rajan 1992; Dhaliwal et al 2011; Kale and Meneghetti 2011; Yosha 1995; Krishnaswami et al. 1999; Leland and Pyle 1977; Ross 1977; Heinkel 1982; Harris and Raviv 1990; Diamond 1991; Cantillo and Wright 2000; Rauh and Sufi 2010). Although in practice the concepts of transparency, disclosure, and regulatory quality are not necessarily unrelated or mutually exclusive, it is useful to examine each concept separately.

Box 4.1 Bangladesh's Contractibility

Bangladesh does not presently meet the conditions for SNG bond issuance, but it is concerned with improving the regulatory environment for its corporate bond market (GuarantCo 2019). Issuers note high transaction costs due to regulatory compliance. Experts identified the weak market and regulatory environment as impediment to corporations raising funds through bond capital markets. "An absence of a centralised database management system hinders issuers and investors from accessing authentic information. As a result, lack of information prevents issuers and investors from entering into the bond market. Privately placed bonds are traded over the phone by the companies. Such old-fashioned trading techniques bring in transparency issues in the bond market" (GurantCo 2019: 55). Among other recommendations, experts encourage Bangladesh to streamline "the information sharing process to ensure access is transparent and information is authentic" on the basis that "investors require detailed, authentic and transparent information about the companies issuing bonds before investing into them. However, there is a poor system of disclosure of accounting information to the public. A central database with such information is missing in the country and different sources represent different data points. The government needs to ensure formulation and strict implementation of policies regarding the disclosure of such information to enable investors to make quick, informed decisions regarding investment in bonds" (GuartCo 2019: 73). Such efforts would improve Bangladesh's system contractibility and begin the development of a capital market with arm's length transactions.

Transparency

Without a doubt, the transparency of information affects markets, including municipal bond markets (Stiglitz 1977a, 1977b; Downing and Zhang 2004; Harris and Piwowar 2006; Green et al. 2010; Sharma and Knight 2016). Capital markets in non-transparent environments result in price distortions and segmented investors (Grossman and Stiglitz 1980; Green et al. 2010). Transparency also impacts capital structure (Easterwood and Kadapakkam 1991; Melnik and Plaut 1995; Krishnaswami et al. 1999). Melnik and Plaut (1995) attribute the expansion of privately placed debt to information asymmetries. To do so, they model type of debt as a decision to minimize borrowing costs, where market segmentation equilibrates based on competing costs. At the same time, the choice of debt placement is a function of the costs of information asymmetries relative to the costs of regulatory compliance. Krishnaswami et al. (1999) echo these findings; they find an association between firms with higher contracting costs due to moral hazard issues and higher proportions of private debt. They also find that firms that operate under conditions of information asymmetry, even when they have favorable information on future profitability, disproportionately use private debt. When information asymmetries obscure the transparency of how firms enter and exit capital markets, the firm's lender selection becomes more distinct: Large firms with cash and collateral are likely to use credit markets over direct bank financing. By applying these findings to SNG capital markets, we expect that SNGs are more likely to have a broader array of financing options and to make greater use of capital market debt when there is greater transparency in the credit environment.

Disclosure

In addition to the influence of transparency on the information environment and capital structure, disclosure policy has its own role. Early research demonstrated that low disclosure relates negatively to a firm's information environment (Lang and Lundolm 1996; Bamber and Cheon 1998). Environments rich in information disclosure enhance market efficiency, particularly when technologies mitigate the limitations of geographic space (O'Brien 1992). Disclosure lessens information asymmetries and future risk, thus improving market liquidity (Diamond and Verrecchia 1991). It is no surprise, then, that disclosure policy is an important factor contributing to capital volume and structure (Yosha 1995; Melnik and Plaut 1995; Dhaliwal et al. 2011). By analogy to SNG capital markets, SNGs in greater disclosure contexts are more likely to use capital market debt.

Regulatory Quality

Keeping at the fore the importance of the information environment on capital structure, regulatory quality impacts the debt placement of firms (Melnik and Plaut 1995; Krishnaswami et al. 1999). Regulatory quality refers to the value that market actors get from regulatory structures. While regulation can improve the information environment, it does so at a cost. When the advantage of an improved information environment outweighs the additional costs, regulatory structures can foster market growth. However, when the costs of regulation exceed the information benefits, regulatory structures can impede capital market growth and drive borrowers to options that limit the costs of regulatory compliance (Krishnaswami et al. 1999). Privately placed debt is subject to less regulation than public debt, allowing borrowers to lower their regulatory costs, but at the expense of information asymmetry. These regulatory costs, as well as borrowers' responses to them, result in the segmentation between public and private placements and a higher default rate due to the information asymmetries associated with privately placed debt (Melnik and Plaut 1995). In application to SNG capital markets, as regulatory policy works to improve information relative to the cost, the greater the likelihood of SNGs to use capital market debt.

Economic Institutions

While the three facets of information resolution are critical to contractibility, subnational capital markets require other key governance institutions as well. First are economic institutions, which attend to the economic base and prudent economic policies of the base. At the macroeconomic level, institutional capacity requires the sovereign to direct a healthy economy and achieve macro stability through fiscal management and control (Laeven 2014). At this level, there is a positive relationship between inflation and public domestic debt risk (Mehl and Reynaud 2010). Macroeconomic policies are important, for with stability comes access to external capital finance, and with that increased market scrutiny and improved fiscal discipline (de Mello 2005). Also, economic size, entrepreneurial and investment base, and soundness of economic policy bear upon public debt risk (Mehl and Reynaud 2010). Macroeconomic policies and subnational credit are intertwined, as the former allow SNGs to operate in environments with sufficient economic activity; and subnational credit risks relate to macroeconomic stability and institutional reforms (Canuto and Liu 2010, 2013).

Financial and Market Institutions

The financial management and market institutions broadly refer to market governance, such as policies on investor protection, risk assessment, and information management that affect the financial market's breadth and depth. The institutional capacities for financial management and market governance also include the organizational and structural features of credit markets. Governance policies define legal rights; the parameters on investments, instruments, frameworks for debt issuance and conduct, monitoring and reporting protocols, clearing and settlement processes; and parameters of trading platforms and settlement systems for primary and secondary capital markets (Kehew et al. 2005; Laeven 2014; Gorelick 2018).

Political Institutions

The political institutions refer to government stability, political accountability, and government effectiveness. Research shows that weaker governments and fragmented political power increase fiscal imbalances at all levels of government (Roubini and Sachs 1989). Furthermore, political ideology and political cycles impact fiscal conditions, though comparative empirical evidence is mixed (Roubini et al. 1989; Borrelli and Royed 1995; Blais et al. 1993; Seitz 2000; Alesina et al. 1993; Schneider 2006). However, Saez (2016) and Benton and Smith (2019) empirically support that politics and electoral cycles shape the allocation of capital resources at the local level in India's regions and among Mexico's municipalities, respectively.

Legal Institutions

The last fundamental institution, in practical terms highly related to political and financial and market institutions, is the legal one. This is based on legal rules and norms that govern capital financing both in private and public sectors, including the degree to which the rule of law facilitates transactions

(Awadzi 2015). Legal origins are also important for setting the parameters for financial transactions, as well as the roles that the public sector plays in access to credit and its distribution (LaPorta et al. 2008). The legal institutions set the parameters for borrowing, including the enforcement of those parameters and the types of SNGs that are allowed or prohibited to utilize the borrowing function (Freire 2013; de Mello 2001; Webb 2004; Aldasaro and Seiferling 2014; de Mello and Barenstein 2001; Bird and Smart 2002; Lewis 2003; Ahmad et al. 2005). Finally, the legal dimension determines the extent to which the rules are enforced and upheld. Blatant disregard of rules or their excessive fluidity, in the extreme resulting in corruption, have a direct impact on SNG borrowing (Butler et al. 2009; Depken and LaFountain 2006; Moldogaziev et al. 2017; Liu et al. 2017).

Building on the existing literature (Akerlof 1970; Stiglitz and Weiss 1981; Diamond 1984; Ramakrishnan and Thakor 1984; Leland and Pyle 1977; Bertomeu and Marinovic 2016; Liberti and Petersen 2017) we posit that, conditional on fundamental governance institutions, information resolution institutions are critical for market development and are especially valuable for infrastructure finance in their role of reducing the costs associated with information asymmetries. When information costs are reduced, the speed and scale of financial transactions increase, thereby reducing geographic boundaries and improving capital flow (O'Brien 1992). The value of information resolution is even greater for the growth in infrastructure, as this asset class is characterized as having "persistent, localized, and opaque characteristics . . . which make the information dense" (Sharma and Knight 2016: 2). Under weak information resolution mechanisms, the liquidity of securities for infrastructure decreases and may result in multiple equilibriums involving informed versus uninformed investors (Green et al. 2007).

Information is important not just for private sector capital markets—it is also significant for capital in the public sector. It holds that, within the same national system, the supply and demand dynamics for capital are conditional on the same institutions of governance. The explicit extension and expectation is that market-based transactions of capital between lenders and borrowers, both in private and public sectors, are exchanges between parties that rely on the same set of institutions of information resolution. Therefore, a system's capacity to resolve information asymmetry is critical to the enhancement of SNG credit contractibility and is paramount for SNG access to capital markets as well.

While the pertinent literature discusses a range of institutional prerequisites and conditions for SNG capital market development, it is often based on single country or single region studies and fails to systematically develop and test hypotheses across countries. This is somewhat problematic as these studies--while rich in detail and informative about individual markets--neglect to account for variations in national institutional contexts and their impact on fiscal governance outcomes. A more comprehensive analytical approach would help when evaluating whether public policy practices and public finance theories are portable to dissimilar institutional environments.

Inquiry and Data

A number of relevant questions have not been addressed in the existing literature: What is the activity and size of SNG capital market debt around the world? What do we know about how national institutional contexts impact SNG capital markets? Does information resolution matter, and how does it matter? Several hypotheses can be formulated at this point: SNG capital market activity is greater when the system-level information resolution—made up of transparency and depth of credit information, extent of disclosure, and regulatory quality—is greater. This chapter addresses these questions and empirically tests the hypotheses by examining SNG capital market debt.

The following descriptive statistics derive primarily from unbalanced panel data from 52 countries, for the years 2007–2014, unless otherwise noted. The data draw from all countries that authorize and have activity in SNG—whether regional, local, or both—capital markets.[1] Of the 126 countries in the world that allow some form of SNG debt, only 52 have recorded levels of SNG debt during the study period. In some countries, such as Argentina or India, SNG debt originates at the regional (provincial) level. In other countries, such as Bulgaria or Colombia, SNG debt originates at the local (municipal) level. Yet in other countries, such as Austria or Mexico, SNG debt originates at both the regional and local levels. Figure 4.1 shows the levels of aggregate SNG debt around the world in 2014, while Table 4.1 delineates these countries by the level of government where debt originated in 2014. Data from these countries allow for some observations about the important relationships between informational resolution and SNG debt.

---

[1] The Technical Appendix describes the data measurement and processing and shows the results of regression analyses.

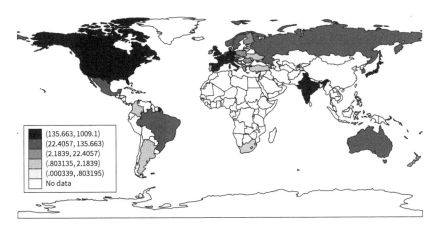

Figure 4.1 Distribution of aggregate SNG debt by country in USD billions in 2014

Note: Color intensity for shaded areas corresponds to greater levels of aggregate SNG borrowing. Blank areas represent absence of borrowing activity or omitted cases.

Table 4.1 Countries and level of government for subnational debt origination, 2014

Countries with SNG debt originating from regional or provincial level	Countries with SNG debt originating from local or municipal level		Countries with SNG debt originating from regional or provincial and local or municipal levels
Argentina, ARG*	Bulgaria, BGR	Lithuania, LTU	Australia, AUS*
India, IND*	Colombia, COL	N. Macedonia, MKD	Austria, AUT*
Mexico, MEX*	Costa Rica, CRI	The Netherlands, NLD	Belgium, BEL*
Uruguay, URY	Croatia, HRV	New Zealand, NZL	Bolivia, BOL
	Cyprus, CYP	Norway, NOR	Brazil, BRA*
	Czechia, CZE	Poland, POL	Canada, CAN*
	Denmark, DNK	Portugal, PRT	Germany, DEU*
	El Salvador, SLV	Romania, ROM	Japan, JPN
	Estonia, EST	Serbia, SRB	Peru, PER
	Finland, FIN	Slovakia, SVK	The Philippines, PHL
	France, FRA	Slovenia, SVN	Russian Federation, RUS*
	Greece, GRC	South Africa, ZAF	South Korea, KOR
	Hungary, HUN	Sweden, SWE	Spain, ESP
	Ireland, IRL	Thailand, THA	Switzerland, CHE
	Italy, ITA	Turkey, TUR	Ukraine, UKR
	Latvia, LVA	The UK, GBR	United States, USA*

Note: * denotes federal countries.

Table 4.2 Descriptive statistics, unbalanced country-year panel, $N = 377$, 2007–2014

Variables	Mean	Std. Dev.	Min	Max
Aggregate SNG debt size, USD bln	97.41	213.72	0.00	1036.06
Aggregate SNG debt per capita, USD thou	2282.52	3884.83	0.01	22943.07
Aggregate SNG debt as % GDP	5.60	7.43	0.00	45.67
Information institutions index	0.57	0.51	−1.13	1.53
Transparency and depth of credit info	4.67	1.48	0.00	6.00
Extent of disclosure	5.98	2.73	0.00	10.00
Regulatory quality	0.83	0.73	−1.08	1.97
Economic institutions	0.85	0.80	−0.99	2.74
GDP	1.1E+12	2.37E+12	6.86E+09	1.74E+13
GNI	1.1E+12	2.41E+12	6.83E+09	1.78E+13
GS	2.27E+11	4.09E+11	1.47E+09	2.95E+12
GNE	1.06E+12	2.31E+12	8.03E+09	1.73E+13
Financial and market institutions	0.38	0.71	−1.39	2.38
Investor legal rights	6.35	2.19	0.00	10.00
Investor protections	5.73	1.49	2.70	9.70
Ease of investor suits	6.41	1.67	2.00	10.00
Political institutions	0.76	0.75	−0.78	2.01
Government effectiveness	0.81	0.78	−0.81	2.36
Political stability	0.34	0.77	−1.93	1.50
Voice and accountability	0.34	0.77	−1.93	1.50
Legal institutions	0.70	0.95	−1.00	2.29
Corruption control	0.67	0.99	−1.09	2.55
Rule of law	0.70	0.91	−1.14	2.12
Population density	124.38	127.47	2.69	517.35
Unemployment rate	8.77	5.88	0.70	36.00

SNG Capital Market Debt Size

SNG capital market debt includes all long-term capital market debt issued by subnational general-purpose governments. While the aggregated data obscure the nuances between regional- and local-level debt, the construct allows us to understand how the information environment affects SNG borrowing. The size of SNG capital market debt is measured in three ways. In each case, the data violate the assumption of normal distribution. Consequently, the following statistics include both raw and natural logarithmic values.

The first measure is the aggregate level of SNG debt in the country in billions of constant US dollars. For the sample period, the mean debt size in the sample of 52 countries is $97 billion, with a standard deviation of $200 billion. This distributional abnormality is largely due to the SNG capital markets of the United States, Germany, Japan, Canada, and recently Spain and is expected given the historic use of SNG borrowing in the five relatively well-established SNG debt markets. Over time, the amount of SNG capital market debt remained steady, averaging $95b per country in 1995 and $92b in 2015. At least three trends are clear, nevertheless. The number of new SNGs that have joined the market has grown and been driven by the dominant borrowing countries (USA, Germany, Japan, and Canada; with Spain coming to lead the remaining cluster of countries by 2015). Country-level details of legal origins, OECD membership as of 2014, levels of debt, and sources for SNG debt information are in Table A4.1 in the appendix to this chapter. In the aggregate, those countries have significantly increased their levels of SNG capital market debt.

When limiting discussion to the non-dominant borrowers or excluding the top-five SNG debt-issuing countries, as Figure 4.2 illustrates, since 1995 the number of issuing countries increased from about 10 countries to almost 50 countries. About a dozen of the relatively more developed countries—such as Italy, France, Switzerland, United Kingdom, and Brazil to name the leading issuers depicted in the figure—account for the increase in volume. The newcomers to the SNG market, those that experienced SNG debt market activity since late 2000s, have had positive, but negligible, levels of SNG capital market borrowing.

The second measure is SNG capital market debt per capita. The mean SNG debt per capita in the sample of 52 countries is $2,328, with a standard deviation of $3,992. In terms of per capita SNG debt levels, Canada and Germany continue to have larger SNG debt levels compared to other countries in the sample. Norway, Belgium, Switzerland, the Netherlands, and Spain are other countries that have been or are lately above the $5,000 per capita level. In terms of per capita SNG debt, the United States and Japan fall out of the cluster of dominant SNG debt-issuing countries. Figure 4.3 shows the distribution of SNG debt per capita, with the top-five countries excluded. In this cluster of countries, about a dozen countries such as Japan, Australia, Austria, and the Netherlands reached SNG per capita debt levels of $2,000 by 2015, the rest of the countries remained at relatively low levels of SNG debt, below $1,000 per capita.

The third measure is the aggregate SNG capital market debt as a percentage of GDP. This measure captures the size of the market relative to the economy. The mean SNG debt to GDP ratio is 7.6 percent, with a standard deviation of 11.2 percent. By 2015, Canada and Germany remain as countries with the

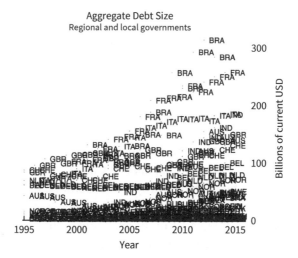

Figure 4.2 Aggregate SNG debt levels by country in USD billions in 1995–2015
Note: Dominant top-five countries excluded = Canada, Germany, Spain, Japan, and United States.

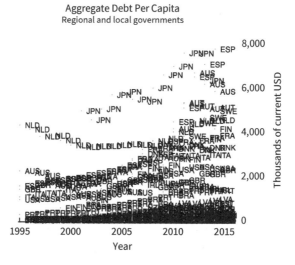

Figure 4.3 Aggregate SNG debt per capita levels by country in USD in 1995–2015
Note: Dominant top-five countries excluded = Canada, Germany, Switzerland, Norway, and Belgium.

largest SNG debt to GDP ratios, followed by Belgium, Switzerland, Norway, and Spain. This distribution is in line with SNG per capita debt figures. The vast majority of countries have SNG debt levels that remain fairly low with respect to the size of GDP, as Figure 4.4 shows.

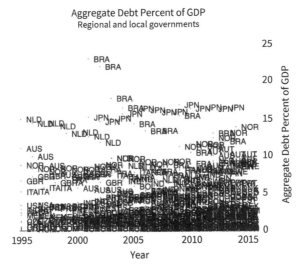

Figure 4.4 Aggregate SNG debt to GDP ratio by country in percentage points in 1995–2015
Note: Dominant top-five excluded countries = Canada, Germany, Switzerland, Spain, and Belgium.

Fundamental Institutions

The data show that SNG debt levels vary by country and, to date, the best predictors of these differences in the literature have been economic institutions, financial and market institutions, political institutions, and legal institutions. Details of institutional variables and their sources are in Table A4.2 in the appendix located at the end of the chapter. The first governance factor relates to economic institutions, which is measured by an index consisting of four widely accepted proxies of country level economic strength: gross domestic product (GDP), gross national income (GNI), gross savings (GS), and gross national expense (GNE), all in current USD. A positive value indicates a stronger economic capacity. For this sample, the mean value of the economic capacity index is approximately 0.85, with a standard deviation of 0.80, ranging from −0.99 to 2.74.[2]

---

[2] The factor indices constructed for the study are based on principal component factors for the items included in each index. There are **three reasons** why factor indices must be preferred. The first one has to do with the recognition that economic, financial and market, political, and legal institutions are multifaceted phenomena. Therefore, using multidimensional constructs is methodologically appropriate. The second one has to do with a need to capture each control factor as broadly as possible in order to accurately describe the associations of items within the construct of information institutions, as well as the overall construct of information institutions, with SNG debt market outcomes. Hence, the interest is in robust control measures and not unique coefficients for each item in the control constructs. The third reason relates to the fact that severe levels of multicollinearity are present when variables capturing different dimensions of the economic, financial and market, political, and legal institutions are included in the same regression models. When faced with multidimensionality of constructs, which by definition will be collinear, building indices from multiple items is the most appropriate statistical solution.

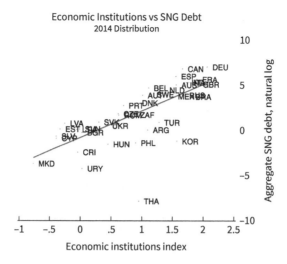

Figure 4.5 Economic institutions index vs. aggregate SNG debt levels, natural log transformation, in 2014

Figure 4.5 displays a positive relationship between the economic capacity index and SNG debt levels in 2014.

The second fundamental governance factor relates to financial and market institutions, which is measured as an index consisting of variables for investor protections in credit provision in each country—extent of investors' legal rights, strength of investor protections, and ease with which investors can file lawsuits to protect their capital. Investor-friendly market environments will be conducive toward capital markets, broadly speaking, including the SNG debt market activity and levels. Existing research utilized these measures in studies of private credit and debt enforcement, and access to credit, and banking crises around the world (Djankov et al. 2007; Djankov et al. 2008; Bae et al. 2009; Büyükkarabacak and Valev 2012; Giannetti and Jentzsch 2013). A positive value in the index indicates greater financial and market capacity. For this sample, the mean score is 0.38, with a standard deviation of 0.71 and a range from −1.39 to 2.38. The expectation is that the financial and market capacity index correlates with greater levels of SNG debt market borrowing, all else held constant. Figure 4.6 depicts the bivariate relationship between financial and market institutions and SNG debt levels in 2014.

The third fundamental governance factor relates to political institutions, operationalized as an index built using three items—levels of government effectiveness, political stability and violence, and citizens' voice and government accountability. The three items capture overall political climates in the countries under review (Kaufmann et al. 2007, 2010) and are a part of the

World Governance Indicators (WGI) project, an affiliate of the World Bank. Positive values indicate greater political capacity. The average level of political capacity index in the sample is 0.76, with a standard deviation of 0.75 and a range from −0.78 to 2.01. Favorable political capacities are expected to be conducive to SNG debt markets, all else held constant. Figure 4.7 shows the bivariate relationship between political institutions and SNG debt in 2014.

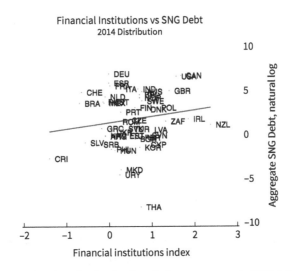

Figure 4.6 Financial and market institutions index vs. aggregate SNG debt levels, natural log transformation, in 2014

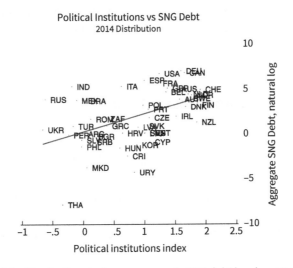

Figure 4.7 Political institutions index vs. aggregate SNG debt levels, natural log transformation, in 2014

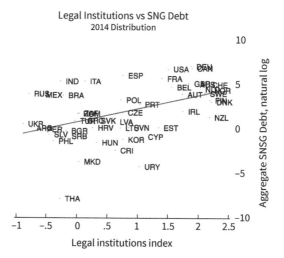

Figure 4.8 Legal institutions index vs. aggregate SNG debt levels, natural log transformation, in 2014

The last fundamental governance factor relates to legal institutions, estimated as an index made up of two variables measuring the rule of law and corruption control at the country level of analysis. The two items are also from the WGI project and are expected to proxy for legal climates in the countries in the sample. Positive values indicate greater legal capacity. The mean and standard deviation for legal capacity index are 0.70 and 0.95, respectively, while the range varies between −1.00 and 2.29. Conditions with favorable legal institutions are expected to positively relate to SNG debt market activity, as the 2014 bivariate distribution between these two measures in Figure 4.8 displays.

Information Resolution Institutions

The preceding bivariate statistics support existing knowledge that governance institutions affect SNG debt but do not exhaustively explain SNG capital market debt levels. Do those fundamental governance institutions account for all the variation? What is the role for information resolution institutions to bear upon SNG debt markets? To explore the relationships between information resolution and SNG debt, we operationalized a three-component information resolution index—consisting of transparency and depth of credit information, extent of disclosure, and regulatory quality. These components combined represent the strength of contractibility in the SNG capital market.

The first component of information resolution is "transparency and depth of credit information." This measure derives from an index constructed by the World Bank's "Doing Business" project.[3] It consists of eight subcomponents that measure multiple facets of credit information availability in the country: distribution of information on both individuals and firms; availability of both positive and negative information on credit-market participants; distribution of data from both retail and utility firms above and beyond financial institutions; the length of data storage for both good and bad credit performance information; data distribution on very small loans (less than 1 percent of per capita debt); availability of credit bureaus and registries and their cost; availability of multiple electronic access points to credit information; and, finally, availability of credit-scoring entities, be they public or private. The index varies from 0 to 8, with higher values in the index representing greater access to credit information. The mean level of the index in our sample is 4.67, with a standard deviation of 1.48.

The second component of information resolution is the extent of disclosure, which is also an index constructed by the "Doing Business" project. This measure evaluates country-level disclosure quality for private firms that obtain credit from investors. The index ranges from 0 to 10 and represents the capacity of the capital market system to regulate the conflict of interests within major private sector corporate firms. This component is important not only for accountability of financial intermediation between investors and firms but also between firms and government entities. The five facets of the "extent of disclosure" measure are variations in internal controls on management power to approve transactions within firms; variations in whether external actors have a say in internal firm transactions; disclosure transparency between firm management and the boards; requirements of immediate disclosure of firm transactions to relevant external parties; and requirements on annual activity disclosures, including conflict of interest disclosures of corporate management. The mean value of the "extent of disclosure" index in the sample is 5.98, with a standard deviation of 2.73.

The final component of information resolution is "regulatory quality." The multidimensional measure is developed by the WGI project. First applied in mid-1990s, this measure has remained in use ever since, after going through rounds of validation and fine-tuning. According to WGI's definition, the measure of "regulatory quality captures perceptions of the ability of the

---

[3] The "Doing Business" project aims at collecting measures on regulations that enhance or diminish private sector business activity, including regulations of private and corporate credit, in the countries around the world. More details about this project are available at http://www.doingbusiness.org.

government to formulate and implement sound policies and regulations that permit and promote private sector development."[4] This final component of information resolution in the capital market system captures the qualities of regulatory capacity that are necessary for resolving information asymmetry problems. Regulatory quality holds information resolution of the financial system together by bridging information provision and monitoring credit transactions of major firms in the financial system. Since "regulatory quality" is a standardized index, it ranges in our sample between −1.08 and 1.97, with a mean and standard deviation of 0.83 and 0.73, respectively.

Using a principal-component approach, the three individual components are drawn into a construct of information resolution, which ranges from −1.13 to 1.53. Its mean is 0.57, with a standard deviation of 0.51.[5] Using both the individual items of information resolution––transparency and depth of credit information, extent of disclosure, regulatory quality–– and the construct of information resolution, we evaluate their association with SNG debt levels in countries that experienced SNG debt activity, conditional on the fundamental governance institutions and a set of control factors, in an unbalanced sample of 52 countries in 2007–2014. Figure 4.9 shows the distribution of information resolution vs. SNG debt levels in 2014.

Control Variables

In addition to the fundamental governance institutions discussed in this chapter and information resolution, empirical studies account for a number of control measures. Population density and unemployment rates are proxies for service and social policy pressures. While population captures the demands for public capital infrastructure at the subnational level, the unemployment rates appraise whether SNG capital-financing policies respond to social burdens. The average population density in the sample is 124 persons per square kilometer, with a standard deviation of 127. Average unemployment rate is about 8.77 percent, with a standard deviation of 5.88 percent.

---

[4] WGI has seen critical reviews of its data quality in peer-reviewed and non-peer reviewed outlets (e.g.,, Thomas 2010; Arndt and Oman 2006). However, this data source is by far the most standardized and carefully constructed study of governance indicators for the past two decades (Arndt and Oman 2006; Kaufmann et al. 2007, 2010; Andrews 2010). Additional details on the WGI project, data, and data sources are available at http://info.worldbank.org/governance/wgi/index.aspx#home.

[5] The principal-component approach employs the correlation matrix of the selected items in the measure and produces factor loadings based on the squared multiple correlations as estimates of communality between the items.

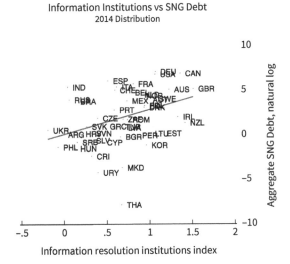

Figure 4.9 Information resolution institutions index vs. aggregate SNG debt levels, natural log transformation, in 2014

Modeling SNG Capital Market Debt

A central tenet in this chapter is that fundamental institutions are necessary, but not sufficient, for the development of SNG capital markets. To expand from existing approaches, we construct statistical models that allow us to assess the relationship between information resolution as well as its three components critical for credit contractibility—transparency and depth of credit information, extent of disclosure, and regulatory quality—on the level of SNG debt, while taking into account institutional contexts.[6] Based on the theoretical framework regarding information resolution and its components, as well as the review of empirical literature on SNG debt, we expect information resolution institutions to have a positive relationship with SNG debt. Our models evaluate the link between information resolution and SNG capital market borrowing in 52 countries during 2007–2014.

The models utilize three measures of SNG capital market debt—the natural log of the SNG debt (in USD billions), the natural log of SNG debt per capita (in USD thousands), and the natural log of SNG debt as percent of GDP. We ran regression models to control for a number of fixed effects, including type of government, legal origin, OECD membership, and World Bank regional groups. Regardless of the controls used, the results for information resolution

---

[6] The material on empirical analyses in this chapter is based on Moldogaziev et al. 2018.

consistently remained significant. Full technical information about data sources, measurement, data processing, variable specification, model specification, and results of regression analyses are presented in this chapter's appendix. Using a sample of 52 countries with various degrees of market-based approaches to public debt finance, the study evaluates whether and how information resolution covaries with the measures of SNG borrowing. Six important implications follow from the observed results.

First, information resolution institutions matter. The inclusion of information resolution measures, over fundamental governance institutions, improves the strength of the model. Of the three items in the information resolution index, it appears that transparency and depth of credit information and extent of disclosure are the main drivers of the association with SNG borrowing. The more transparent the system and the greater the depth of credit information, which is measured along a 7-point scale from 0 to 6, SNG debt experiences a 12–13 percent compounded increase, all else equal. Thus, a country around the mean level of transparency and depth of credit information could gain about $12 billion in market size (from an existing average of $97 billion) when transparency and depth of credit information improve, all else held constant. At the same time, as the extent of disclosure in the system improves, which is measured using an 11-point scale from 0 to 10, SNG debt sees a compounded increase of about 39–41 percent. In monetary terms, this impact would add about $40 billion to an average SNG market size of $97 billion. These results are significant both statistically and substantively. Regulatory quality is positively related to SNG capital market size as well, but the coefficients are not significant at conventional levels.

Second, the relationship holds regardless of the measurement for SNG borrowing. Information resolution is strongly associated with aggregate SNG debt levels, SNG debt per capita levels, and SNG debt per GDP.

Third, of the four measures for the fundamental governance institutions—economic, financial and market, political, and legal institutions—the legal dimension appears to be significant for aggregate SNG debt size, SNG debt per capita, and SNG debt per GDP, all else equal. This result suggests that strong legal institutions in the nation's system are conducive to greater levels of SNG borrowing. Consequently, enhancements in the rule of law and policies tackling accountability are expected to be important tools for SNG market activity.

Fourth, economic institutions have a negative association with SNG debt as percentage of GDP. This may be an indication that countries with advanced economic contexts, all else held constant, are in lesser need for SNG debt as far as the percentage of GDP is concerned. Economic institutions have no significant effect on the other measures of SNG capital market debt, however.

Fifth, the results show that population, a proxy for service pressure levels, is positively and significantly related to SNG debt size. Unemployment rates, however, do not bear upon SNG borrowing. We must conclude that while the levels of SNG borrowing appear to be insensitive to unemployment, SNG debt levels appear to respond to greater population density.

Finally, the models explored whether a form of government or legal origins matter for to SNG debt. These findings suggest that SNGs in federal countries incur greater levels of debt compared to their counterparts in unitary states, which is consistent with existing literature. SNGs in federal countries, especially in countries with relatively more open economies, have greater levels of both administrative and fiscal autonomy (Liu and Sun 2016). Results also show that countries with a French legal origin are likely to issue lower levels of SNG debt compared to countries with an English legal origin, while countries with German and Scandinavian legal origins are on par with countries with an English legal original. This lends evidence to the argument that legal origin may have important consequences for national credit systems (La Porta et al. 2008).

Discussion

The empirical results support the argument that a nation's ability to resolve information problems--subject to economic, financial and market, political, and legal institutions--directly relates to SNG capital market. This finding has important implications to both theory and practice. Consistent with our expectations, greater levels of information resolution indeed matter for SNG debt levels. In particular, measures for transparency and depth of credit information and extent of disclosure drive the levels of SNG debt. Regulatory quality, while positively associated, is not statistically significant. From a practical perspective, efforts to build better platforms for information generation and provision as well as disclosure on the firms, borrowing entities, and transactions in the system may be an essential and missing piece of institutional reforms, in concert with other aspects of governance institutions.

In terms of the fundamental governance institutions, the results of our analysis indicate that legal institutions are significant, suggesting that the rule of law and control of corruption facilitate greater capital market activity. This finding is consistent with evidence in existing studies that, when left unchecked, greater levels of public sector corruption and substandard levels of the rule of law result in costs in a number of areas of capital market activity.

These costs are linked to a deterioration of SNG credit quality, increases in borrowing costs, and swelling of overall levels of borrowing (Depken and LaFountain 2006; Butler et al. 2009; Moldogaziev et al. 2017; Liu et al. 2017). The positive coefficient also supports the argument that legal institutions are important for SNG capital markets, thus underscoring their importance in supporting credit contractibility.

As the coefficients for other factors governance institutions are generally not statistically significant, does it mean that they do not matter? Questions remain about whether the economic, financial and market, and political institutions are truly insignificant or simply overwhelmed by the dominance of information institutions. Our theoretical framework and post-estimation results suggest these explanations are unlikely. Alternatively, the countries included in the study sample may offer clues. The 52 countries we evaluate are among the most advanced in the world along the key dimensions of governance institutions and are likely more homogenous along these factors than statistically desired.

Development of capital markets must be viewed as a complex governance task, where a broad range of actors may be capable of co-providing capital-financing services. Efficiencies are achievable by allowing SNGs and external actors to participate in this fiscal governance objective. The findings reported in this chapter suggest that the resolution of information problems is fundamental to successfully utilizing a range of internal and external resources. Specifically, findings suggest that transparency and depth of credit information resolution and extent of disclosure, factors central to private and corporate credit, are also the dominant drivers of SNG capital market size, other governance institutions held constant.

Lessons for Policy and Practice

Prior to this demonstration of the important role of system-level information resolution in SNG capital markets, no empirical research has explicitly examined how a nation's information resolution institutions bear upon SNG debt levels. Yet, national-level information resolution is critical to SNG capital markets, particularly along the dimensions of transparency and depth of credit information, as well as financial disclosure. Furthermore, the magnitude of this impact is greatest in countries with English, as well as German and Scandinavian, legal origins. These results complement recent studies of SNG capital markets by focusing not just on fundamental governance institutions but also on information resolution institutions.

Despite the potential of SNG capital markets, the vast majority of SNGs authorized to borrow from capital markets continue to rely on non-capital market, internal sources of finance. The results suggest that governments can improve information resolution to leverage the benefits that SNG capital markets can offer. Given the importance of transparency and disclosure, policymakers must pay attention to systems of information management and provision to overcome problems of information asymmetry to leverage a full range of actors—including SNGs, financial firms, and individual investors—in the provision of and financing of infrastructure. Doing so has the potential to increase SNG access to billions of dollars from external sources.

The central government has a role in building information resolution institutions in the country in support of SNG access to capital financing, as Box 4.2 summarizes. Policy at the national level can focus first and foremost on efforts to improve the transparency and depth of credit information

---

Box 4.2 Central Government Activities for SNG Access to Capital Financing

Central governments can activate SNG capital markets by improving the climate for transparency and depth of credit information and extent of financial disclosure. Discrete activities include the following:

- Establish clear bankruptcy procedures and insolvency rules
- Develop standards for self-regulatory organizations
- Govern access to, longevity of, and quality of government, industry, and self-regulatory organization data
- Publicize positive and negative credit information
- Provide timely and relevant information about trading interest in market prices, volume, and participants
- Post payment and settlement information of securities
- Manage government data by requiring management systems that control inconsistencies and hold the data producers accountable for quality data
- Establish disclosure requirements regarding types of information, entities responsible for dissemination, and disclosure points along the stages of the debt-issuance process
- Disclose pricing information from various actors in the financial system for financial service costs
- Disclose monitoring processes and evaluation results

for all market actors. Transparency should begin with the establishment of clear bankruptcy procedures and insolvency rules for all types of borrowers, as well as standards for self-regulatory organizations. The environment for transparency should address the rules governing access to, longevity of, and quality of government, industry, and self-regulatory organization data. This includes increasing the visibility of positive and negative credit information; timely and relevant information about trading interest in prices, including pre-trade price and volume, post-trade price and volume, and the identity of market participants; and payment and settlement information of securities. Additionally, transparency should address the government's ability to manage its own data, to require management systems that control inconsistencies and hold the data producers accountable for quality data, including accounting and debt information. In these instances, transparency refers predominantly to information flows to firms, investors, and market actors.

These efforts would go hand in hand with improvements to disclosure requirements. Disclosure should begin by establishing what types of information must be disclosed by whom at what stages of the debt-issuance process. That includes information that flows predominantly from firms, borrowing entities, and market actors and might include information about financial, accounting, and managerial practices so that investors can assess risk. Disclosure also refers to the dissemination of pricing information from various actors in the financial system, including financial service costs. Disclosure efforts can also extend to monitoring and evaluation, accurate data reporting, and self-certification. Emphasis on reducing the relative cost of information will also shift the balance between the costs of information and regulation, ultimately rendering regulatory compliance less costly.

Given that legal institutions are especially significant for SNG capital markets, it is also important for national level policies to enforce rules and uphold contract law. Legal processes should be clearly understood and implemented in a timely fashion. Policies must also consider how they serve to facilitate, or retard, access to market participants.

The results of this chapter provide critical information about the role of institutions in the development of SNG capital markets. They underscore the role of information resolution institutions at the national or system level. They do not, however, address information resolution mechanisms available at the subnational level. The results in this chapter spawn additional questions. Among them is how information resolution bears out at the subnational level. Given that more SNGs seek to borrow, two facts remain: the

SNG is embedded in an intergovernmental arrangement with higher level governments; yet within the confines of national governance institutions, SNGs have options that can facilitate their access to an array of capital financing options. The next chapter deals with these issues by examining one level of SNGs, the city.

Technical Appendix

Data and Measurement

Data on SNG debt variables are collected from a variety of sources. The sampling strategy is designed to identify all the countries where SNGs—either at the regional level, the local level, or both—have capital market debt-issuance authority and activity during the study period. Capital market debt refers to debt from private lenders, including private banks and bond markets; it excludes debt provided or guaranteed by the central government. The single largest source of SNG debt data for 26 countries in our sample is Eurostat, an informational portal of the European Commission.[7] However, for a number of these countries, SNG debt data are available only from 2011 and on. To complete data on missing observations, when possible, SNG debt measures are collected from respective countries' governing institutions that are directly responsible for monitoring SNGs or for collecting and disseminating SNG fiscal and financial data. The details are presented in Table A4.1. According to regulations of accounting classifications stipulated for the European Union countries,[8] general-purpose government capital market debt consists of "debt securities" and "loans."

Data on SNG debt for the remaining 26 countries with debt-issuance authority and activity are collected on an individual country basis using accounting classifications comparable to the Eurostat categories. In each country, the laws and statutes that govern SNG debt-issuance authority, if any, are evaluated, and governing institutions at a country level that are responsible for SNG units are identified. We then collected data on SNG debt (debt securities and loans) in these countries issued by regions (such as states and

---

[7] All information from this source is standardized to EMUs (European monetary units) until the end of 1999 and switched to euros as EMU was retired in 1999.

[8] *Official Journal of the European Union*, L 174, June 26, 2013. Available in multiple languages at http://eur-lex.europa.eu/legal-content/EN/ALL/?uri=OJ%3AL%3A2013%3A174%3ATOC. Debt is reported for four sectors, two of which--state governments (S.1312) and local governments (S.1313)--are directly relevant for this study.

Table A4.1 Aggregate levels of SNG debt by country and data sources, means and standard deviations, 2005–2014

Country, abbreviation	Legal origins, OECD member (as of 2014)	Mean debt size, USD mln	Std. dev. debt size, USD mln	SNG units in the analysis; SNG debt data source
Argentina, ARG*	French, non-OECD	$723.12	$574.39	Province; Ministerio de Hacienda y Finanzas Públicas
Australia, AUS*	Anglo-Saxon, OECD	$55,999.27	$44,445.97	State and local; Australian Bureau of Statistics
Austria, AUT*	German, OECD	$43,231.94	$735.57	Lander and local; Eurostat and Statistics Austria
Belgium, BEL*	French, OECD	$65,038.83	$13,855.82	Regional and local; Eurostat
Bolivia, BOL	French, non-OECD	$533.16	$42.80	Department and local; Ministerio de Economía y Finanzas Públicas
Brazil, BRA*	French, non-OECD	$173,325.20	$82,865.77	State and local; Tesouro Nacional
Bulgaria, BGR	French, non-OECD	$530.27	$168.47	Local; Eurostat and Ministry of Finance
Canada, CAN*	Anglo-Saxon, OECD	$583,154.96	$81,268.30	Province and local; Bank of Canada
Colombia, COL	French, non-OECD	$1,623.54	$138.76	Local; National Department of Planning
Costa Rica, CRI	French, non-OECD	$60.68	$16.98	Local; National Institute of Statistics and Censuses
Croatia, HRV	German, non-OECD	$512.70	$270.87	Local; National Bank of Croatia
Cyprus, CYP	French, non-OECD	$397.39	$34.06	Local; Eurostat
Czechia, CZE	German, OECD	$2,964.42	$2,097.62	Local; Eurostat and Czech National Bank
Denmark, DNK	Scandinavian, OECD	$18,051.85	$827.22	Local; Eurostat and StatBank Denmark
El Salvador, SLV	French, non-OECD	$240.16	$115.23	Local; Ministerio de Hacienda
Estonia, EST	German, OECD	$539.65	$288.76	Local; Eurostat and Statistics Estonia
Finland, FIN	Scandinavian, OECD	$10,903.01	$6,037.68	Local; Eurostat and Statistics Finland
France, FRA	French, OECD	$176,230.71	$55,332.24	Local; Eurostat
Germany, DEU*	German, OECD	$740,375.77	$210,946.65	Lander and local and Eurostat; DeStatis
Greece, GRC	French, OECD	$1,566.34	$822.08	Local; Eurostat
Hungary, HUN	German, OECD	$2,273.33	$1,952.94	Local; Eurostat

Country	Tradition	Value 1	Value 2	Source/Notes
India, IND*	Anglo-Saxon, non-OECD	$62,731.24	$54,912.52	State; Ministry of Finance and Reserve Bank of India
Ireland, IRL	Anglo-Saxon, OECD	$7,110.41	$486.34	Local; Eurostat and Comptroller and Auditor General
Italy, ITA	French, OECD	$126,454.33	$44,652.95	Local; Eurostat
Japan, JPN	German, OECD	$757,073.19	$122,805.87	Prefecture and local; Local Government Bond Association
Korea, Rep., KOR	German, OECD	$193.71	$46.54	Province and local; Ministry of the Interior
Latvia, LVA	German, OECD	$960.19	$697.90	Local; Eurostat and Central Statistical Bureau of Latvia
Lithuania, LTU	German, OECD	$361.80	$302.19	Local; Eurostat and Statistics Lithuania
Mexico, MEX*	French, OECD	$17,067.20	$10,416.73	State; Secretaría de Hacienda y Crédito Público
The Netherlands, NLD	French, OECD	$61,060.37	$7,851.47	Local; Eurostat
New Zealand, NZL	Anglo-Saxon, OECD	$2,001.79	$1,012.74	Local; Government Statistical Office
Norway, NOR	Scandinavian, OECD	$31,643.55	$19,624.76	Local; Eurostat and Statistics Norway
N. Macedonia, MKD	French, non-OECD	$6.06	$8.65	Local; Ministry of Finance
Peru, PER	French, non-OECD	$646.59	$157.04	Regional and local; Ministerio de Economía y Finanzas
The Philippines, PHL	French, non-OECD	$236.61	$35.98	Provincial and local; Bureau of Local Government Finance
Poland, POL	German, OECD	$11,398.75	$7,293.81	Local; Eurostat and Ministry of State Treasury
Portugal, PRT	French, OECD	$8,137.83	$4,368.24	Local; Eurostat
Romania, ROM	French, non-OECD	$1,874.53	$1,883.72	Local; Eurostat
Russian Federation, RUS*	French, non-OECD	$28,237.27	$10,919.77	Regional and local; Ministry of Finance
Serbia, SRB	French, non-OECD	$245.67	$105.59	Local; National Bank of Serbia
Slovakia, SVK	German, OECD	$2,175.66	$42.01	Local; Eurostat
Slovenia, SVN	German, OECD	$494.34	$342.53	Local; Eurostat

(continued)

Table A4.1 Continued

Country, abbreviation	Legal origins, OECD member (as of 2014)	Mean debt size, USD mln	Std. dev. debt size, USD mln	SNG units in the analysis; SNG debt data source
South Africa, ZAF	Anglo-Saxon, non-OECD	$4,858.51	$1,465.27	Local; Statistics South Africa
Spain, ESP	French, OECD	$141,923.85	$92,718.45	Regional and local; Eurostat
Sweden, SWE	Scandinavian, OECD	$42,208.16	$5,003.04	Local; Eurostat
Switzerland, CHE*	German, OECD	$89,235.36	$16,575.02	Canton and local; Federal Department of Finance
Thailand, THA	Anglo-Saxon, non-OECD	$10.13	$7.39	Local; Bank of Thailand
Turkey, TUR	French, OECD	$1,820.35	$864.43	Local; Statistic Turkey
Ukraine, UKR	French, non-OECD	$2,217.20	$2,646.65	Regional and local; Ministry of Finance
The UK, GBR*	Anglo-Saxon, OECD	$108,088.84	$15,977.68	Local; Eurostat
United States, USA*	Anglo-Saxon, OECD	$491,141.48	$189,501.47	State and local; The Bond Buyer
Uruguay, URY	French, non-OECD	$12.88	$7.95	Department; Ministerio de Economía y Finanzas

Notes: * denotes federal countries. Source for legal origins is La Porta et al. (2008). OECD membership status as of 2014 is available from https://www.oecd.org/about/members-and-partners/.

provinces) and general-purpose local governments (such as municipalities, cities, towns, or counties). Consequently, data were collected on a country by country basis from whatever sources available, including ministries of finance, ministries of regional or local self-governance, central banks, offices of statistics, auditors offices, and/or treasuries.

Data Processing

The chapter evaluates general government (general-purpose) SNG long-term debt levels that are obtained/issued using market mechanisms of capital financing. General-purpose governments are entities with a broader spectrum of public service responsibilities such as cities, counties, and municipalities (the specific name for the jurisdiction depends upon the political organization of each country), or states/provinces (often labeled regional entities), as well as the hybrids between these two major classifications (city-states, cities with an equivalent of a federal region status, or metropolitan regions). There are two primary reasons for focusing on general-purpose SNGs. The first has to do with accounting conventions and standards governing debt around the world. In the countries where regional and local governments access credit directly, general-purpose debt (debt securities, loans, and other direct overlapping debt or co-guarantees) are the most standardized way of accounting and reporting debt data.[9] The second reason is the availability of reliable and comparable data.

Thus, the data on the aggregate of regional and local government general-purpose long-term debt directly attributable to SNG governments and created through capital market mechanisms are collected. The aggregate debt measures are all regional and local debt (usually reported in local currencies), which are converted to US dollars (USD) based on official currency exchange rates of the US Federal Reserve Bank. During the period under evaluation, we observe that the countries that authorized market-based capital financing to their SNGs also

[9] There are also classifications for non-market and indirect general-purpose debt available to SNGs, such as debt securities or loans with a full guarantee of the central government, loans from other governments (both higher level governments and horizontal loan arrangements with other "peer" governments) or government authorities and enterprises, or direct and indirect non-debt guarantees, sometimes including liabilities of public funds. These non-autonomous and non-market arrangements will predominantly exist as a major source of SNG capital financing in countries that do not possess sufficient levels of information capacity, conditional on fundamental institutions of governance. We also find that in a number of countries debt is issued by special purpose SNG authorities or vehicles and public-private partnership (PPP) projects with distinct SNG benefits but is not always properly recognized, monitored, regulated, and reported as SNG debt. At the same time, non-debt liabilities (non-debt security and non-loan guarantees) are outside of the scope of the study.

had freely floating currencies; thus, using official currency exchange rates is not expected to mask the effects of any currency control mechanisms that may often still exist in emerging economies. Critically, the data for the measures of governance institutions that we evaluate in this chapter are collected from various fiscal and governance quality assessment projects. Table A4.2 offers details for each item in the institutional measures we use and their sources.

Table A4.2 Key variables of interest and data sources

Information institutions	
Transparency and depth of credit information	Doing Business project: http://www.doingbusiness.org/methodology/getting-credit.
Extent of disclosure	Doing Business project: http://www.doingbusiness.org/methodology/protecting-minority-investors.
Regulatory quality	Worldwide Governance Indicators project: http://info.worldbank.org/governance/wgi/index.aspx#doc.
Economic institutions	
GDP, USD current	World Bank Economy & Growth indicators: http://data.worldbank.org/indicator.
GNI, USD current	World Bank Economy & Growth indicators: http://data.worldbank.org/indicator.
GS, USD current	World Bank Economy & Growth indicators: http://data.worldbank.org/indicator.
GNE, USD current	World Bank Economy & Growth indicators: http://data.worldbank.org/indicator.
Financial and market institutions	
Legal rights	Doing Business project: http://www.doingbusiness.org/methodology/getting-credit.
Investor protections	Doing Business project: http://www.doingbusiness.org/methodology/getting-credit.
Ease of investor suits	Doing Business project: http://www.doingbusiness.org/methodology/getting-credit.
Political institutions	
Government effectiveness	Worldwide Governance Indicators project: http://info.worldbank.org/governance/wgi/index.aspx#doc.
Political stability and violence	Worldwide Governance Indicators project: http://info.worldbank.org/governance/wgi/index.aspx#doc.
Voice and accountability	Worldwide Governance Indicators project: http://info.worldbank.org/governance/wgi/index.aspx#doc.
Legal institutions	
Corruption control	Worldwide Governance Indicators project: http://info.worldbank.org/governance/wgi/index.aspx#doc.
Rule of law	Worldwide Governance Indicators project: http://info.worldbank.org/governance/wgi/index.aspx#doc.

Regression Results

Tables A4.3, A4.4, and A4.5 show the regression results. Models 1.1–1.3 are two-way year-country fixed-effects models for the covariates of SNG borrowing, where information resolution is measured as a multifaceted index consisting of three items. Model 1.1 is the baseline regression of debt size on information resolution index along with year-country fixed effects. In Models 1.2 and 1.3, covariates are added to the baseline model and the interpretations focus on coefficients from these models with additional covariates.[10] The coefficients for the index of information resolution have the expected direction and are statistically significant in Models 1.2–1.3 ($\hat{\beta}_{ICF} = 1.194$ & 1.169; $p < 0.001$). Therefore, as the resolution of information asymmetry problems improves, the compounded increase in SNG debt size is roughly equal to 122–130 percent ($e^{\hat{\beta}_{ICF}} - 1$). Alternatively, a one standard deviation increase in the measure of information resolution is expected to result in about a 210–223 percent increase in SNG debt size ($e^{\hat{\beta}_{ICF}*s_{IGF}}$).

To further scrutinize the items in the index of information resolution, each of the three items is individually assessed in Models 2.1–2.3. Of the three items, transparency and depth of credit information and extent of disclosure are the main drivers of the positive coefficient in Models 2.2–2.3. Improvements in transparency and depth of credit information are found to result in a compounded increase in SNG debt size of about 12–13 percent ($\hat{\beta}_{DCI} = 0.115$ & 0.120; $p < 0.01$). For a standard deviation change in transparency and depth of credit information, the expected change in SNG debt size is 20–21 percent ($e^{\hat{\beta}_{DCI}*s_{DCI}}$). At the same time, enhancements in the extent of disclosure appear to result in a compounded increase in SNG debt size of about 39–41 percent ($\hat{\beta}_{ED} = 0.341$ & 0.329; $p < 0.01$). A standard deviation change in the extent of disclosure, translates to a 195–209 percent expected change in SNG debt size ($e^{\hat{\beta}_{ED}*s_{ED}}$). The coefficient for regulatory quality, while positive, becomes statistically insignificant when we move from the baseline regression in Model 2.1 to regressions with covariates in Models 2.2 and 2.3. Table A4.3 displays results for Models 1.1–1.3 and 2.1–2.3.

Empirical findings for the associations between information resolution and two other specifications for the outcome of interest—SNG debt per capita and SNG debt per GDP—are almost identical to the coefficients reported for SNG

---

[10] Models 1.2 and 1.3 differ in that the former includes political institutions, while the latter includes legal institutions. Measures of political and legal institutions exhibited high correlation in the data set; therefore, to avoid multicollinearity issues, they are included in separate regression models. This concern for multicollinearity between political and legal institution indices separates Models 2.2 vs. 2.3, 3.2 vs. 3.3, 4.2 vs. 4.3, 5.2 vs. 5.3, and 6.2 vs. 6.3.

Table A4.3 Regression results for Models 1.1–1.3 and Models 2.1–2.3

Variables	Outcome Variable = ln(SNG Debt)					
	Model 1.1	Model 1.2	Model 1.3	Model 2.1	Model 2.2	Model 2.3
	Baseline	M1.1 + Controls	M1.2—Political + Legal	Baseline	M2.1 + Controls	M2.2—Political + Legal
L1. Information capacity index	0.916***	1.194***	1.169***			
	(3.37)	(3.40)	(3.47)			
L1. Transparency and depth of credit information				0.0799*	0.115**	0.120**
				(2.36)	(2.77)	(2.91)
L1. Extent of disclosure				0.223*	0.341**	0.329**
				(2.28)	(2.79)	(2.64)
L1. Regulatory quality				0.600*	0.555	0.385
				(2.24)	(1.63)	(1.33)
L1. Economic capacity		-0.196	-0.395		0.094	-0.011
		(-0.32)	(-0.62)		(0.17)	(-0.02)
L1. Financial and market capacity		-0.299	-0.242		-1.048	-0.969
		(-0.48)	(-0.39)		(-1.45)	(-1.35)
L1. Political capacity		-0.179			0.007	
		(-0.40)			(0.02)	
L1. Legal capacity			0.799*			0.702+
			(2.00)			(1.83)
L1. Population density, ln		4.453*	4.970*		4.220*	4.713*
		(2.23)	(2.40)		(2.25)	(2.37)

L1.Unemployment rate						
	−0.516**	0.0008	0.0063		−0.0041	−0.0017
	(−2.63)	(0.05)	(0.45)		(−0.25)	(−0.10)
Year effects	Yes	Yes	Yes	Yes	Yes	Yes
Country effects	Yes	Yes	Yes	Yes	Yes	Yes
Constant		−12.38*	−13.19*	−1.990**	−14.59**	−15.53**
		(−2.33)	(−2.47)	(−2.83)	(−2.69)	(−2.80)
N observations (2007 = base year)	377	377	377	377	377	377
N countries (Argentina = base country)	51	51	51	51	51	51
AIC	573.00	573.00	567.70	566.80	560.50	556.50
BIC	809.20	828.60	823.30	810.90	824.00	819.90
R-squared	0.979	0.980	0.980	0.980	0.981	0.981
Adjusted R-squared	0.975	0.976	0.976	0.976	0.977	0.977

Notes: t statistics in parentheses (robust standard errors)

Level of significance: $+ p < 0.10$, $* p < 0.05$, $** p < 0.01$, $*** p < 0.001$

Table A4.4 Regression results for Models 3.1–3.3 and Models 4.1–4.3

| | Outcome Variable = ln(SNG Debt Per Capita) | | | | | |
| | Model 3.1 | Model 3.2 | Model 3.3 | Model 4.1 | Model 4.2 | Model 4.3 |
Variables	Baseline	M3.1 + Controls	M3.2—Political + Legal	Baseline	M4.1 + Controls	M4.2—Political + Legal
L1.Information capacity index	0.961***	1.195***	1.169***			
	(3.56)	(3.40)	(3.47)			
L1.Transparency and depth of credit information				0.0878**	0.115**	0.120**
				(2.62)	(2.77)	(2.91)
L1.Extent of disclosure				0.226*	0.341**	0.329**
				(2.32)	(2.79)	(2.64)
L1.Regulatory quality				0.580*	0.554	0.384
				(2.18)	(1.63)	(1.33)
L1.Economic capacity		-0.200	-0.399		0.091	-0.015
		(-0.33)	(-0.62)		(0.16)	(-0.03)
L1.Financial and market capacity		-0.299	-0.241		-1.049	-0.968
		(-0.48)	(-0.38)		(-1.45)	(-1.35)
L1.Political capacity		-0.177			0.010	
		(-0.40)			(0.02)	
L1.Legal capacity			0.804*			0.707+
			(2.01)			(1.84)
L1.Population density, ln		3.518+	4.037+		3.285+	3.782+
		(1.76)	(1.95)		(1.75)	(1.91)
L1.Unemployment rate		0.0014	0.0070		-0.0035	-0.0010
		(0.10)	(0.50)		(-0.21)	(-0.06)

Year effects	Yes	Yes	Yes	Yes	Yes	Yes
Country effects	Yes	Yes	Yes	Yes	Yes	Yes
Constant	2.683***	−6.662	−7.482	1.129	−8.881	−9.826+
	(13.93)	(−1.26)	(−1.40)	(1.61)	(−1.64)	(−1.77)
N observations (2007 = base year)	377	377	377	377	377	377
N countries (Argentina = base country)	51	51	51	51	51	51
AIC	569.80	573.20	567.80	563.80	560.60	556.60
BIC	806.00	828.80	823.40	807.90	824.10	820.00
R-squared	0.974	0.974	0.975	0.974	0.975	0.976
Adjusted R-squared	0.969	0.969	0.969	0.969	0.970	0.970

Notes: t statistics in parentheses (robust standard errors)

Level of significance: + $p < 0.10$, * $p < 0.05$, ** $p < 0.01$, *** $p < 0.001$

Table A4.5 Regression results for Models 5.1–5.3 and Models 6.1–6.3

	Outcome Variable = ln(SNG Debt as % GDP)					
	Model 5.1	Model 5.2	Model 5.3	Model 6.1	Model 6.2	Model 6.3
Variables	Baseline	M5.1 + Controls	M5.2—Political + Legal	Baseline	M6.1 + Controls	M6.2—Political + Legal
L1.Information capacity index	0.893**	1.161**	1.137**			
	(3.27)	(3.22)	(3.26)			
L1.Transparency and depth of credit information				0.0783*	0.110*	0.113**
				(2.37)	(2.56)	(2.66)
L1.Extent of disclosure				0.255**	0.344**	0.338**
				(2.63)	(2.74)	(2.64)
L1.Regulatory quality				0.161	0.529	0.332
				(0.59)	(1.51)	(1.12)
L1.Economic capacity		−1.353*	−1.560*		−1.051+	−1.150+
		(−2.11)	(−2.31)		(−1.79)	(−1.93)
L1.Financial and market capacity		−0.325	−0.275		−1.092	−1.036
		(−0.51)	(−0.43)		(−1.48)	(−1.41)
L1.Political capacity		−0.352			−0.148	
		(−0.77)			(−0.34)	
L1.Legal capacity			0.688+			0.597
			(1.67)			(1.48)
L1.Population density, ln		3.408+	3.884+		3.185+	3.632+
		(1.69)	(1.86)		(1.67)	(1.81)
L1.Unemployment rate		0.0116	0.0170		0.0066	0.0083
		(0.77)	(1.16)		(0.38)	(0.47)

	(1)	(2)	(3)	(4)	(5)	(6)
Year effects	Yes	Yes	Yes	Yes	Yes	Yes
Country effects	Yes	Yes	Yes	Yes	Yes	Yes
Constant	−1.959***	−10.07+	−10.83*	−3.999***	−12.33*	−13.27*
	(−12.92)	(−1.88)	(−2.01)	(−5.81)	(−2.24)	(−2.36)
N observations (2007 = base year)	376	376	376	376	376	376
N countries (Argentina = base country)	51	51	51	51	51	51
AIC	592.10	587.60	584.50	582.20	575.10	572.50
BIC	827.90	843.00	839.90	825.90	838.40	835.80
R-squared	0.952	0.954	0.954	0.954	0.956	0.956
Adjusted R-squared	0.943	0.944	0.945	0.945	0.946	0.947

Notes: t statistics in parentheses (robust standard errors)

Level of significance: + $p < 0.10$, * $p < 0.05$, ** $p < 0.01$, *** $p < 0.001$

debt size regressions. The association of information resolution with SNG debt per capita and SNG debt per GDP remains positive and significant in Models 3.2–3.3 and Models 5.2–5.3 ($\hat{\beta}_{ICF} = 1.195$ & 1.169 and $\hat{\beta}_{ICF} = 1.161$ & 1.137, respectively, all significant at conventional levels). The same is true for the associations between individual items of information resolution. The association of transparency and depth of credit information with SNG debt per capita and SNG debt per GDP is positive and significant in Models 4.2–4.3 and Models 6.2–6.3 ($\hat{\beta}_{DCI} = 1.115$ & 1.120 and $\hat{\beta}_{DCI} = 1.110$ & 1.113, respectively, all significant at conventional levels). The association of extent of disclosure with SNG debt per capita and SNG debt per GDP also remains positive and significant in Models 4.2–4.3 and Models 6.2–6.3 ($\hat{\beta}_{ED} = 1.341$ & 1.329 and $\hat{\beta}_{ED} = 1.344$ & 1.338, respectively, again significant at conventional levels). Finally, the association of regulatory quality with SNG debt per capita and SNG debt per GDP is positive but insignificant in Models 4.2–4.3 and 6.2–6.3. Regression results for these models are shown in Tables A4.4 and A4.5.

5

Information Resolution, Information Content, and City Debt

This chapter explores how information resolution tools at the city level bear upon the levels and composition of their debt. SNGs are often subject to statutes and policies governing access to capital financing that are established at the national level. Although SNGs operate within a national system of governance institutions and are constrained by their external environment, they also operate within their own decision environment.

The city is an understudied level of government in cross-country comparative debt analyses. Yet, it is the unit of government that can benefit the most from SNG capital market expansion. Cities increasingly have various tools available to them to communicate information about their underlying credit fundamentals, borrowing instruments, or contracts. The city's credit rating, a signal of a borrower's likelihood of repayment, has become a widely used tool of information provision about credit risk to financial sector firms and investors.

This chapter critically evaluates long-term debt levels and debt composition for cities from diverse governance settings, emphasizing the role of credit quality and its components as a mechanism of information resolution or signaling, conditional on information institutions in the system. In this way, this study extends to the city level of analysis the hypotheses that information resolution affects debt issuance and debt structure.

The theoretical underpinnings hold that information allows for improved credit contractibility and that the composition of debt responds to informational content of a borrower's credit quality. Credit ratings, a tool for assessing underlying informational components about issuing entities, are based on a well-recognized, standardized scale developed by global firms such as Moody's, Fitch, or Standard & Poor's. Despite the proliferation of research on corporate debt, there is a dearth of critical comparative analysis of local governance issues, including issues related to SNG borrowing and access to capital market financing (Alm 2015; da Cruz et al. 2018; Pierre 2005; Halbert and Attuyer 2016). Specifically, how SNGs resolve information asymmetries to participate more fully in capital-financing arrangements, especially when

Information Resolution and Subnational Capital Markets. Christine R. Martell, Tima T. Moldogaziev, and Salvador Espinosa, Oxford University Press. © Oxford University Press 2021. DOI: 10.1093/oso/9780190089337.003.0005

financing processes are laden with complexity and uncertainty, are unknown. We posit that credit ratings, reflecting the fundamentals components of credit quality (economic fundamentals, fiscal fundamentals, debt and financial fundamentals, and governance fundamentals), are important for SNG capital market levels and composition, conditional on other country and city-level covariates. We test this expectation on a panel of cities from diverse governance settings for 2007–2016. This chapter adds to comparative governance literature by assessing city debt outcomes, conditional on national governance institutions, based on city-level credit ratings and the subcomponents of underlying city credit quality.

The next section reviews the capital market literature, which is most developed for corporate markets, with an emphasis on information resolution mechanisms and debt features, particularly borrowing levels and debt composition. Based on our theoretical framework and literature review, we then present the empirical inquiry approach and data. This is followed by a display of what we know about city debt levels and composition, credit ratings, and the information components of credit quality. Based on results of regression analyses, we continue with a discussion of the importance of credit ratings as a mechanism for information certification and signaling at the city level, above and beyond the quality of information resolution institutions at the system level. The last section reviews policy implications and recommendations both for national- and city-level policymakers to improve intergovernmental relations and the context for SNG borrowing. This section also offers insights for city policymakers to improve their understanding of the informational components of underlying credit quality and the role of credit ratings as a mechanism for information certification and signaling.

Literature on Information, Borrowing, and Debt Composition

SNG capital markets depend on a degree of institutional maturity along economic, financial and market, political, and legal dimensions. In the preceding chapter, we highlighted the added importance of information institutions, more specifically those at the system level, for creating an environment of credit contractibility where SNG capital markets can operate and expand. Maintaining the tenor of the book's theme that successful access to capital markets is desirable in contexts with robust information resolution institutions, in this chapter we scale down to explore the tools in play at the city level and their relationship with borrowing and composition of debt.

Information, Debt Levels, and Debt Composition

Theories of information are fundamental to understanding SNG credit markets as they pertain to debt outcomes: levels and composition of debt. While governments and corporations differ in significant ways, the principles of capital markets remain constant, allowing lessons of corporate capital markets to be useful in understanding SNG capital markets. Capital structure and capital market access, far from static, respond to information on credit quality. In the presence of information asymmetries, capital levels and capital structure signal firm performance to investors, and firm borrowing options are shaped by the content of the borrower's credit quality information (Leland and Pyle 1977; Ross 1977; Heinkel 1982; Harris and Raviv 1990; Bharath et al. 2009; Krishnaswami et al. 1999). Disclosure of information affects capital volume (Yosha 1995; Melnik and Plaut 1995; Dhaliwal et al. 2011). Early work on the subject found that better firm credit quality resulted in greater and wider access to borrowing, and that firms with riskier returns had fewer and costlier options in the capital market (Leland and Pyle 1977). Debt levels may relate to firms' unobserved value and through signaling serve to resolve information problems (Heinkel 1982). Information also signals investors about the quality of management (Harris and Raviv 1990), but contracting costs may be higher in the face of moral hazard concerns (Krishnaswami et al. 1999).

The market's assessment of adverse selection risk affects capital structure, where firms with greater levels of adverse selection risk issue more debt (Bharath et al. 2009). This result is consistent with the theory that a firm's choice for greater debt exposure, over equity, is a tool to signal to investors that the firm is open to public scrutiny (Harris and Raviv 1990). Higher debt levels follow when information is useful. From this perspective, firm debt mitigates the information asymmetry problems between the firm and investors, as investors can design debt payment timing and levels to "exploit the ability of debt to generate useful information" (Harris and Raviv 1990: 322). Specifically, investors "use debt to generate information and monitor management. They gather information signals from the firm's ability to make payments and from a costly investigation in the event of default. Debtholders use their legal rights to force management to provide information and to implement the resulting efficient liquidation decision. The optimal amount of debt is determined by trading off the value of information and opportunities for disciplining management against the probability of incurring investigation costs" (Harris and Raviv 1990: 322–3). Empirically, increases in debt levels accompany increases in firm value (Harris and Raviv 1990).

In addition to explaining debt levels, theories of information are fundamental to understanding SNG credit markets as they pertain to debt composition. In the private sector, there is a direct relationship between information—be it transparent, translucent, or opaque—and the type of debt that borrowers hold (Sharma and Knight 2016; Liberti and Petersen 2017; Kwan and Carleton 2010; Rajan and Zingales 1998; Rajan 1992). Transparent information is associated with market-based debt, whereas opaque information is associated with relationship-based debt. That is, in an environment of information asymmetries, market debt is thin and lending is largely limited to relationship-based debt.

A city government typically can choose between bank lending (financial institutions) or from subnational bond markets (Peterson 2002; Alm 2015). The characteristics of bank lending are that it is relationship based, monitors performance, and bundles both services and prices (Peterson 2002). One of the lender's functions is to perform an internal assessment of a borrower's credit quality. Local governments in some countries can borrow from a government-created financial intermediary (such as a development bank). These types of lending institutions spread the credit risk over many borrowers, often with top-down (vertical) subsidies, resulting in interjurisdiction (horizontal) cross-subsidization of borrowing costs. They are advantageous for small borrowers. Yet, political bias can distort project selection, and the arrangement fails to fully differentiate the central or local governments' liabilities. In contrast to bank loans or credit pools, municipal bonds are market based; rely on public monitoring; and typically do not bundle risks, services, and support features. The borrowing rate is set based on the borrower's credit quality, as determined by an independent third party. These instruments, while offering direct access to capital markets, can offer efficient pricing and remove the central government as an implicit guarantor.

The agency theory of debt holds that a principal-agent problem may exist between borrowers and lenders, whereby, in an effort to maximize their utility, borrowers may have an incentive to engage in moral hazard behavior against the best interests of the lenders (see Jensen and Meckling 1976 for a more formal definition). For example, debt composition heavily dependent on relationship-based debt reduces borrower effort as the bank shares the surplus rents (Rajan 1992). Information asymmetries between the borrowers and lenders exacerbate the agency problems. In response, credit quality resolution and credit-monitoring mechanisms can resolve information asymmetry problems between borrowers and lenders (Berlin and Loeys 1988; Diamond 1991; Berlin and Mester 1992; Chemmanuer and Fulghieri 1994). Furthermore, providing contract incentives, employed through contract design, and monitoring the borrower can mitigate divergent behavior. Although costly, credit-monitoring arrangements have the added value of developing a borrower's reputation (Diamond 1991).

A central finding of studies that focus on the firm's choice between privately placed bonds and public debt is that "the greater monitoring and the more restrictive covenants in privately placed debt helps [*sic*] mitigate costs that arise due to conflict between bondholders and shareholders" (Krishnaswami et al. 1999: 432). Put another way, intermediaries impose costs but offer better organizational functions (Cantillo and Wright 2000). Diamond (1991) finds that monitoring services, via bank loans, are used relatively more often for medium-quality borrowers and in periods of high interest rates. Krishnaswami et al. (1999) find that firms with higher contracting costs due to both adverse selection and moral hazard concerns depend on greater levels of private debt. Conversely, Cantillo and Wright (2000) show that public debt is associated with issuance size, cash, and collaterals. In a study on private placements versus public bonds, Kwan and Carleton (2010) find that relative to public bonds, private placement bonds require more investor input in the bond covenant design, more credit monitoring, but offer greater ease to renegotiate bond terms, if and when necessary. Therefore, private placement debt has key features of relationship-based credit compared to market-based public bonds (Rajan and Zingales 1998). In the presence of high agency costs of debt, borrowers demand financial contracting and monitoring to control incentive problems. Private debt and bank debt, with greater monitoring provisions, are well suited for lower quality borrowers with high agency costs (Kwan and Carleton 2010).

While both bank and private debt can be modified throughout the life cycle of the contract by mutual agreement, the choice to issue bank debt, over private debt, can benefit lower credit quality borrowers. "Bank debt potentially mitigates costs of information asymmetry better than traditional private debt because banks tend to maintain long-term relationships with borrowing firms and accumulate soft information about them . . . In addition, banks are able to quickly renegotiate loans and therefore could have superior ability to contain financial losses in case of borrowers' financial distress than nonbank traditional private lenders" (Arena 2011: 396).

It follows that information and information resolution are at the heart of overcoming agency problems, and the quality of information signals bears upon capital structure. By extension of this argument to the public sector, the ability to resolve information problems affects SNG capital markets, both its size and debt structure. The previous chapter showed a positive relationship between information resolution institutions, which ensure contractibility—transparency and depth of credit information, extent of disclosure, and regulatory quality—and aggregate SNG capital market size. Countries that are able to resolve information problems reduce the information asymmetries between borrowers and creditors, and therefore yield more capital flow. Corporate research finds that firms with greater information problems (lower disclosure, greater inability to resolve moral hazard or agency problems) rely more heavily on private, or relationship-based, debt.

Urban Governance and Financialization

A shift toward debt finance and capital market use does not come easily for cities in some countries, including those with well-developed mechanisms for regional and urban infrastructure financing, due to functional constraints and concerns over the use of capital markets. Often, this is based on distrust of fiscal policy incentives and preferences at the local level. Mechanisms of information certification and monitoring at the city level would contribute to lessen these concerns.

Cities face a number of functional constraints. The lack of local government autonomy and borrowing authority, soft budget constraints, poor ability to assess credit risk, inadequate accounting and reporting practices, low own-source revenue generation, nonexistent or inadequate legal mechanisms for default, and morally hazardous fiscal behavior have thwarted the use of capital finance at the local level in many countries.

Aside from these functional constraints owing to lack of institutional maturity, concerns over the potential negative implications of using capital finance also underpin the use of market debt by SNGs. Studies of urban governance note the integrated relationship between capital finance and urban space, and they use the term *financialization* to refer broadly to a process of engaging with capital market actors and commodification of urban land use. "Income streams from a wide range of assets are converted into new investment products for dispersed investors through techniques that disaggregate and continually reassign ownership to allow for more and faster-paced exchanges. *Financialization* is the term used to describe both this institutional form and the processes that lead to it" (Weber 2010: 252).

The negative view of capital finance in urban governance maintains that financialization undermines democratic urban governance through a com-modification process, resulting in socio-spatial inequalities, such as gen-trification, abandonment, and disparate outcomes (Halbert and Attuyer

2016). Moreover, critics argue that exposure to risky financial instruments and volatility of financial markets exacerbate socio-spatial exclusory patterns (Weber 2010; Halbert and Attuyer 2016). This view takes financial markets as monolithic, driven by profit motives that unilaterally act upon city governments.

A supportive view argues that "financial integration is both variegated and locally embedded" (Weber 2010: 253), and that local governments act on financial circuits through local property markets as much as financial markets act on local governments. Urban governance, thus, also influences the shape of local finance in the following three ways (Weber 2010): by creating new investments and identifying assets for collateral; by protecting income streams deriving from the assets; and by preserving public provision (though not necessarily production) of public goods. This counter-perspective views capital as a tool of local public finance that local governments can leverage. Fiscal governance proponents hold the position that cities need to work with markets to finance capital-intensive projects, if and when appropriate and available.

Irrespective of the view of financialization, capital markets have a transformative effect on urban production. By situating the local government squarely in the center of the debate, the issue boils down to one of not whether financing tools should be used, but how they can be utilized to efficiently, effectively, and equitably address key governance tasks. Financial instruments or financial intermediaries are not inherently pro- or anti-public sector—it is a policy task to ensure that financial solutions are not misapplied, which requires policymakers to have adequate competence in governance and vis-à-vis financial sector firms. Ashton et al. (2016) demonstrate the trade-offs with a case analysis of Chicago. They show that the financialization of assets through leasing mechanisms can require shifts in governance, with increased financial constraints and the city finance office coordinating more urban management functions; but that the arrangements allow the city to "increase its capacity to govern urban problems through financial markets" (Ashton et al. 2016: 1397).

As emphasized, credit quality assessment and monitoring mechanisms improve information resolution and influence debt size and structure (Berlin and Loeys 1988; Diamond 1991; Berlin and Mester 1992; Chemmanuer and Fulghieri 1994). While the providers of credit quality information resolution mechanisms can range from governments to third parties, the rapidly growing and recognized standard for evaluating and monitoring SNG credit quality is through assessment by an independent credit-rating agency, often summarized in a credit report or opinion and encapsulated in a credit rating. Credit ratings, therefore, contain information about a borrower's credit quality by encompassing the black box of various components of SNG creditworthiness.

Despite the merits of credit-rating systems, they are underused in many countries; instead the information on the creditworthiness of local governments is seldom useful and not precisely known (Alm 2015). The categories that generally explain underlying city credit quality are economic fundamentals, fiscal fundamentals, debt and financial fundamentals, and governance fundamentals (Hildreth and Miller 2002; Moody's 2013; Standard & Poor's 2010). As Freire (2014) argues, financial sector firms—from information intermediaries to capital intermediaries—have unique economies of scale and expertise that they can offer to the services of city policymakers. The imbalance between capital market actors and cities can be actively overcome by national and subnational policymakers by understanding not only how credit quality is related to debt size or composition but also by looking into the black box of credit ratings and learning about their constituent parts. To come full circle, the SNG must resolve its own information problems to increase its agency vis-à-vis financial markets and its use of capital markets to fulfill its key fiscal governance task. The credit rating is a signal of this capacity. Therefore, we argue that for the growing role of cities in addressing core, urban governance tasks, where capital markets are now a critical source of financing, becoming competent in how credit quality assessment works is the most direct way for policymakers to maintain parity with financial sector firms.

Inquiry and Data

This background leaves us seeking to know more about borrowing by cities across the globe, especially among diverse institutional settings and sociopolitical contexts. What debt levels do cities have, and what is the composition of city debt? How does information resolution, both of institutions at the national level and the tools available to subnational borrowers, influence debt outcomes? Despite being enmeshed in higher level government policies and institutions, do city governments select debt levels and composition based on information principles similar to corporate credit markets? The literature guides several hypotheses: City-level debt and the share of debt securities are greater with information resolution institutions and the informational content of credit quality.

We use data for the three most populous cities in 51 countries that permit SNG capital market borrowing.[1] We collected annual data for the 10-year period (2007–2016) from a variety of sources. Data on debt levels were taken from financial sections in credit-rating reports (where available from Fitch, Moody's, and/or Standard & Poor's), directly from city annual financial reports, from national repositories of local government data, ministries of finance, and from our requests for information. The final sample, represented by an unbalanced panel of 73 cities from 37 countries for a maximum of 10 years, has 653 observations. Table 5.1 presents the cities in the sample and identifies broad patterns of debt level over time. The cities exhibit a variety of patterns, though at first blush there is no discernable rationale for the patterns of debt levels.

City Borrowing, Debt Composition, and Credit Quality

The descriptive statistics highlight a number of important observations about city debt levels. First, there is substantial variation in debt levels across cities. Second, city debt levels have positive correlations with key variables of interest—city credit quality and the system-level information resolution institutions. As the city credit quality improves, the levels of city debt also increase. The relationship is not linear, however. Similarly, as contractibility improves with information resolution institutions, city debt levels increase. Third, the trends hold even when we omit outliers in the distribution. Table 5.2 presents univariate descriptive statistics for the variables of interest. They include debt levels, shares of debt securities, city credit ratings, the components of city credit quality, and other relevant covariates.

The cities under scrutiny exhibit variation in socioeconomic characteristics, debt profiles, fiscal health, and credit ratings, as demonstrated by the large standard deviations and wide ranges. The average city in the sample has a population of 2.5 million, an unemployment rate of 8.39 percent, and a per capita GDP of $30,066. It has $4.1 billion in total long-term debt, of which 44 percent is from debt securities, and carries a debt service of 9.9 percent of operating revenues. The average city spends $4 billion in operations and about $1 billion in capital expenditures a year and raises $4.8 billion in operating revenues. Finally, the mean city had a credit rating of AA/Aa between 2007–2016.

---

[1] We draw from the sample presented in the previous chapter, but exclude the US cities (New York, Los Angeles, and Chicago) as the debt size and composition of these cities, all from US municipal capital markets, dwarf any other city in the sample.

Table 5.1 City sample information and city debt patterns, 2007–2016

Increasing debt	Constant debt	Increasing and decreasing, or decreasing and increasing	No discernable debt trend	Decreasing debt
Birmingham, GBR (2007–10)	Berlin, DEU (2007–15)	Athens, GRC (2007–16)	Auckland, NZL (2007–16)	Cali, COL (2009–16)
Buenos Aires, ARG (2007–16)	Bucharest, ROM (2007–16)	Basel, CHE (2007–16)	Barcelona, ESP (2007–16)	La Plata, ARG (2007–16)
Bursa, TUR (2007–15)	Hamburg, DEU (2008–15)	Belgrade, SRB (2010–16)	Lima, PER (2007–16)	Porto, PRT (2007–14)
Christchurch, NZL (2007–16)	Milan, ITA (2007–16)	Bogota, COL (2007–16)	Lyon, FRA (2007–16)	Rome, ITA (2007–14)
Córdoba, ARG (2010–16)	Montreal, CAN (2007–16)	Brno, CZE (2007–16)	Novosibirsk, RUS (2007–15)	São Paulo, BRA (2010–16)
Izmir, TUR (2007–15)	Naples, ITA (2007–15)	Budapest, HUN (2007–16)	Prague, CZE (2007–16)	Tokyo, JPN (2007–16)
Lisbon, PRT (2007–11)	Vienna, AUT (2009–16)	Calgary, CAN (2007–16)	Puebla, MEX (2007–14)	
Lviv, UKR (2007–16)		Cape Town, ZAF (2007–16)	St. Petersburg, RUS (2007–15)	
Johannesburg, ZAF (2007–16)		Gdansk, POL (2007–16)		
Kosice, SVK (2007–10)		Geneva, CHE (2007–16)		
Kyiv, UKR (2007–16)		Gothenburg, SWE (2007–16)		
Odessa, UKR (2007–12)		Guadalajara, MEX (2009–15)		
Oslo, NOR (2007–16)		Istanbul, TUR (2007–15)		
Madrid, ESP (2007–14)		Marseille, FRA (2007–16)		
Medellin, COL (2007–16)		Monterrey, MEX (2007–15)		
Paris, FRA (2007–16)		Moscow, RUS (2007–15)		
Plovdiv, BGR (2007–14)		Novi Sad, SRB (2007; 2011–16)		
Presov, SVK (2007–12)		Osaka, JPN (2007–16)		
Rio de Janeiro, BRA (2012–14)		Poznan, POL (2008–16)		
San José, CRI (2008–16)		Riga, LVA (2007–16)		
Seoul, KOR (2007–16)		Toronto, CAN (2007–16)		
Sofia, BGR (2007–16)		Warsaw, POL (2007–16)		
Tallinn, EST (2007–16)		Wellington, NZL (2007–16)		
Tshwane/Pretoria, ZAF (2007–16)		Yokohama, JPN (2007–16)		
Varna, BGR (2007–14)		Zagreb, HRV (2007–16)		
Vilnius, LTU (2007–10)				

Table 5.2 Descriptive statistics, unbalanced city-year panel, 2007–2016

Variable	Obs.	Mean	Std. Dev.	Min	Max
Total city debt, USD mln	653	$4,110.33	$9,897.93	$1.57	$72,456.88
Percent debt securities	160	44.38	37.13	0.00	100.00
City population	637	2.5 million	3.1 million	91.4 thousand	14.7 million
City unemployment rate	637	8.39	5.05	0.70	26.50
GCP per capita, USD mln	637	$30,066.24	$29,019.98	$604.00	$178,608.10
Operating expenditure, USD mln	612	$3,990.22	$7,501.37	$29.33	$56,145.81
Capital expenditure, USD mln	612	$1,038.70	$2,210.20	$0.00	$21,717.69
Operating revenue, USD mln	612	$4,792.86	$9,313.75	$32.35	$67,643.99
Debt service % operating revenue	625	9.91	9.78	0.00	99.30
Budget and fiscal practices	353	0.21	0.14	0.06	0.75
Management of cash flows and accounting quality	353	0.24	0.13	0.04	0.63
Long-term planning	353	0.18	0.11	0.04	0.58
Government openness and transparency	353	0.19	0.11	0.05	0.65
Political and administrative stability	353	0.18	0.11	0.05	0.69
Rating AAA/Aaa	653	0.08	0.27	0.00	1.00
Rating AA/Aa range	653	0.23	0.42	0.00	1.00
Rating A range	653	0.17	0.37	0.00	1.00
Rating BBB/Baa range	653	0.22	0.42	0.00	1.00
Rating BB/Ba range	653	0.15	0.36	0.00	1.00
Rating B range	653	0.07	0.26	0.00	1.00
Rating CCC/Caa range	653	0.03	0.18	0.00	1.00
Unrated	653	0.05	0.22	0.00	1.00
System info resolution institutions	653	0.02	0.54	−2.11	1.37

City Debt Levels

City debt level is measured by the total direct debt outstanding. The data were classified, according to the EU and OECD debt classifications, as general government and revenue debt securities, other debt-securities, private loans, and public loans (OJOTEU 2013).[2]. The data pertain only to

[2] *Official Journal of the European Union*, L 174, 26 June 2013. The significance of this source is that it makes accounting terminology available in numerous languages. Details are available at http://eur-lex.europa.eu/legal-content/EN/ALL/?uri=OJ%3AL%3A2013%3A174%3ATOC.

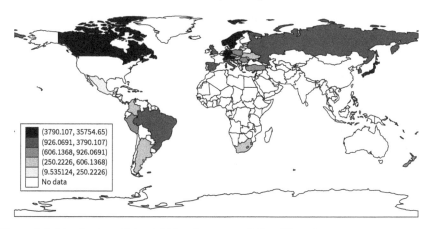

Figure 5.1 Distribution of city debt levels, average USD millions in 2005–2016
Note: Color intensity for shaded areas corresponds to higher levels of city debt levels. Blank areas represent absence of debt activity or debt data.

the selected city governments, and not to public authorities, entities, or public-private partnerships affiliated with the city. All data were converted from national currencies to millions of USD based on official currency exchange rates.[3] City debt levels range from $1.6 million to more than $72.4 billion, but the distribution departs significantly from normality. Figure 5.1 illustrates the magnitude of sample city debt levels across the globe. Cities with the highest levels of borrowing are in Scandinavian countries, Japan, and Canada. While the overall average debt trends upward over time, there is tremendous variation in debt levels across cities, and, in many cases, within cities over time.

It is instructive to view cities and their debt levels in a comparative perspective along select measures. It is natural that cities with larger populations or greater population densities require greater levels of capital financing. Figure 5.2 is a bivariate plot of city debt levels across population size. Overall, on average between 2005 and 2016, it appears that larger cities required greater levels of debt compared to smaller ones. In these figures, cities

---

[3] During the period under evaluation, the countries that authorized market-based capital financing to their SNGs also had freely floating currencies; thus, using their official currency exchange rates is not expected to mask the effects of any currency control monetary tools that are often used in several emerging economies. For robustness analyses, we also normalize city debt levels by city population (city debt per capita) and GCP (city debt per GCP). The results are consistent with the core findings reported in the chapter, and therefore are omitted for brevity.

Figure 5.2 Total city debt levels vs. city population, average in 2005–2016, natural log transformations

also appear to cluster according to OECD membership (wealthier economies versus less well-off ones) and legal origins (whether English, French, German, or Scandinavian). Such clustering may be shaped by economic resources available to local governments and approaches to the regulation of financial markets in distinct legal systems (La Porta et al. 1997; Ginannetti and Jentzsch 2013). On average in 2010–2016, we observe spatial proximity for cities from OECD member countries (generally above the fitted line) versus cities in non-OECD member countries (generally below the fitted line). In terms of legal origins, cities from English, German, and Scandinavian legal origins are predominantly above the fitted line compared to cities from a French legal origin.

Relatedly, when looking at city economic indicators directly, gross city product (GCP) per capita and city debt exhibit a steep and positive trend in Figure 5.3. Therefore, cities with higher GCP appear to have greater levels of per capita debt compared to cities with lower GCP. At the same time, there appears to be a certain level of clustering by legal origins once again. Countries with a French legal origin, primarily from Latin America and Eastern Europe, are located toward the lower left part of the figure, with countries from other legal origins mixed across the right-hand side of the bivariate distribution.

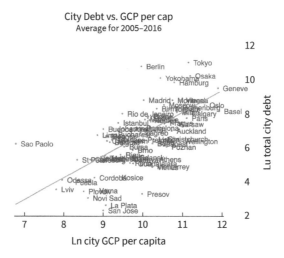

Figure 5.3 Total city debt levels vs. city GCP per capita, average in 2005–2016, natural log transformations

City Debt Composition

The share of debt securities refers to the percentage of city debt issued using capital market arrangements through general securities, revenue securities, and other (private loan) securities. Share of debt securities ranges from 0 percent to 100 percent, with a mean of 44 percent. Data for this measure are available for only 160 city-years, however, representing 25 percent of the sample. As Figure 5.4 shows, there is considerable variation in debt composition across cities. For summary purposes, we also broadly categorize percent of debt securities by three clusters—below 20 percent, between 20 percent and 80 percent, and above 80 percent.

We observe that cities with an English legal origin have levels of debt dominated by debt securities, cities with a French legal origin have the lowest share of debt securities, and cities from a German legal origin placed in between. Moreover, even among the 160 observations, variations are mainly between cities' debt composition, not within cities: just a few cities move between debt composition categories. Figure 5.4 shows the distributions of percent of debt securities by city, including years, during the decade under analysis. A few cities, such as St. Petersburg, Tshwane/Pretoria, and Kiev—all from emerging economies—have moved between the three categories of percent debt securities measure, while most others, such as Auckland, Calgary, and Tallinn, remained in the same category. Overall, there is a strong level of stability with regards to percent of debt securities at the city level.

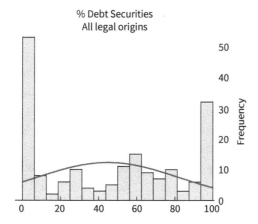

Percent debt securities categories:

Below 20%	**20%–80%**	**Above 80%**
Cape Town 2007–14	Auckland 2007–14	Calgary 2008–14
Kiev 2014	Berlin 2007–14	Johannesburg 2008,
Monterrey 2007–14	Christchurch 2007–14	2011–14
Novosibirsk 2009–12	Johannesburg 2007,	Kiev 2012–13
Porto 2012–14	2009–10	Montreal 2007–16
Puebla 2007–14	Moscow 2007–12, 2014	Moscow 2013
Rio de Janeiro	Novosibirsk 2008,	Novosibirsk 2007
2007–12, 2013–14	2013–14	St Petersburg 2007–08
Sao Paolo 2010–16	Paris 2013–14	Toronto 2007–16
Seoul 2010–13	Seoul 2007–08, 2014	
St Petersburg 2009	St Petersburg 2010–14	
Tshwane/Pretoria	Tallinn 2008–14	
2007–12	Tshwane/Pretoria 2013–14	
	Wellington 2007–14	

Figure 5.4 Distribution of debt composition for percent of debt securities and sorting cities by three debt composition categories, years included

Credit Ratings: Information Bases of Underlying City Credit Quality

Credit ratings are an important tool for assessing and communicating the underlying credit quality of a city in order to gain access to capital financing. They contain information about the context in which the city is located and, importantly, about the underlying city-level credit quality fundamentals. Empirical evidence shows that credit ratings are a reasonable mechanism for assessing, certifying, and communicating the informational content of credit quality of subnational-level governments (Palumbo and Zaporowski 2012; Moldogaziev and Guzman 2015; Loviscek and Crowley 1988; Martell et al.2013; Jimenez 2011; Peng and Brucato 2004).

Where credit ratings were available, we collected credit-rating data for the cities in the sample. Of the 653 city-year observations, 32 are unrated cases; 165 are non-investment grade cases with ratings in the CCC/Caa, B, and BB/Ba credit notches; 405 are investment grade cases with ratings in the BBB/Baa, A, and AA/Aa credit notches; and 51 are the highest credit quality class cases with a AAA/Aaa rating. The credit ratings are collected from the three global credit rating firms—Fitch, Moody's, and Standard & Poor's. Several cities in the sample obtained ratings from more than one of these credit rating firms. Generally, however, cities appear to obtain only one credit rating. Figure 5.5

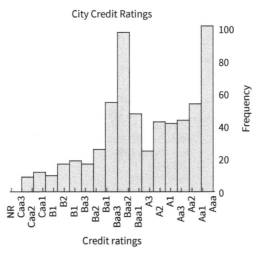

Unrated cities: Belgrade 2010–11; Birmingham 2007–09; Cali 2009–2013; Cape Town 2007; Cordoba 2010–11; Izmir 2007; Lima 2007–09; Marseille 2007–08; Novi Sad 2007; Odessa 2012; San Jose 2008; São Paolo 2010–16; Wellington 2007–09.

Non-investment grade cities: Athens 2011–16; Belgrade 2012–16; Buenos Aires 2007–16; Bursa 2007–15; Cordoba 2012–16; Guadalajara 2014–16; Istanbul 2007–08; Izmir 2008–10; Kiev 2007–16; La Plata 2007–16; Lisbon 2010–11; Lviv 2007–16; Monterrey 2012–15; Novi Sad 2012–16; Novosibirsk 2007–12; Odessa 2007–11; Puebla 2007–15; Rio de Janeiro 2007–09; Varna 2010–12; Zagreb 2016.

Investment grade cities: Athens 2007–10; Auckland 2007–16; Barcelona 2007–16; Basel 2007–16; Bogota 2008–16; Brno 2007–16; Bucharest 2007–16; Budapest 2007, 2011–16; Calgary 2007–16; Cali 2014–16; Cape Town 2008–16; Christchurch 2007–16; Gdansk 2007–16; Genève 2007–16; Istanbul 2012–16; Izmir 2013–15; Johannesburg 2007–16; Kosice 2007–10; Lima 2012–15; Lisbon 2007–09; Lyon 2007–16; Madrid 2007–14; Marseille 2009–16; Medellin 2007–16; Milan 2007–16; Monterrey 2010; Montreal 2007–16; Moscow 2007–15; Naples 2007–15; Osaka 2007–16; Ostrava 2007–16; Paris 2013–16; Porto 2007–11; Poznan 2008–16; Prague 2007–16; Presov 2007–12; Riga 2007–16; Rio de Janeiro 2010–11, 2013–15; Rome 2007–14; San Jose 2009–16; Seoul 2007–16; Sofia 2010–12; St Petersburg 2007–15; Tallinn 2007–16; Tokyo 2007–16; Toronto 2007–16; Tshwane/Pretoria 2007–16; Vienna 2016; Vilnius 2007–10; Warsaw 2007–16; Wellington 2010–16; Yokohama 2007–16; Zagreb 2007–13.

Highest investment grade cities: Berlin 2007–15; Birmingham 2010; Gothenburg 2007–16; Hamburg 2008-15; Oslo 2007–16; Paris 2007-12; Vienna 2009-15.

Figure 5.5 Distribution of city credit ratings, information on credit class, years included
Note: Sample size for city credit ratings $N = 653$ (unrated $N = 32$; non-investment grade observations [Ba/B/Caa] $N = 165$; investment grade observations [Aa/Baa] $N = 405$; highest investment grade observations [Aaa] $N = 51$).

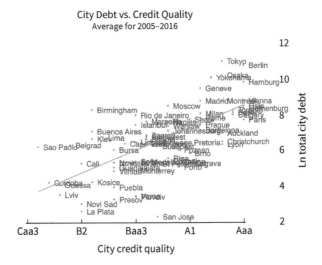

Figure 5.6 Total city debt levels, natural log transformation vs. city credit quality, averages in 2010–2016

shows the distribution of credit ratings, which ranges from Caa3/CCC– up to Aaa/AAA and has a mean rating of A2/A. The distribution is not normal, with two peaks around the Baa3/BBB– and Aaa/AAA credit notches.

Figure 5.6 shows a bivariate distribution of averages for city debt levels versus city credit ratings in 2005–2016. One can observe here that there is a positive association between the two variables. In addition, there appears to be a significant clustering of cities from OECD countries versus cities from non-OECD countries. Generally, cities in the former cluster have better credit ratings and greater levels of city debt. In terms of legal origins, cities from countries with Scandinavian, German, and English legal origins tend to have better credit ratings and relatively greater levels of city debt. Cities from countries with a French legal origin appear to further separate into two groups— mostly by those that are from OECD versus non-OECD member countries.

The composition of city debt also varies across the sample of cities in our analysis. Although there is a high level of variance around the fitted line for the bivariate distribution of percent debt securities and city credit ratings, primarily due to the non-normal distribution of percent debt securities measure, one can certainly observe a positive slope. Figure 5.7 shows that the data generally, but not exclusively, bear out our expectation that higher quality cities tend to rely on debt securities to a greater extent. There also appears to be a clustering of cities based on a country's OECD membership status, with cities from OECD countries generally enjoying higher levels of credit quality, and therefore, greater tendency to rely on debt securities. The results regarding

Figure 5.7 City debt compositions vs. city credit quality, averages in 2010–2016

the role of the legal origin on clustering of cities along the credit-rating scale is less conclusive, however.

Select Components of City Credit Quality

Existing research shows that the informational content of regional and local government credit quality is constructed around four broad classes of underlying credit fundamentals—economic, fiscal, debt and financial, and governance fundamentals. Holding governance institutions constant, it is possible to select generalizable and robust measures for each of the classes at the SNG level (Palumbo and Zaporowski 2012; Loviscek and Crowley 1988, Moldogaziev and Guzman 2015). From a comparative perspective, empirical evidence for city-level credit quality factors has been largely nonexistent, however.

While credit ratings are an excellent mechanism for informational resolution of city credit quality, it is also instructive to understand the components of credit ratings that can serve as relatively robust and generalizable information tools. Doing so is desirable for a number of reasons—cities without a rating may evaluate themselves along a list of core credit quality measures at their disposal (World Bank 2016; Eichler et al. 2012); city policymakers may compare themselves to other cities using both their credit ratings and the subcomponents; city policymakers may better interact with financial intermediaries, including credit-rating firms; and, most importantly, they may manage and address their credit quality fundamentals by focusing on key components of underlying credit quality both in medium-term and long-term horizons. By doing so, city policymakers can also better assess what they can afford, as exemplified in Northern Macedonia (see Box 5.1).

We present cases for each of the component classes of underlying credit fundamentals. Among typical measures that the empirical literature identifies for economic base are city population, GCP, or GCP per capita (as discussed in Figure 5.3). Given our sample, where we focus on the largest cities in each country, one can also look at the relative standing of these cities with respect to their national economies through measures of relative shares—whether the city's unemployment rate is above the national average as well as the relative size of city population and GCP over national levels.

For fiscal base measures, the most often used measures are city revenue and expenditure trends, as well as the net balance between the two. Revenue levels, their volatility, and the net balance convey information on a city's ability to pay not only for operating needs but also recurring long-term liabilities. Greater levels of revenues, especially own-source revenues, and lower levels of revenue volatility are positively related to credit quality. On the one hand, Padovani et al. (2018) argue that operating revenues are particularly relevant to credit quality in developing bond markets. Expenditure levels and

---

Box 5.1 Analytical Tools to Assess Municipal Bond Market Readiness in Northern Macedonia

Analytical tools can be useful for a jurisdiction to understand its ability and willingness to issue municipal bonds. These may include a comprehensive identification and analysis to identify internal and external contexts and regression analysis of fiscal and financial data. Such analyses, applied to Stip, Northern Macedonia, identified conditions in the internal and external contexts, both informing what efforts needed to be taken to shore up weak points (Gogovana Saminikov et al. 2017). Northern Macedonia has poorly developed financial markets, and municipalities rely on loans from commercial banks for financing. However, the regression analysis conducted for Stip revealed Stip's potential to carry a debt burden by examining trends in revenues, expenditures, balances, and debt service. The results of this assessment suggested that Stip could enjoy access to additional debt, and that municipal bond payment risks would remain lower if the bonds' repayment sources were linked to and guaranteed by specific revenues.

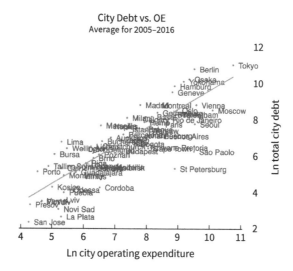

Figure 5.8 City debt levels vs. operating expenditures, averages in 2010–2016, natural log transformations

their volatility, on the other hand, show resources that are already committed to service delivery and service pressures. Greater spending levels, as well as greater spending volatility, are negative signs of underlying credit quality. Moreover, related to infrastructure financing more directly is spending on capital projects—the greater capital expenditures are at the city level, the need for overall reliance on debt is lower. At the same time, special compartmentalized or dedicated lines for capital expenditures may mean fewer maintenance delays and lower pressures on overall operating spending needs down the road. Figure 5.8 displays the positive relationship between city debt levels and operating expenditures. The debt to operating expenditures seems insensitive to OECD membership and legal origin, however.

Existing debt or financial burden is a factor directly relevant for city credit quality. Often used measures here are debt outstanding or the size of debt service, both as a percent of either operating revenues or own-source revenues. The logic is that if greater levels of revenue are already potentially in play to service existing levels of debt, a city may have fewer resources to operate within other areas central to its task responsibilities. Figure 5.9 shows the relationship between city debt service per operating expenditure and total city debt, averages in 2010–2016. The positive relationship highlights the ongoing debt service burden that cities face in exchange for acquiring capital upfront, though these ratios seem to be insensitive to OECD membership and legal origin. Existing research discusses relatively safe levels of debt burden that SNGs may wish to keep (Liu and Pradelli 2012), though Greer et al. (2018) caution

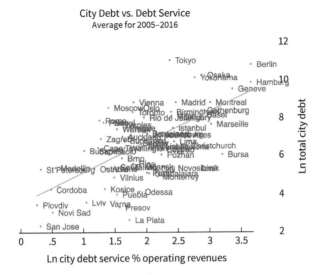

Figure 5.9 City debt levels vs. debt service as percent of operating revenues, averages in 2010–2016, natural log transformations

that jurisdictions may circumvent prescribed limits such as debt levels as a percentage of locally assessed property tax base through special purpose vehicles.

Finally, measures of city governance have to do with several management- and policy-related variables. Despite their importance, the financial management literature does not quantify governance measures as extensively as it does the preceding components of credit quality. The usual issue here is that there are no easily generalizable variables, such as GCP per capita or dollars of operating revenue, which one could utilize to measure governance fundamentals (an exception is Andersen et al.'s [2010] study, which operationalizes governance as on-time budget approval).

To assess measures of governance, we go directly to the official credit-rating reports produced by credit-rating firms to extract governance topics and their proportional weights in each credit report using computational text analysis techniques.[4] Generally, five governance factors are associated with city debt levels. These five measures are government openness and transparency; management of cash flows and accounting quality; political and administrative stability; budget and fiscal practices; and long-term planning. The topic model

---

[4] We partition text corpora in each credit-rating report using a five-topic model. Five topics are synthesized from methodologies of three global credit rating firms—Fitch, Moody's, and Standard & Poor's. Details of text partitioning and fit tests are presented in Ivonchyk and Moldogaziev (2021).

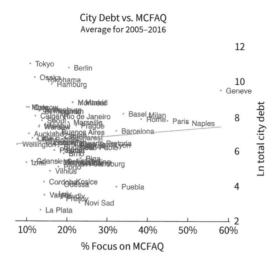

Figure 5.10 City debt levels, natural log transformation vs. management of cash flows and accounting quality (MCFAQ), averages in 2010–2016

measures identify the proportions given to each governance topic in credit reports. This method distinguishes the relative importance of each governance base within and between cities and assesses how this importance relates to our outcomes of interest. In a bivariate distribution, for instance, management of cash flows and accounting quality (MCFAQ) has a positive slope. One can observe in Figure 5.10 that MCFAQ positively relates to city debt levels, though the roles of OECD membership and legal origin are uncertain.

System Information Resolution Institutions and Controls

Among control measures for levels of city debt and city debt composition, system-level information resolution institutions remain a key factor of interest. As discussed in detail in Chapter 4, we operationalize a system's information resolution institutions along Rajan and Zingales's (1998) continuum of contractibility based on an index made up of transparency and depth of credit information, extent of disclosure, and regulatory quality. We remind the reader that, first, transparency and depth of credit information refers to the country's availability and distribution of information on individuals and firms that affect credit-market participants. Second, the extent of disclosure represents a country's quality of disclosure from firms to investors, serving an important accountability function for financial intermediation. Finally, regulatory quality captures the ability of governments to adopt and implement policies critical to fiscal policy and governance. The previous chapter showed that aggregate SNG debt levels relate positively with information resolution institutions in the country, especially to transparency and depth of credit information and extent of disclosure.

Figure 5.11 continues to show information resolution institutions are also positively related to debt levels and debt composition at the city level. We also observe the interplay between country levels of information resolution versus city levels of debt by OECD membership and legal origins. Non-OECD countries and countries with a French legal origin report lower levels of city debt. Similar conclusions hold for the bivariate association between a country's information resolution institutions and city-level debt composition. Variances around the fitted lines in Figure 5.12 are wide, but general trends remain largely the same. Of note is that, regardless of OECD classification or legal origin, city debt levels and debt composition exhibit the same association with informational content of city credit ratings and information resolution institutions. This means that while some classes of cities may have an inherent wealth or institutional advantage that gives them a head start, even those cities with less favorable credit quality or information contexts may command access to capital market financing alternatives.

Overall, the descriptive statistics lay a firm foundation for testing empirically our primary theoretical expectation in this chapter regarding the informational content of city credit quality and city levels of debt and debt composition. As

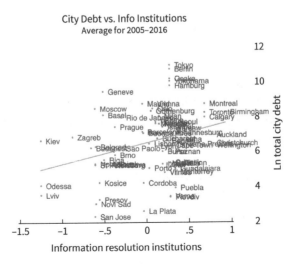

Figure 5.11 City debt levels, natural log transformation vs. system information resolution institutions, averages in 2010–2016

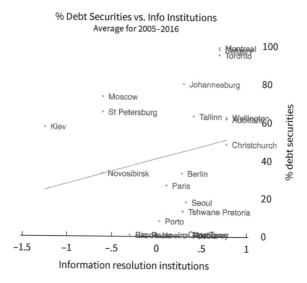

Figure 5.12 City debt composition vs. system information resolution institutions, averages in 2010–2016

a secondary objective, we empirically test the relationship between a country's ability to resolve information problems and city levels of debt.

Modeling City Borrowing and Debt Composition

Factors reflecting institutional maturity at the national level affect the development of SNG credit markets (Martell and Guess 2006; Canuto and Liu 2013; Freire and Petersen 2004). Holding these factors constant, no comparative research exists on the extent to which information resolution mechanisms available to cities, beyond the broader information resolution institutions at the macro level, affect the size and composition of SNG debt. Extrapolating the lessons of corporate finance to SNG capital markets, this section presents empirical results from multivariate regression models to answer the following research questions:

1. Is there a relationship between informational content of credit quality and city debt level, holding other factors constant?
2. Is there a relationship between informational content of credit quality and city debt composition, holding other factors constant?

Scarce evidence, generally from single-country studies (e.g., Blackwell and Kidwell 1988; Greer and Denison 2016), predicts that the answers to these research questions will be affirmative. This analysis expands such inquiries to a cross-country context. In multivariate regression models that control for city and year fixed effects, we estimate the relationship that outcomes of interest—debt levels and composition—relate to the informational content of credit quality, above and beyond the system's information resolution institutions. The models test whether debt size and share of debt securities are a function of city credit quality, system information capacity, other control variables, and an error term.[5] Technical details about core measures of interest, their descriptions, regression models, and expanded empirical results are presented in the chapter's appendix.

Overall, credit quality is associated with both city debt levels and the share of debt securities. The relationship is not linear, however. In terms of debt levels, the results separate cities in a concave function into three groups: those with the highest credit quality, or triple-A rated cities; those cities with investment grade credit quality, or with ratings of BBB/Baa to AA/Aa; and those cities with below investment grade credit quality, or ratings of BB or less. Investment grade cities represent the group with the greatest level of debt, followed by triple-A rated cities. Non-investment grade cities carry the least amount of debt.

The results allow us to drill down beyond overall credit quality to the components of credit quality: economic, fiscal, debt and financial, and city governance fundamentals. Among the economic components of credit quality, overall city population, as well as city's share of national population, are significant covariates of city debt levels. Thus, larger populations naturally require and gain access to more debt. The fact that the size of the city relative to the nation is significant for debt levels suggests that large, primary cities either behave differently, or that the national government and/or markets treat them differently. Due to their importance—economic, political, or otherwise—they may manage to access capital markets with ease relative to secondary cities. Stronger GCP per capita levels are positively, but only marginally, significant for city debt levels.

Among fiscal measures, operating expenditures, capital expenditures, and per capita operating expenditures are significantly related to city debt levels. These show both the ability and willingness to pay at the city level for both current and capital needs. The same result holds for debt-service levels: more debt service comports with higher debt levels. One of the governance measures,

---

[5] A number of other control measures are present in the study, which are utilized as necessary in a listwise approach due to concerns for multicollinearity and model degrees of freedom. At the same time, all models incorporate two-way fixed-effects models, for city and year, to take advantage of the panel data structure. We employ cluster robust error terms due to the presence of heteroskedasticity.

budget and fiscal practices, is significantly less relevant in our cross-country sample of cities in comparison to other governance topics—government openness and transparency, management of cash flows and accounting quality, political and administrative stability, and long-term planning. This suggests that policies to improve governance are as, if not more, important than those promoting budget practices.

In terms of debt composition, results of both linear and ordered functional forms of percent debt securities models show that credit quality impacts debt composition, and that the impact is nonlinear. Evidence suggests that debt securities are utilized the most by highest rated triple-A cities. Other investment grade cities, relative to triple-A cities, appear to rely on less debt from securities. Therefore, highest quality cities appear to opt heavily for debt securities, while cities with relatively lower, but still investment grade credit qualities, issue higher levels of debt using a mix of capital market options.

Also, consider how the decomposed components of credit quality affect debt composition. For economic bases of credit quality, city population and its size relative to the country population, respectively, are significant, albeit in different directions. While greater population size may require or facilitate greater access to debt securities, the most populous cities per national population rely on a lower share of debt from securities. The reasons for this are unknown but may have to do with their historical relationships as dominant cities, having both city-level and national-level roles. Similarly, for fiscal base measures, greater levels of capital expenditures may diminish the need for debt securities, albeit marginally so. The remaining fiscal measures, as well as the debt profile measure, are insignificant in the debt composition models. For city governance measures, management of cash flows and accounting quality and long-term planning are significant drivers of debt securities relative to other city governance topics. Therefore, disciplined fiscal management approaches and planning for long-term horizons appear to be associated with greater reliance on debt securities.

Finally, even while testing the relationships between city credit quality and debt outcomes, previous results that the system's information resolution institutions have a positive association with debt levels and composition remain relevant. The more the country is able to resolve information problems, particularly transparency and depth of credit information and extent of disclosure of financial information, the more likely cities are to access market capital. When combined with the results that city credit quality also affects debt levels and composition, the clear message is that information resolution at both the national and subnational levels is critical to SNG capital market development.

Lessons for Policy and Practice

These results matter for policymakers in cities around the globe, whose goal is to realize a higher standard of living and economic opportunity through the local government's provision of basic infrastructure. With an ongoing process of city investment in its community, facilitated by infrastructure provision, cities can provide the services that the citizens need to improve their communities. The results show that city size and debt levels correlate, allowing for more investment opportunities but at the same time posing more exposure and risk to the national government. Like a fulcrum, debt management calls for a city to balance its investment for the purposes of meeting citizens' infrastructure needs with responsible fiscal constraints to avoid creating negative fiscal externalities. Decisions about how a city finances its infrastructure are a critical component of a fiscal governance task.

To reiterate the main findings, information about credit quality matters. It matters externally for investors to have reasonable expectation of repayment; it matters internally to national governments to ensure that subnational borrowing will not derail fiscal balance and pose negative outcomes to other governments and/or across levels of government; and it matters to city policymakers to gain competence in the process of financing. City borrowing and debt composition covary with informational components of city credit quality as well as national-level information resolution institutions, particularly those regarding transparency and depth of credit information and extent of disclosure of financial information.

The results presented in this chapter suggest a policy approach to the management of and access to external resources by examining debt in the face of city credit quality. Figure 5.13 presents a quadrant that groups cities along two dimensions: debt levels and credit quality. This quadrant guides policy decisions for the four groups of cities. As the empirical patterns we presented are similar for debt levels and debt composition, the discussion holds for both.

Beginning with the lower left quadrant are cities with low credit quality and low debt. For a city to have better credit quality and more access to debt, policy should affect both city credit quality, along the horizontal axis, and access to capital, along the vertical axis. These are cities like Lviv, Cordoba, or Belgrade from the sample. The policies desired include city policies to internally enhance their own credit quality or any national government policies that may enhance, rather than inhibit, city credit quality. After these policies bear fruit, cities may begin leveraging a range of capital market financing options where and when necessary.

In Figure 5.13, moving to the upper left quadrant are cities with low credit quality but high debt levels. In addition to the first set of policy concerns, an additional policy set is required to ensure that relatively low exposure of over-indebtedness exist to other governments, both vertically and horizontally speaking. For these jurisdictions, rules of fiscal responsibility offer a policy tool to constrain debt. In the sample, the lower credit quality cities with relatively higher levels of debt are Buenos Aires and Rio de Janeiro. It is no coincidence that these cities bump up against rules of fiscal responsibility, constraints designed to, among other objectives, rein in over-indebtedness.

Moving to the lower right quadrant are cities with high credit quality but low debt levels. Policy objectives for these jurisdictions may be to encourage greater capital market access. Thus, in our sample, cities such as Cali, Poznan, Paris, and Wellington are potentially underutilizing the benefits that capital markets can offer.

Finally, in Figure 5.13, there are cities with high credit quality and relatively higher levels of debt in the upper right quadrant. With highest credit quality the most efficiencies can be gained from capital market financing, including that from debt securities. The cities in the sample that fall in this quadrant are Geneva, Montreal, and Yokohama. Though cities in this quandrant may have high debt, they also can draw from a strong credit quality base with relative ease.

In sum, the policy questions are as follows: What needs to happen, by internal or external incentives, for cities to raise their credit quality? And, what institutional arrangements should be used to reduce the debt of low-credit

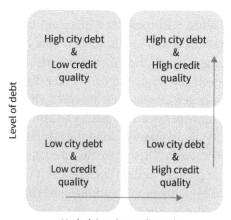

Underlying city credit quality

Figure 5.13 Policy quadrants for decision considerations between credit quality and city debt

quality cities and raise the debt, specifically debt from securities, for higher credit quality cities?

The empirical results also introduce the question of whether OECD status and legal origin matter. Examination of the key variables by OECD membership and legal origin suggest two clusters. The first cluster contains cities characterized by non-OECD countries, French legal origin, low wealth, low credit quality, and low use of debt securities. The second cluster contains cities characterized by OECD membership, non-French legal origin, high wealth, high credit quality, and greater use of debt securities. Whether OECD status (economic wealth) or legal origin account for these discrepancies is beyond the scope of this book. It is fair to conclude, however, that there are interactions between these two variables and other factors important to SNG borrowing that call for future research. How can a city move from one cluster to another? Upon examination of the legal origin, what systematic constraints or opportunities exist for cities? Do features of the legal system systematically inhibit wealth and credit quality, thus ultimately inhibiting SNG market development? Or, is legal origin simply spurious? The pattern of legal origin is less clear when considering both economic factors and legal origin (primarily the cities from a French legal origin), suggesting that policy measures can overcome any constraint imposed by a legal system, suggesting the legal system is pliable. For example, when controlling for city credit quality, the cities from French legal-origin countries can be found in both OECD and non-OECD member clusters along the capital market utilization measures.

An important result of this research is that city access to capital finance is not, nor need be, limited to the wealthiest countries. Rather, attention to information resolution mechanisms as well as information institutions is important for expanding capital market access to a broader range of cities. Although only a small portion of sample cities uses debt securities, the results provide a roadmap for all city policymakers to follow as they build their competency to engage in capital market financing. Even smaller, less wealthy cities can benefit from mastering the principles of information resolution.

Understanding what policy measures *should* be taken by what level of government can be challenging, as a conceptual issue to tackle pertains to what policy issues constitute the domain of the central government versus SNG. While ultimately the financing choices at the city level depend on both national information resolution institutions and the informational components of underlying credit quality, there appear to be cases of both capital market financing over- and under-utilization in our sample of cities, leaving policy space for both national and subnational leaders.

All the recommendations for policy at the national level discussed in Chapter 4 remain in force here. They are to build the architecture for information flow from borrowers to investors. Particular attention should be given to creating the transparency and depth of credit information and extent of financial disclosure for all market actors as one of the key components of contractibility. The recommendation complements those of the Committee on the Global Financial System (2019), which target the development of capital markets writ large. Moreover, national policy can improve the quality and transparency of national and subnational fiscal and debt data via mechanisms of monitoring, coordination, and accountability. Efforts in these areas include the use of independent accounting and auditing standards; collection of subnational fiscal and debt data; and the production and dissemination of financial management ratios and budget data. Policies that support disclosure requirements of borrowers, investment projects, and prices further advance information flow.

Beyond the system-level efforts of the national government to establish credit contractibility, the national government's policy should be to help SNGs enhance their own credit quality (see Box 5.2). The first measure may be for the national government to set credit quality standards. Systematic analysis of

---

Box 5.2 Recommended National-Level Policy Measures to Improve Information Resolution Institutions

- Establish credit assessment standards that subnational borrowers may use as a reference point to self-assess readiness to access capital markets, including the enactment of regulations to harmonize accounting standards across levels of government.
- Encourage assessment and certification—either by self-, third-party, or public entities—of SNGs' credit quality based on widely accepted standards, and introduce mechanisms for the continuous monitoring of SNGs' credit fundamentals.
- Initiate disclosure platforms regarding fiscal, financial and debt, capital investment, and governance information; update or introduce legislation and implementation mechanisms to ensure timely and full disclosure of material information about potential subnational borrowers; and create centralized and publicly available repositories with relevant information about SNGs' financial condition and outstanding debt.

city credit fundamentals, monitoring of such, and dissemination of the results can add to the information environment. A second effort should be for the national government to evaluate how fiscal federal arrangements encourage or hamper city credit quality, with a willingness to revise policies that inhibit SNG capital market growth. A system that encourages SNGs to improve their credit quality may require changes to the distribution of revenues and resources, which undoubtedly would necessitate painful deliberations, but the enhanced credit quality and SNG fiscal health could be a worthy exchange for the cost of modifying a fiscal governance system. A third effort would be to set and politically support fiscal rules that constrain over-indebtedness and enforce bankruptcy proceedings in the event of default.

No amount of national effort to enhance SNG credit quality will have much effect if the efforts do not pair with incentives for public sector borrowers to comply. Thus, credit quality efforts should be met with rewards for good performance (Martell and Guess 2006). One type of reward for SNGs with good credit quality is to have the authority to borrow from capital markets. The national government, in consultation with subnational policymakers, would thus be responsible for establishing clear-cut thresholds of creditworthiness, whereby any SNG that meets the thresholds can attain the defined benefit without facing burdensome regulations and obstacles only overcome by subjective judgment and political whim.

The recommendations for policy at the regional and local level are to adopt measures and mechanisms to enhance credit quality (see Box 5.3). The first step is for cities to inventory and evaluate their credit quality. Even those

---

Box 5.3 Recommended Subnational Policy Measures to Improve Information Resolution Mechanisms

- Establish clear short- and long-term capital improvement plans and budgets based on prioritization criteria.
- Self-assess credit risk fundamentals to identify factors affecting credit quality strengths and weaknesses; adopt means of comparative data analysis over time and across jurisdictions; and use information to improve credit quality.
- Adopt practices to develop accurate fiscal and financial data and accounting review processes.
- Invest in human resources, processes, and technologies to address fiscal and financial transparency, production, analysis, and dissemination of information.

borrowers that do not choose to undergo a formal credit evaluation from an independent party can conduct an analysis of their credit quality by using tools such as those provided by the World Bank, the German Gessellshaft für Internationale Zusammanerbeit, and others (World Bank 2016; Eichler et al. 2012; Farvacque-Vitkovic and Kopanyi 2019). City policymakers can compare the results to historical data and benchmark themselves against peers in the country and across borders. To improve the climate of transparency and disclosure, city policymakers should disseminate the results, at a minimum to their citizens and to relevant stakeholders. Once policymakers evaluate city credit quality, they can identify areas for improvement.

The results of this study show that a city's economic base (population, GCP); fiscal position (operating expenditures, capital expenditures); existing debt burden (debt service); governance quality of budget and fiscal practices (for debt levels); and management of cash flows and accounting quality and long-term planning topics (for debt securities) are particularly salient for city debt. City governments should prioritize improvements in these areas. Finally, city policymakers can track performance over time to highlight improvements and guide additional policy choices. Ultimately, a city should exhibit credit quality improvements and be able to prepare for a formal credit quality analysis. Policymakers must come to own, embrace, and manage city fiscal and debt affairs, and the dissemination of this information to all public and private stakeholders.

Despite these recommendations at the national and subnational levels, a few issues remain outstanding. First, whether the national or subnational level should have domain for guidance on SNG debt policies is not determined a priori, and it is valuable for national and local policymakers to delineate which level should be responsible for setting which policies. Second, while we advise cities to inventory and improve their credit quality, there has been little guidance of how to get inside the black box of credit quality assessment and its component parts. Chapter 6 takes up this issue by exploring the fundamental components of underlying credit quality. Finally, recall that one of the goals of SNG access to capital markets is to reduce the need for SNG dependence on national governments to finance infrastructure. This and the previous chapter have spoken about the need to improve the information resolution environment and fundamentals bases of SNG credit quality. But there is an additional angle: financial instruments and financial contracts available to SNGs may be structured or used in ways that can limit credit risk. Alm (2015: 253) writes that "policymakers need to encourage the development of financial institutions and instruments that can surmount information problems and relieve the government of the need to provide subsidies and interest guarantees." Chapter 8 addresses this issue in the discussion of enhancements.

The results in this chapter are consistent with the findings from studies on public and corporate finance that information resolution and information certification and signaling tools impact the levels and type of capital-financing options. As such, the underlying relationships identified in corporate financial management literature hold for SNG capital markets as well. Credit contractibility in a system and information evaluation tools available to cities are critical for capital market development.

Technical Appendix

This section specifies the model and analytical results from the multivariate regression analyses. It begins with a presentation of the model and descriptions of key variables and continues with the results of how covariates affect city debt levels and debt composition.

Data and Measurement

The variables for our multivariate regression models are from an unbalanced panel data set, with i = cities and t = years from 2007 to 2016. The two outcomes of interest are aggregate city debt levels, in USD converted to natural log values, and aggregate annual percent of city debt securities, 0 percent to 100 percent, which is represented using two competing functional forms—linear and ordered categorical specifications. The main measures of interest are city credit rating, and key underlying factors of credit ratings, as well as a system's information resolution institutions. Credit ratings are represented by ordinal and binary categories. A number of variables are utilized to test for informational components of city credit ratings and their individual associations with city debt levels and debt composition. The details for all variables of interest are summarized in Table A5.1.

Regression Results

Models 1.1 and 1.2 are for the covariates of debt levels, with two-way city-year fixed effects, focusing on the role of city-level credit ratings. The coefficient for credit rating is statistically significant in Model 1 and provides evidence

Table A5.1 Key variables of interest and measurement

DV	Where the outcomes of interest are city debt level and city debt composition (dependent variables—DV):
	DV1: ln(Debt level) = aggregate annual direct city debt in USD, ln
	DV2a: Debt composition = aggregate annual percent of city debt securities, 0% to 100%
	DV2b: Debt composition = categorical functional form of aggregate annual percent of city debt securities, category 1 = below 20%, category 2 = 20%–80%, category 3 = above 80%
IV	The variable of interest is credit rating. Competing functional forms of city-level credit rating are the following:
	IV1: Credit rating = city credit rating from Fitch, Moody's, and/or Standard & Poor's, unrated = 1, else = 0; Caa/CCC- = 2, . . . Aaa/AAA = 20
	IV2: Credit rating = binary functional form of city credit rating from Fitch, Moody's, and/or Standard & Poor's, unrated = 1, else = 0; Caa/CCC- = 1, else = 0; . . . Aaa/AAA = 1, else = 0
	To assess the relative dimensions of credit ratings, we decompose credit quality further into the four component parts of economic, fiscal, debt and financial, and governance fundamentals per IV-E, IV-F, IV-D, and IV-G.
IV-E	The city-level economic measures are (component of city credit quality) the following:
	IV-E1: Unemployment rate = annual city unemployment rate
	IV-E2: GCP per capita = annual GCP per capita in USD, ln
	IV-E3: Population = annual city population, ln
	IV-E4: Ratio city population over country population = relative city population size vs. country population size, represented in percent
IV-F	The city-level fiscal measures are (component of city credit quality) the following:
	IV-F1: Operating expenditure = annual city operating expenditure in USD, ln
	IV-F2: Capital expenditure = annual city capital expenditure in USD, ln
	IV-F3: Operating expenditure per capita = annual city operating expenditure per capita in USD, ln
IV-D	The city-level debt and financial measure is (component of city credit quality) the following:
	IV-D: Debt service = ratio of annual city long-term debt service over city operating revenues, ln
IV-G	The city-level governance measures are (component of city credit quality) the following:
	IV-G1: Government openness and transparency = proportion of attention to city-level government openness and transparency topic, LDA extracted measure from Fitch, Moody's, and/or Standard & Poor's reports, governance/management sections
	IV-G2: Management of cash flows and accounting quality = proportion of attention to city-level management of cash flows and accounting quality topic, LDA extracted measure from Fitch, Moody's, and/or Standard & Poor's reports, governance/management sections
	IV-G3: Political and administrative stability = proportion of attention to city-level political and administrative stability topic, LDA extracted measure from Fitch, Moody's, and/or Standard & Poor's reports, governance/management sections

Table A5.1 *Continued*

	IV-G4: Budget and fiscal practices = proportion of attention to city-level budget and fiscal practices topic, LDA extracted measure from Fitch, Moody's, and/or Standard & Poor's reports, governance/management sections
	IV-G5: Long-term planning = proportion of attention to city-level long-term planning topic, LDA extracted measure from Fitch, Moody's, and/or Standard & Poor's reports, governance/management sections
	We control for the system level information resolution institutions. The country (macro) level measure of information resolution institutions is the following:
CV	CV-IRI: Information resolution institutions = annual country level information resolution index (see Chapter 4 for details)

Several other measures of macro-level governance are excluded for brevity, due to scope and relevance. Core conclusions regarding city credit ratings, credit quality components, and the outcomes of interest remain unaffected from such omission.

in favor of our hypothesis that cities with higher levels of credit quality tend to have greater levels of city debt, all else equal. The relationship, as shown in Model 1.2, does not appear to be linear, however. With the highest credit quality measure as an omitted category, we can observe that investment grade quality cities—those in double-A, single-A, and triple-B/Baa range—are the ones that generally drive the statistical difference. On the flip side, unrated cities and those in non-investment grade credit quality range (Ba and lower) all appear to be associated with relatively lower levels of city debt. Table A5.2 presents the findings.

In Models 2.1–2.5, presented in Table A5.3, instead of a measure of credit rating, we focus on individual components of credit quality. Due to multicollinearity and degrees of freedom concerns, we do not include all economic, fiscal, debt and finance, and city governance measures in the same equation. Instead, we tackle these in a list-wise fashion. In Model 2.1 the focus is on city unemployment rates, city GDP per capita, city population size, and the relative population size of a city vis-à-vis a country's population size. Of these measures, city population size is the most prominent, showing a statistically significant positive relationship with city levels of debt, all else constant. Relative city population size versus overall country population size is negatively related to city debt levels, however. This is plausible because as a city becomes more prominent due to its population size, its fiscal position becomes more important to higher levels of government, including in capital financing. This phenomenon is known as "too big to fail" (Wildasin 1997). GCP per capita is marginally significant and positive.

Table A5.2 Models 1.1–1.2 for the covariates of city debt levels, linear and binary credit-rating functional forms, two-way city-year fixed-effects models

Variables	Model 1.1	Model 1.2
DV1: ln(Total city debt)—Ordinary Least Squares (OLS)		
L1.Credit rating	0.0224*	
	(2.56)	
L1.System info resolution	0.337*	0.362**
	(2.47)	(2.59)
Rating AA/Aa range		0.434**
		(3.15)
Rating A range		0.616***
		(3.47)
Rating BBB/Baa rang		0.477**
		(2.70)
Rating BB/Ba range		0.356+
		(1.78)
Rating B range		0.460+
		(1.85)
Rating CCC/Caa range		0.367
		(1.49)
Unrated		0.195
		(1.08)
City FE	Yes	Yes
Year FE	Yes	Yes
Constant	6.799***	6.491***
	(30.98)	(20.07)
N	653	653
AIC	795.20	801.90
BIC	1171.60	1205.30
Log-likelihood	–313.60	–311.00
R-squared	0.959	0.960

Notes: Rating Aaa/AAA = omitted rating category

t statistics (robust standard errors) in parentheses

Level of significance: + p <0.10, * p <0.05, ** p <0.01, *** p <0.001

Model 2.2 presents results for the association between city fiscal measures and city levels of debt. One can observe here that the levels of both operating expenditures and capital expenditures are significantly and positively related to levels of city debt, all else equal. Model 2.3 swaps the measure of total city operating expenditures to per capita levels. Results suggest that, all else held

Table A5.3 Models 2.1–2.5 for the covariates of city debt levels, individual credit quality components, two-way city-year fixed-effects models

Variables	Model 2.1	Model 2.2	Model 2.3	Model 2.4	Model 2.5
DV1: ln(Total city debt)—Ordinary Least Squares (OLS)					
City unemp. rate	−0.00373				
	(−0.46)				
ln(GDP per cap)	0.231+				
	(1.90)				
ln(City population)	3.072***				
	(3.75)				
r(CityPop/CountryPop)	−0.291***				
	(−3.93)				
L1.System info resolution	0.368**	0.449**	0.451***	0.132	0.229
	(2.75)	(3.23)	(3.33)	(1.08)	(1.41)
ln(Oper. expend.)		0.262*			
		(2.47)			
ln(Capit. expend.)		0.175**	0.199***		
		(3.23)	(3.61)		
ln(Oper. expend.pc.)			0.207**		
			(2.87)		
ln(Debt serv.)				0.159**	
				(2.98)	
Management of cash flows and accounting quality					0.387
					(0.67)
Budget and fiscal practices					−1.004*
					(−2.08)
Political and admin. stability					−0.958
					(−1.51)
Long-term planning					−0.354
					(−0.95)
City FE	Yes	Yes	Yes	Yes	Yes
Year FE	Yes	Yes	Yes	Yes	Yes
Constant	−38.85**	3.497***	4.049***	6.524***	7.517***
	(−3.20)	(−4.19)	(−7.17)	(−27.79)	(−18.21)
N	637	612	612	625	353
AIC	763.70	699.10	689.40	708.20	353.20
BIC	1151.40	1074.50	1064.80	1081.00	631.60
Log-likelihood	−294.80	−264.50	−259.70	−270.10	−104.60
R-squared	0.961	0.962	0.963	0.963	0.970

Notes: Gov. openness and transparency = omitted governance topic

t statistics (robust standard errors) in parentheses

Level of significance: + p <0.10, * p <0.05, ** p <0.01, *** p <0.001

equal, per capita city operating expenditures are also positively associated with city debt levels.

Model 2.4 evaluates the measure of debt burden. One can find here that the ratio of city-level debt service over city-level operating revenues is significantly and positively associated with city levels of debt. This is reasonable, as the more debt one has, the more debt service there is. The policy issue is "how much" debt is optimal or sustainable, a concern often discussed in the fiscal position and debt affordability literatures.

Finally, Model 2.5 evaluates which of the five city governance factors are associated with city debt levels. These five measures, based on extant literature and credit-rating methodologies for city-level governance or management components, are government openness and transparency, management of cash flows and accounting quality, political and administrative stability, budget and fiscal practices, and long-term planning. We extract the five governance factors directly from the governance and management discussion sections of Fitch, Moody's, and Standard & Poor's using topic models for text analysis. Doing so allows for within and between city analyses of governance measures that are discussed significantly by credit-rating firms as important.

Topic models identify the proportions given to each topic within a corpus of a document. Consequently, we can distinguish how important each city governance measure is within and between cities and assess how this importance is related to our outcomes of interest. Of the five governance measures, four stand out as being equally important: One of the governance measures, budget and fiscal practices, is significant in our cross-country sample of cities in comparison to other governance themes that appear to be equally more important— government openness and transparency, management of cash flows and accounting quality, political and administrative stability, and long-term planning.

We now turn our attention to the covariates of debt composition. Recall that the distribution for the percent of debt securities measure is not normal. Consequently, in addition to a linear functional form of debt composition, we test for an ordered functional form of this measure, where the outcome of interest has three choice categories.

Table A5.4 presents the results for a linear functional form of debt composition and its covariates of interest. Notice that the sample sizes in Model 3.1 and 3.2 both shrink significantly compared to models of debt levels. The primary reason is lack of data on debt composition at the city level of analysis. While we encourage the readers to approach these results with caution, our results continue to offer important implications to theory and practice of SNG capital financing from a cross-country comparative perspective.

Table A5.4 Models 3.1–3.2 for the covariates of the linear functional form of city debt composition, linear and binary credit quality functional forms, two-way city-year fixed effects models

Variables	Model 3.1	Model 3.2
DV2a: Percent debt securities—Ordinary Least Squares (OLS)		
Credit rating	–0.0379	
	(–0.19)	
System info resolution	23.94*	24.37*
	(2.26)	(2.28)
Rating AA/Aa range		–51.79***
		(–6.27)
Rating A range		–62.39***
		(–6.32)
Rating BBB/Baa range		–51.43***
		(–6.00)
Non-investment grade		–53.28***
		(–6.28)
Unrated		–50.36***
		(–6.75)
City FE	Yes	Yes
Year FE	Yes	Yes
Constant	–10.92	38.75***
	(–1.61)	(7.02)
N	173	173
AIC	1395.30	1399.30
BIC	1502.50	1516.00
Log-likelihood	–663.60	–662.70
R-squared	0.908	0.909

Notes: Rating AAA/Aaa = omitted credit rating category

t statistics (robust standard errors) in parentheses

Level of significance: $+ p < 0.10$, $* p < 0.05$, $** p < 0.01$, $*** < 0.001$

Overall, two results stand out from Models 3.1 and 3.2. First, the relationship with city credit ratings and city debt composition is nonlinear. It appears that all credit-rating categories differ from the Aaa/AAA sample of cities. All else equal, triple-A rated cities in our sample tend to use significantly greater levels of debt securities. Notice, however, that due to scarcity of observations, the lowest credit quality categories below investment grade level are collapsed to a single category of non-investment grade cities. Second, a system's informational resolution institutions remain a significant factor even for city-level debt composition, all else equal.

We replicate the linear debt composition models using ordered specification of debt composition by estimating ordered logit (Models 4.1 and 4.3) and ordered probit (Models 4.2. and 4.4) regression models, also with two-way city-year fixed effects. Table A5.5 displays these results. By and large, the findings from these models confirm the conclusions from the models with a

Table A5.5 Models 4.1–4.4 for the covariates of ordered functional form of city debt composition, linear and binary credit quality functional forms, two-way city-year fixed-effects models

Variables	Model 4.1 OLM	Model 4.2 OPM	Model 4.3 OLM	Model 4.4 OPM
DV2b: Percent debt securities—Ordered Logit (OLM) and Probit (OPM) Models				
Credit rating	−0.128*	−0.0634*		
	(−2.04)	(−2.24)		
System info capacity	5.558**	3.001***	5.582**	3.056***
	(2.76)	(3.54)	(2.89)	(3.63)
Rating AA/Aa range			−28.11***	−11.22***
			(−10.95)	(−9.71)
Rating A range			−30.58***	−12.46***
			(−9.13)	(−8.07)
Rating BBB/Baa range			−28.26***	−11.18***
			(−8.68)	(−9.13)
Non-investment grade			−27.15***	−10.16***
			(−21.00)	(−21.41)
Unrated			−26.62***	−10.41***
			(−15.14)	(−12.27)
City FE	Yes	Yes	Yes	Yes
Year FE	Yes	Yes	Yes	Yes
Constant cut 1	24.03***	8.511***	−2.966**	−1.620***
	(13.62)	(10.54)	(−3.23)	(−3.54)
Constant cut 2	31.58***	12.60***	4.462***	2.426***
	(15.07)	(11.15)	(4.25)	(4.70)
N	173	173	173	173
AIC	106.00	146.50	119.90	136.30
BIC	150.20	253.70	186.10	227.70
Log-likelihood	−39.01	−39.24	−38.96	−39.15

Notes: Rating AAA/Aaa = omitted credit rating category
t statistics (robust standard errors) in parentheses
Level of significance: + p <0.10, * p <0.05, ** p <0.01, *** p <0.001

Table A5.6 Models 5.1–5.5 for the covariates of the ordered functional form of city debt composition, individual components of credit quality, two-way city-year fixed-effects models

Variables	Model 5.1	Model 5.2	Model 5.3	Model 5.4	Model 5.5
DV2b: Ordered percent debt securities–Ordered Logit Models (OLM)					
City unemp. rate	−0.00287				
	(−0.01)				
ln(GDP per cap.)	0.972				
	(0.93)				
ln(City pop.)	79.57***				
	(3.53)				
r(CityPop/CountryPop)	−1.709*				
	(−2.16)				
System info resolution	−7.744***	−6.346***	−6.133***	−4.844*	−14.26**
	(−3.56)	(−3.65)	(−3.42)	(−2.56)	(−3.07)
ln(Oper. expend.)		3.957**			
		(2.76)			
ln(Oper. expend.)		−4.220**	−3.818**		
		(−2.77)	(−2.63)		
ln(Oper. expend. per cap.)			3.315*		
			(2.51)		
ln(Debt serv.)				−0.162	
				(−0.22)	
Budget and fiscal practices					9.498
					(0.30)
Political and admin. stability					47.91
					(1.51)
Management of cash flows and accounting quality					84.99*
					(2.00)
Long-term planning					92.50**
					(2.89)
City FE	Yes	Yes	Yes	Yes	Yes
Year FE	Yes	Yes	Yes	Yes	Yes
Constant cut 1	1313.0***	31.73***	19.68***	21.53***	93.59
	(3.58)	(4.32)	(3.75)	(12.17)	(1.49)
Constant cut 2	1321.8***	39.49***	27.30***	28.71***	112
	(3.60)	(5.33)	(5.59)	(11.41)	(1.52)
N	158	145	145	151	86
AIC	123.30	107.30	122.90	123.60	51.31
BIC	218.30	166.90	203.30	196.00	85.67
Log-likelihood	−30.66	−33.66	−34.44	−37.81	−11.66

Notes: Gov. openness and transparency = omitted governance topic

t statistics (robust standard errors) in parentheses

Level of significance: + $p <0.10$, * $p <0.05$, ** $p <0.01$, *** $p <0.001$

linear functional form of debt composition. Overall fit statistics suggest that ordered outcome regression results must be preferred over linear regressions.

As to the individual components of credit quality and their association with debt composition, we go directly to the results from the ordered logit regressions in Models 5.1 to 5.5. This output is presented in Table A5.6. Regarding the economic base in Model 5.1, regression results here suggest that city population size is the most prominent covariate of percent debt securities that a city will have, while a relative size of the city over a country's population is marginally and negatively related to percent of debt from securities. GCP per capita is also significantly and positively associated with percent debt securities, all held equal.

Models 5.2 and 5.3 show that greater levels of capital expenditures at the city level are negatively, albeit marginally, related to percent of debt securities that cities borrow. This is reasonable because, as cities commit greater resources of their own on capital projects, there is less need to rely on debt securities for investment projects, all else equal. There is no discernible association between debt burden and debt composition, however, as Model 5.4 shows. Finally, of the city governance factors, as shown in Model 5.5, management of cash flows and accounting quality and long-term planning appear to be of relative importance compared to other remaining governance factors. This is also reasonable as cash-flow management and long-term planning concerns are usually related to multiyear projects, often requiring meaningful capital plans with a long-term horizon.

6
Understanding, Managing, and Communicating Credit Fundamentals

The previous chapters provide support that information resolution institutions increase the likelihood of access to and use of capital markets by subnational governments (SNGs) by enhancing levels of contractibility in the capital market. In addition to this, city credit ratings, as a signal of underlying credit quality, influence capital market debt at the city level. This chapter probes more deeply about *what* the credit ratings are and their role in fiscal decisions, *why* city policymakers should care about credit ratings, and *how* city policymakers may evaluate and make use of the informational content of credit ratings. By explicitly showcasing 12 cities from different contexts, this chapter conducts a comparative evaluation of core credit quality fundamentals for these cases. This analysis looks at the economic, fiscal, debt and financial management, and governance factors that policymakers may leverage to proactively manage the city's underlying credit quality. The results give tools to city policymakers to signal their market readiness, regardless of, and perhaps even undeterred by, the context of governance institutions in which the city is nested.

Agency and tools are timely, given a growing degree of recognition that key metropolitan cities require access to an array of capital-financing options to manage their fiscal governance task. Policy scholars suggest that urban governance and capital finance go hand in hand in the era of decentralized governance approaches under resource constraint, both in developed and developing contexts (Alm 2015; Pagano and Perry 2008; Bahl et al. 2013; Bahl and Linn 2014; Freire 2014). Pagano and Perry (2008: 22) write: "Urban policy makers today find themselves in the position of negotiating with neighboring communities, competitive markets, and citizens in a fragmented governance system. What appears to be a little more than organized chaos has evolved over decades into the complex, if not always rational, system of infrastructure finance and governance in which cities and other local governments find themselves today." Policymakers may not ignore the realities in which SNGs must interact with a variety of stakeholders when addressing capital-financing constraints. Rather, they must be astute about these realities and

Information Resolution and Subnational Capital Markets. Christine R. Martell, Tima T. Moldogaziev, and Salvador Espinosa, Oxford University Press. © Oxford University Press 2021. DOI: 10.1093/oso/9780190089337.003.0006

position themselves to increase their agency in their fiscal and capital-financing functions.

As a reminder, SNG access to financial markets for the sake of accessing capital is an insufficient justification to pursue that channel. Two key concerns should always be paramount for city policymakers with regards to a decision to access capital market financing. Capital financing can be particularly useful for projects that have substantial initial financing costs such as critical infrastructure assets or large-scale programs with clear investment-like features. Attempting to pay for large-ticket items from annual budgets may be infeasible or fiscally questionable. Capital financing is also appropriate for a more equitable distribution of costs and benefits, especially when capital projects or programs have impacts that are clearly intergenerational. The flipside of capital financing is that long-term repayment pledges become contractually obligated and protected from annual budgetary risks. Such long-term certainty is required by financial actors but can also serve as a disciplining mechanism whereby cities will need to practice fiscal prudence and maintain credit quality to ensure their continued access to financial capital (Freire 2014). Therefore, the objective is not access to market capital per se, but to secure capital and consciously address the distribution of costs and benefits among stakeholders, both of which are conditional on their willingness and ability to pay. This chapter bears upon the efficiency, effectiveness, and equity considerations of the fiscal governance task with regards to public capital financing.

The first section of the chapter discusses credit ratings, their information certification and monitoring role, how they are intertwined in the global capital order, and their fiscal impact. The next section frames why city policymakers should care about credit-rating fundamentals. Following that, we introduce how city policymakers may evaluate and leverage the informational content of credit ratings. In that section, we explore the cases along core themes to showcase how city policymakers could enhance their agency to gain access to capital market financing. Policy recommendations conclude the chapter.

Credit Ratings and Fiscal Impact

Subnational credit ratings, including city-level underlying credit quality, are a well-studied theme in the literature. However, even the most comprehensive studies are often assessed in a context of a single country and mostly from a US SNG perspective (Ederington et al. 1987; Loviscek and Crowley 1990; Zandi and Perna 1994; Ammar et al. 2001; Palumbo and Zaporowski 2012; Depken and LaFountaine 2006). Performance of city credit quality fundamentals in a comparative, multi-country, perspective presents a knowledge gap. Such dearth of systematic research is puzzling as the world of practice already approaches city credit ratings using both underlying and contextual factors of default risk.

By their nature and design, global credit-rating firms and credit ratings operate without hard borders when linking cities and their local service and resource bases to financial circuits around the world. This increasing involvement of global financial actors in localities from multiple contexts is referred to as *glocalization* of urban governance (Torrance 2008, 2009). Such glocalization has become possible as more and more cities in developed and developing contexts have sought to leverage a range of resources that are available to them. Those that are able to show and communicate underlying credit quality are more likely to enjoy access to capital financing as an additional channel to raise resources for public sector projects (Liu and Tan 2009; Freire 2014). To fully understand these dynamics, a comparison of cities from distinct contexts is necessary. Borrowing from Fitzpatrick et al. (2011: 821) a comparative approach "can help scholars and practitioners recognize how differences in governance contexts—institutions, administrative processes, and culture—can present opportunities and challenges for effectively adopting uniform 'best practice' solutions."

For SNGs, the three global credit-rating firms utilize an international public finance credit-rating schedule (where in financial industry parlance the units of which may be referred to as credit notches). In terms of capital financing, the key objective for rating firms is to offer an opinion with regards to long-term underlying city credit quality along an easily recognizable spectrum of creditworthiness. The long-term view captures both the willingness and ability of an SNG to repay debt on time and in full through the lifetime of the capital project, which may often span through an economic cycle. Fitch and Standard & Poor's utilize an identical rating scale, while Moody's rating scale is comparable to the other two firms' rating scales. As seen in Table 6.1, using these credit ratings, borrowers can be broadly classified into two categories—investment grade versus non-investment grade SNGs. Investment grade borrowers—those with ratings ranging from AAA/Aaa to BBB−/Baa3 credit notches—are generally thought to have low levels of risk for invested principal, but an increasing risk of interest nonpayment moving down along the investment grade credit notches. At the same time, non-investment grade borrowers are SNGs with ratings ranging from BB+/Ba1 to C−/C3. Such SNGs are also known as speculative or junk grade borrowers, where both the principal and interest are at risk of nonpayment.

Table 6.1 SNG (regional and local governments) credit-rating scales by firm

Credit-rating firm	Investment grade	Non-investment (speculative) grade	Credit outlook & credit watch
Fitch and Standard & Poor's	AAA AA+/AA/AA– A+/A/A– BBB+/BBB/BBB–	BB+/BB/BB– B+/B/B– CCC+/CCC/CCC– CC+/CC/CC– C+/C/C-	Outlook: positive, stable, negative, developing On watch for: upgrade, downgrade, uncertain
Moody's	Aaa Aa1/Aa2/Aa3 A1/A2/A3 Baa1/Baa2/Baa3	Ba1/Ba2/Ba3 B1/B2/B3 Caa1/Caa2/Caa3 Ca1/Ca2/Ca3 C1/C2/C3	Outlook: positive, stable, negative, developing On watch for: upgrade, downgrade, uncertain

Sources: Fitch, "Rating Definitions," https://www.fitchratings.com/site/definitions (accessed November 20, 2019);

Moody's, "Rating Symbols and Definitions," https://www.moodys.com/sites/products/AboutMoodysRatingsAttachments/MoodysRatingSymbolsandDefinitions.pdf (accessed November 20, 2019);

Standard & Poor's, "S&P Global Ratings Definitions," https://www.standardandpoors.com/en_US/web/guest/article/-/view/sourceId/504352 (accessed November 20, 2019).

When underlying credit quality fundamentals experience changes of sufficient magnitude, they may be put under a process known as a credit watch by a rating firm. Subsequently, a city's credit rating may be put on watch for a possible upgrade, downgrade, or re-affirmation. Standard & Poor's (2014: 5) writes that a credit watch is warranted "when we believe there has been a material change in performance of an issue or issuer, but the magnitude of the rating impact has not been fully determined, and we believe that a rating change is likely in the short term." While the city is under a credit watch, a rating firm will enter a process of re-evaluating its credit opinion and will report a potential direction of a rating outlook. The outlooks can be positive, negative, stable, or developing if credit quality is uncertain. Unlike the information resolution and certification roles of credit ratings, credit watches and outlooks are often assumed to act as continued monitoring and disciplining levers that the rating firms may exert on borrowers.

Sinclair (1994b) argued that credit-rating firms were behind the "emerging world order" characterized by an oversized role for these financial information intermediaries as regulatory mechanisms of governance. A decade later Sinclair (2005: 47) wrote: "Rating involves an admixture of quantitative and qualitative data, and it is thus inherently a process of judgment. The form of knowledge that dominates the rating process is narrowly analytical and largely avoids long-run issues of development." Hackworth (2007) links the growing role of credit-rating firms in subnational governance to general tendencies of central governments to move away from centralized consumption to decentralized provision of regional and urban infrastructure.

This process of financialized subnational governance (regional, local, and special service authorities) has resulted in both intended and unintended outcomes, the latter manifested in unequal inter- and intra-local development and social inequities (Hackworth 2007; Pacewicz 2016; Weber 2010; Sawyer 2014; Rolnik 2013; Christophers 2015; Bayliss 2014; Rosenman 2019. Hackworth (2007) continues that bond-rating agencies have exerted more pressure on local governments in recent years because the financial industry has moved away from traditional financing mechanisms (mostly bank loans) to direct investor-based forms of capital provision. This means that with many more financial players in search of investment opportunities, the costs of market-based borrowing for SNGs have declined as well. However, such an increase of both suppliers of capital and SNGs willing to borrow from them has created layers of additional informational challenges, which make the role of credit-rating firms even more pronounced.

The view in Sinclair (1994a, 1994b, 2005) and Hackworth (2007), nevertheless, is somewhat pessimistic about the role of SNGs as they deal with credit-rating firms. According to this view, the overall observation is that SNGs may have traded top-down control by public sector organizations for private sector control, where financial sector firms may have gained an advantage over subnational (perhaps, even over national) governments. While this may certainly be true for some cities, we argue that by understanding the key components of their underlying credit quality, city policymakers should and can gain agency vis-a-vis capital market financial intermediaries, including credit-rating firms. Freire (2014), for instance, suggests that management of external resources, of which capital financing is now a critical component, is rapidly improving with many policies and tools ensuring discipline among SNGs and financial sector firms. She writes: "Fortunately, the financial sector of most emerging economies has developed rapidly, and local authorities now have access to a number of financing alternatives and to information on what has worked well in the past and what is needed to enter the financing markets. Experiences with local governments' access to external debt have informed local and central governments about potential overborrowing and reinforced the need for prudent policies and close supervision" (Freire 2014: 325). Therefore, our view is that, given the growing role of cities in addressing their core governance tasks, where capital market financing is gaining prominence, becoming competent at managing credit fundamentals is the most direct way for policymakers to maintain parity with financial sector firms.

Specifically, in order to understand how city policymakers could leverage the information certification and monitoring role of credit ratings, we draw on a dozen cities representing diverse contexts from the sample analyzed in the previous chapter. Six cities come from advanced governance contexts (from Europe: Barcelona, Milan, Paris; from Asia/Pacific: Auckland, Osaka, Seoul), while the other six are from emerging contexts (from Latin America: Medellin, Monterrey, Rio de Janeiro; from Eastern/Southeastern Europe: Istanbul, Lviv, Sofia). Several cities are capital cities, several others are large and important metropolitan areas, and almost all of them operate in contexts that underwent varying levels of devolution or delegation of power to SNGs. All of them have a certain degree of experience dealing with one or more of the global credit-rating agencies—Fitch, Moody's, or Standard & Poor's.

Why Cities Should Care About Credit Ratings

The role of credit-rating agencies as a key financial intermediary for public sector capital financing is well documented in the literature. Evidence suggests that credit ratings have significant impact on borrowing costs, especially for those borrowers with ratings toward the lower end of the credit quality spectrum (Ederington et al. 1987; Cantor and Packer 1996; Peng and Brucato 2004; Johnson and Kriz 2005). Research also shows that ratings can serve as a mechanism for fiscal discipline in emerging democracies and developed countries (Block and Vaaler 2004; Hanush and Vaaler 2013; Butler et al. 2009). Not all reviews of credit-rating firms are positive, however. Rating firms have been shown to exacerbate capital market volatility (Kaminsky and Schumkler 2001; White 2010) or influence firm capital structure choices (Kisgen 2006).

The literature on fiscal governance and subnational debt finance recognizes credit-rating firms and their rating services as information providers and certifiers, tiebreakers and gatekeepers to capital finance, regulatory and surveillance agents, and increasingly as private or quasi-public authorities that play a key role in marshaling external resources in internationalized governance environments (Hildreth 1993; Sinclair 1994a, 1994b, 2005; Hackworth 2007; Liu and Tan 2009; White 2010; Bongaerts et al. 2012; Friere 2014).

With regards to capital-financing actors and instruments at the subnational level, Lawrence (2015) argues that urban scholars and practitioners must confront today's realities, where there are many actors in the financial sector with many products and services, who increasingly get plugged into important policy roles in a financial system that is not neutral (see also Freire 2014; Johnson et al. 2014). Furthermore, according to Pike and Pollard (2010), there are three main concerns that city policymakers must heed when operating in financialized governance systems. These concerns are about understanding who the financial intermediaries are and how local interests align with key stakeholder interests, understanding the benefits and risks of services that intermediaries provide, and addressing the potential imbalance in agency between intermediaries and cities.

City governments in several countries, such as the United States and Canada, have decades of experience engaging with capital markets and financial intermediaries (Hildreth and Zorn 2005; Hackworth 2007; Pagano and Perry 2008), while numerous other countries have adopted subnational debt market options in recent years (Freire and Peterson 2004; Martell and Guess 2006; Liu and Tan 2009; Freire 2013; Freire 2014; Liu and Sun 2016; Moldogaziev et al. 2018). During this process of capital market development, more leverage may come to reside with credit-rating firms (e.g., Sinclair 1994b, 2005; Hackworth 2007; Freire 2014).

A city, thus, faces a dilemma. Policymakers can choose not to subject the city to credit evaluation and remain reliant on existing, often limited, resources. Or, they can choose to seek credit ratings and expand financing options to capital markets. Credit-rating firms and their ratings of underlying credit quality are particularly important for a city because without them access to capital-financing markets is often limited. To heed the concerns about operating in a financialized governance system, we argue that city policymakers must pay attention to and seek agency vis-à-vis financial intermediaries and their services, especially credit-rating firms and credit ratings. To do this, city policymakers must understand how city underlying credit quality is formed, how city policy decisions and processes may bear upon credit ratings, and what policy levers policymakers have to manage, perhaps even enhance, city credit ratings. Even though national and, sometimes, regional policymakers may focus on system-level factors to improve access to subnational capital financing, city policymakers will benefit from understanding the core classes of credit fundamentals and take charge of the levers that are directly related to their underlying bases of creditworthiness.

Leveraging Credit Ratings to Expand Access to Capital Financing

In previous chapters, we discussed in detail that cities are nested within their own national contexts. We presented evidence, for instance, that resolution of information problems in a credit system is significantly related to subnational debt levels and debt composition. This is consistent with Sharma and Knight (2016) who argued that information density is critical for urban infrastructure investment. Information availability and flows have "important implications for how infrastructure is located and transacted within and across markets (Sharma and Knight 2016: 2). Furthermore, we posited that resolution of information problems directly supports capital contractibility. We expanded on Rajan and Zingales (1998) that a system's information resolution is grounded on three interrelated factors—transparency or depth of credit information, extent of financial disclosure, and regulatory quality. Combined, these three factors are the foundations of capital contractibility. In Table 6.2, we rank the three cities along each factor of information resolution institutions. It is observed that Lviv and Rio de Janeiro are two cities that consistency ranked lower than other cities in the levels of transparency or depth of credit information, extent of financial disclosure, and regulatory quality. On the other end, Paris and Auckland consistently ranked at the highest level along the same factors. Based on a relative ranking of SNGs such as this, national policymakers could do more to enhance contractibility in their respective capital-financing markets if desired.

Aside from national information resolution institutions that make credit contractibility possible, in earlier chapters we also presented empirical evidence with regards to four fundamental governance institutions or contexts. The first has to do with the economic institutions, where the general expectation is that cities in contexts with stronger economies will tend to have stronger economies themselves, all else equal. Cities such as Paris and Osaka are within developed economic environments, whereas Medellin and Lviv are nested in economic contexts that would be best described as developing. The second governance context pertains to financial and market institutions, with the expectation that they are positively related to SNG credit ratings, all else equal. While the indicators are strong for the likes of Medellin or Auckland, for cities such as Rio de Janeiro or Monterrey it means that they must start from a relatively disadvantaged position. Two other governance context measures are political and legal institutions, which tend to be highly collinear with one another. The expectation generally is that contexts with stronger political and legal institutions will offer stronger credit quality environments to their SNGs. While Auckland and Paris may have the most stable political and legal contexts, the same cannot be said for cities such as Istanbul or Lviv.

Thus, these broader institutional contexts bind cities. Often there is little cities can do, at least in the short term, to effect changes to these contextual governance institutions. However, despite whatever external context within which cities may reside, they can improve their agency and expand their

Table 6.2 Relative distributions of 12 cities along key context dimensions

Variables	Lowest	Lower	Higher	Highest
Information resolution Institutions/ contractibility:	LVI, RIO	IST, MED, BAR, SOF	OSA, MON, MIL, SEO	PAR, AUC
Transparency and depth of credit info	LVI, PAR, SOF, IST	RIO, MED, BAR, AUC	MIL, OSA, SEO	MON
Extent of disclosure	LVI, RIO, BAR	MIL, OSA, SEO	MON, IST	PAR, MED, SOF, AUC
Regulatory quality	LVI, RIO	MED, IST, MON	SOF, MIL, SEO, BAR	OSA, PAR, AUC
Economic institutions	LVI, MED, SOF	IST, MON, SEO	BAR, RIO, MIL	PAR, AUC, OSA
Financial and market institutions	RIO, MON	IST, BAR, PAR, LVI	SOF, MIL, SEO	OSA, MED, AUC
Political institutions	MED, LVI, IST	MON, RIO, SOF	SEO, MIL, BAR	OSA, PAR, AUC
Legal institutions	LVI, MON, MED	RIO, SOF, IST, MIL	SEO, BAR	PAR, OSA, AUC
City credit ratings	LVI	IST, MON, RIO, SOF, MED	BAR, MIL, SEO	AUC, OSA, PAR

Sources: "Transparency/depth of credit information" and "extent of disclosure" are index measures constructed by the World Bank affiliate "Doing Business" project. "Regulatory quality" is a multidimensional measure developed by the Worldwide Governance Indicators project. Measures for economic institutions are from the World Bank. Measures for financial and market institutions are from the "Doing Business" project, while measures for political and legal Institutions are from the Worldwide Governance Indicators project. City credit ratings are from Fitch, Moody's, and Standard & Poor's where and when available.

Note: Selected cities—Auckland (New Zealand), AUC; Barcelona (Spain), BAR; Istanbul (Turkey), IST; Lviv (Ukraine), LVI; Medellin (Colombia), MED; Milan (Italy), MIL; Monterrey (Mexico), MON; Osaka (Japan), OSA; Paris (France), PAR; Rio de Janeiro (Brazil), RIO; Seoul (South Korea), SEO; Sofia (Bulgaria), SOF.

fiscal space by strengthening their credit quality. It is fiscally prudent for them to do so.

Underlying Components of City Credit Quality

When city policymakers seek capital financing, they need to communicate information to market participants about their city's underlying credit quality. A key mechanism to do so is through credit-rating firms, which have become the ultimate information intermediaries in global financial markets. The credit-rating process may not be well understood by all policymakers, and they often may not know how to leverage fiscal and debt management channels to improve city credit quality. The 12 cities in the sample have a credit rating from at least one global credit-rating firm. Lviv is the lowest rated city among them, consistently rated as a non-investment or speculative grade credit quality. Other cities, such as Istanbul or Rio de Janeiro, are rated below but on the cusp of investment grade, and they often spring in and out of the lowest investment grade credit notches. Conversely, cities such as Barcelona or Osaka are consistently rated as an investment grade credit quality borrower. Table 6.2 shows comparative city rankings according to their credit ratings.

The objective, however, is to underscore that city policymakers can and must build technical competencies to evaluate its city credit-risk factors across time and relative to comparable cities within national boundaries, as well as to a set of peer cities globally. At the same time, whether as a short-term adaptation or as a long-term approach, city policymakers may seek credit-enhancement mechanisms to patch up any weaknesses in, or perhaps even upgrade, city credit quality. Of course, any costs of credit enhancement, whether economic or otherwise, should be offset by the benefits that an improved access to credit markets would bring to a city.

Moreover, understanding its city credit quality factors is critical for policymakers because they will gain the capacity to plan for and offer long-term solutions to local demands, an important quality for debt outcomes as established in Chapter 5. To a certain extent this is already happening in a number of countries. Farvacque-Vitkovic and Kopany (2013) summarize that city policymakers in North America, the UK, Australia, and New Zealand are already paying attention to city economic and management fundamentals, primarily through performance management reforms of the 1990s. They also report that European city policymakers are focused on fiscal fundamentals in the framework of unified accounting standards mandated to European Union member states. In recent years, the two approaches began to merge, with US cities adopting best practices in accounting, while performance-based budgeting systems travelled to SNGs outside the UK, US, Australia, and New Zealand (Farvacque-Vitkovic and Kopany 2013).

The objective, however, should be to adopt best examples from successful experiences from a number of countries and implement them more widely to cities from different contexts. This would certainly align well with a set of underlying city credit quality fundamentals that are presented in the methodologies of global credit-rating firms. We discuss four classes of credit

Table 6.3 Underlying city credit quality fundamentals and measurement

Economic fundamentals: potential resources	Fiscal fundamentals: current resources and fiscal institutions	Debt and financial fundamentals: debt affordability, flexibility, and sustainability	Governance fundamentals: quality, stability, and planning
GCP	Fiscal balance	Debt service %	Government
GCP per capita	Own source revenues	revenues	openness and
GCP vs. GDP	Revenue diversity	Debt service	transparency
Economic base and	Revenue/expenditure	per capita	Management of
diversity	stability and	Debt per capita	cash-flows and
Property stock	flexibility	Debt % GCP	accounting
Entrepreneurial/	Revenues % GCP	Debt %	quality
Business activity	Expenditure % GCP	property values	Political and
Unemployment rate	Fiscal rules	Debt structure	administrative
Workforce profile	Fund balances,	Short-term vs. long-	stability
Income	reserves, their	term liabilities	Budget and fiscal
Population profile	fungibility	Capital expenditures	practices
	Liquidity	% revenues	Long-term
		Contingent liabilities	planning

Sources: Underlying city credit fundamentals are summarized from the rating methodologies of three global rating firms: Fitch (2015); Moody's (2013); and Standard & Poor's (2014).

fundamentals, summarized from methodologies of Fitch, Moody's, and Standard & Poor's, and offer examples of how city policymakers could utilize them to understand underlying bases of city credit quality. The four classes of credit fundamentals are economic, fiscal, debt and financial, and governance fundamentals. Table 6.3 summarizes them and provides some core indicators from each class of fundamentals.

Economic Fundamentals

Economic fundamentals show the resource base of the borrower's jurisdiction, which indicates the ability of a city to meet its liabilities when accessing the capital finance markets. Willingness-to-pay pressures may minimize the city's ability to meet liabilities, but creditworthiness is often positive when the economy is strong. All three credit-rating firms highlight their interest in key components of economic activity at the city level and how they add up to form a gross city product (GCP). GCP is the measure of total value of final goods and services produced in a city, which is often normalized by population size or as a ratio to a country's GDP to make reasonable comparisons over time and with other cities within and across countries. Comparing cities in our sample along their GCP per capita levels versus their credit ratings, as depicted in Figure 6.1, there is a significant positive association between the average levels of GCP per capita and credit ratings during 2005–2016 in the sample of 12 cities. We see that Paris, nested at an Aaa/AAA rating category, has the highest GCP per capita; while Lviv, closer to the Caa3/CCC– rating category, has the lowest GCP per capita in the sample.

To have a deeper understanding of the economic context of each city, the profile of the economic base, its diversity and volatility are important as well. Fitch (2015: 8) writes: "A broad, diverse and stable economy is a credit positive, and significant concentration on one or a small group of industry sectors or taxpayers, or a high level of cyclicality, may be a concern." When city policymakers analyze the diversity and strengths of their city's economic bases, they will be able to see where the potential weaknesses to city economic fundamentals may exist.

Furthermore, for cities relying on property taxes as their dominant source of own-source revenue, rating firms consider factors such as the value of property stock for local resource depth. Other factors can also be utilized to gauge city economic fundamentals, such as entrepreneurial activity, employment rates, incomes, labor force participation and labor market characteristics, and/or demographic profiles in the city. All these factors help draw a broader

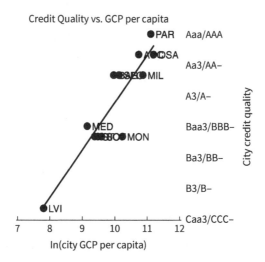

Figure 6.1 Underlying city credit quality vs. GCP per capita, natural log transformation, averages in 2005–2016

Note: Selected cities—Auckland (New Zealand), AUC; Barcelona (Spain), BAR; Istanbul (Turkey), IST; Lviv (Ukraine), LVI; Medellin (Colombia), MED; Milan (Italy), MIL; Monterrey (Mexico), MON; Osaka (Japan), OSA; Paris (France), PAR; Rio de Janeiro (Brazil), RIO; Seoul (South Korea), SEO; and Sofia (Bulgaria), SOF.

picture of what the economic context currently is and what it is likely to be in the long term.

Fiscal Fundamentals

Fiscal fundamentals show the underlying fiscal strength of a city, with the expectation that greater fiscal strength corresponds with higher credit quality. An assessment of revenue and expenditure balances; factors that affect them, such as fiscal rules that limit the ability of a city to raise revenues or require balanced budgets; and fund balances and reserves are the key components of fiscal fundamentals. Many SNGs rely heavily on transfers from higher level governments, the design of which can influence local fiscal choices. Within the constraints of the transfer design, key to the fiscal fundamentals is that the city can manage and leverage its transfers and own-source revenues. Revenue adequacy, flexibility, and diversity over revenue collection are important concerns whether in relation to current or long-term liabilities or in relation to per capita bases or GCP. Thus, ratios such as operating or fiscal balance are a quick proxy for whether a city has sufficient revenues to meet current expenditures. A low operating balance, as Standard & Poor's (2014: 19) reports, "typically indicates less self-financing capacity and suggests the LRG [local and regional governments] would have greater vulnerability to a prolonged recession or to unexpected events. Persistent operating deficits indicate that an LRG would normally need to use debt to fund everyday operations. We note that such a situation is generally not sustainable in the long term and could indicate that the LRG's revenue base may not be sufficient to sustain its range of services, or could indicate management's lack of willingness to address structural imbalances." Accounting ratios for both current and long-term revenue flows also serve as key proxies for city fiscal position.

Consider the ratio of operating revenues to GCP as an example of how fiscal fundamentals affect credit quality. A plot of the ratio of average city operating revenues over GCP by city credit ratings, in Figure 6.2, shows that a heavier burden that operating revenues exert on GCP is generally negatively related to city credit quality. The relationship appears to hold both for cities from developed economies (above the fitted line) and the cities from developing economic contexts (below the fitted line). Using numerous fiscal fundamental indicators such as this one, either in isolation or in relation to other indicators, city policymakers are in a position to better understand the diversity, stability, and flexibility of city fiscal health with respect to credit quality. Furthermore,

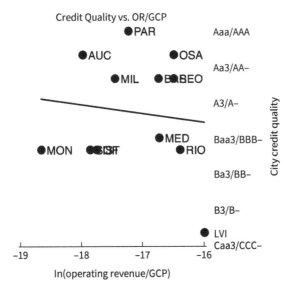

Figure 6.2 Underlying city credit quality vs. ratio of operating revenues over GCP, natural log transformation, averages in 2005–2016

Note: Selected cities—Auckland (New Zealand), AUC; Barcelona (Spain), BAR; Istanbul (Turkey), IST; Lviv (Ukraine), LVI; Medellin (Colombia), MED; Milan (Italy), MIL; Monterrey (Mexico), MON; Osaka (Japan), OSA; Paris (France), PAR; Rio de Janeiro (Brazil), RIO; Seoul (South Korea), SEO; and Sofia (Bulgaria), SOF.

they can integrate that understanding into policy and signal fiscal quality fundamentals to capital markets.

The main point in this area for policymakers is to understand, manage, and communicate city fund balances and reserves to key stakeholders. The evaluation of fiscal fundamentals has to consider two factors: fiscal rules and accounting conventions. All three credit-rating firms report that policies imposing tax and expenditure limitations are important fiscal institutions that influence credit risk. Furthermore, accounting conventions vary across jurisdictions, requiring the standardization of data for effective benchmarking. While European cities operate under relatively more synchronized accounting standards, cities in North America have only recently begun adopting best practices in public sector accounting (Farvacque-Vitkovic and Kopany 2013; Kioko and Zhang 2019). For cities in developing contexts, accounting standards are still evolving. Standard & Poor's (2014: 20) reports: "We have observed that analyses of budgetary performance often suffer from a lack of uniform definition of terms and from other inconsistencies in public-sector accounting standards across countries." Until individual country accounting practices catch up with international accounting standards, cities nevertheless must follow the best practices in accounting standards that are in use.

Debt and Financial Fundamentals

Debt and financial fundamentals show the degree to which resources are committed, governing, in part, the fiscal space for borrowing. Existing levels of debt and contingent liabilities will impact not only the costs of new borrowing but may also constrain a city's ability to gain access to capital market debt. For example, Moody's (2013: 10) writes:

> The government's debt profile includes the amount of debt, the burden it poses, its structure and composition, as well as past trends and future borrowing needs—all important determinants of credit quality. Our assessment of government debt typically includes an analysis of the legal framework for debt issuance and payment, as well as any limits set on the amount or structure of the debt. We relate the government's debt level to measures of the ability to pay, primarily the government's revenue flow, but in some instances relative to the jurisdiction's economic output measured by GDP.

At the city level, debt burden is also often measured relative to revenues (current fiscal burden) or relative to per capita or property tax values (burden on tax base). Of course, the city's debt structure determines how imminent the debt burden is—maturities, interest rate profile, imbedded options, pledged repayment sources, and schedules of debt service all shape a city's ability to continue servicing its debt. In addition, short- and long-term debts are often separately evaluated, because the former has a more direct impact on annual balances and liquidity, while the latter is a proxy for long-term solvency.

In a comparative framework, Figure 6.3 shows that city debt relative to GCP has a negative slope with city credit ratings. This is consistent with an expectation that, all else equal, credit quality decreases with higher levels of debt burden.

At the same time, recent fiscal failures of SNGs have shown that indirect debt levels and contingent liabilities are increasingly an area of concern. Therefore, global rating firms now evaluate guarantees and joint exposures of cities in public or private enterprises, as well as any direct contingent liabilities such as pensions and other workforce insurance plans. Moody's (2013: 11) states: "Contingent liabilities can impinge on credit quality and may arise from debt issued by other entities, whether through guarantees,

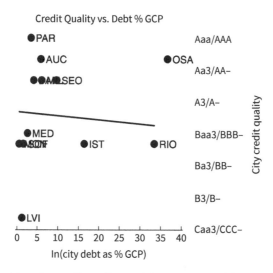

Figure 6.3 Underlying city credit quality vs. debt as percent of GCP, natural log transformation, averages in 2005–2016

Note: Selected cities—Auckland (New Zealand), AUC; Barcelona (Spain), BAR; Istanbul (Turkey), IST; Lviv (Ukraine), LVI; Medellin (Colombia), MED; Milan (Italy), MIL; Monterrey (Mexico), MON; Osaka (Japan), OSA; Paris (France), PAR; Rio de Janeiro (Brazil), RIO; Seoul (South Korea), SEO; and Sofia (Bulgaria), SOF.

ownership, or some other means, even in the absence of debt, if the RLG [regional or local government] considers the entity's operations important enough to support."

Governance Fundamentals

City governance fundamentals are comprised of quality and stability of governance factors at the city level. Often these are referred to as softer and fuzzier factors of underlying city credit quality that do not necessarily lend themselves to quantification. However, global credit-rating firms are becoming more explicit in their reports as to what is contained in their "governance" fundamentals. Governance factors matter because policies and politics can change a city's ability and willingness to pay in critical ways. Fitch (2015: 11) discusses in detail factors such as budget and fiscal policies and political and administrative factors both in short- and long-term horizons. Standard & Poor's (2014: 14) reports: "When reviewing political strength, we focus on a government's strategies for and track record of passing budgets, meeting goals, and effectively implementing public policies. When analyzing management capabilities, we assess the expertise, continuity, and overall capacity of the administration's management. We assess the management's capability to implement the set policies, as well as its ability to maintain financially sustainable policies or adjust the policies as needed despite political pressures." As Figure 6.4 shows, budget and fiscal management practices correlate positively with city credit ratings. Therefore, stability and quality of this factor is of material importance for underlying city credit quality.

Furthermore, at the city level, long-term planning is a critical component of governance quality. Moody's (2013: 13) states that the firm assesses "the extent to which the government clearly articulates a capital plan appropriate to its needs. We also typically assess whether the government makes effective use of multi-year planning for operating and capital spending, and has experience in accessing the debt capital markets." Ultimately, long-term planning is important in that it signals the relationship between annual expenditures and long-term liabilities, shows contingencies for expected spending pressures and potential revenue shortfalls, and matches cash flows to both current and future liabilities. In sum, long-term plans produce roadmaps to how a city may deal with both annual budget deficits and long-term solvency in a balanced manner.

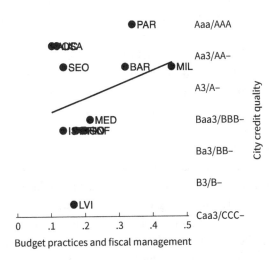

Credit Quality vs. Budget practice

Figure 6.4 Underlying city credit quality vs. budget and fiscal practices (LDA topic model measures, combined for corpora of reports by Fitch, Moody's, and Standard & Poor's), averages in 2005–2016

Note: Selected cities—Auckland (New Zealand), AUC; Barcelona (Spain), BAR; Istanbul (Turkey), IST; Lviv (Ukraine), LVI; Medellin (Colombia), MED; Milan (Italy), MIL; Monterrey (Mexico), MON; Osaka (Japan), OSA; Paris (France), PAR; Rio de Janeiro (Brazil), RIO; Seoul (South Korea), SEO; and Sofia (Bulgaria), SOF.

However, to ensure that key stakeholders, both within a city and in its environment, are able to assess budget and fiscal practices and key components of long-term planning documents, a city must ensure the quality and consistency of accounting practices and financial reports. Information about these practices and the actual reports must be openly available in public domains. Fitch (2014: 5), for example, reminds that it "considers financial statements audited by an independent and reputable accounting firm to be optimum but understands that many LRGs [local and regional governments] do not provide them as it is not a legal requirement. However, where there is a public auditor, Fitch expects audits to be exhaustive and timely."

Policy and Management Implications

Strong underlying credit quality conveys information and is critical for SNGs' access to capital financing. The underlying components of city credit quality are broadly drawn from four classes of fundamentals—economic fundamentals, fiscal fundamentals, debt and financial fundamentals, and city governance fundamentals. Policymakers gain agency with both existing key stakeholders and the financial sector firms by evaluating their underlying credit quality factors. To reiterate, the objective in this chapter is to underscore that cities can build, and some already have, the technical competencies to evaluate credit risk factors over time and relative to comparable cities in the country, as well as to a set of peer cities in other countries. After key credit factors are assessed, both for short- and long-term concerns, city policymakers would know where the most relevant weaknesses are in their underlying credit quality and seek solutions to address them.

Consider a summary of the relative positions of 12 cities in the sample along illustrated measures of underlying credit quality, presented in Table 6.4. One can observe that Lviv has the lowest GCP per capita but relies very significantly on it for operating revenues, and it also has relatively lower levels of debt. Osaka, conversely, enjoys high GCP per capita and exerts a lower pressure on it for its operating revenues. However, the city debt levels as percent of GCP are the highest in the sample for this city. In terms of budget and fiscal practices, Lviv and, especially, Osaka have room for further improvements. Overall, cities that consistently find themselves on the right end of the spectrum would benefit a great deal by signaling and leveraging this information, while cities on the left end of the spectrum would need to seek policies to mitigate these weaknesses or resort to applicable credit enhancements.

Table 6.4 Relative positions of cities along underlying city credit quality factors

Factor	Relative position along select measures of underlying city credit quality		
	Weak	Medium	Strong
GCP per capita	LVI RIO IST MED SOF MON SEO BAR MIL AUC OSA PAR		
Operating revenue as % GCP	LVI RIO SEO OSA MED BAR PAR MIL IST SOF AUC MON		
City debt as % of GCP	OSA RIO IST SEO MIL AUC BAR PAR MED SOF MON LVI		
Budget and fiscal practice	AUC OSA SEO IST RIO LVI MON SOF MED BAR PAR MIL		

Note: Selected cities—Auckland (New Zealand), AUC; Barcelona (Spain), BAR; Istanbul (Turkey), IST; Lviv (Ukraine), LVI; Medellin (Colombia), MED; Milan (Italy), MIL; Monterrey (Mexico), MON; Osaka (Japan), OSA; Paris (France), PAR; Rio de Janeiro (Brazil), RIO; Seoul (South Korea), SEO; Sofia (Bulgaria), SOF.

A holistic view of financial management takes the position that credit quality is more than the sum of the parts. Rather, it goes beyond a series of indicators to an institutionalized set of conventions, policies, and behaviors that commit to continuous monitoring of, evaluation of, and improvement toward the attainment of fiscal policy objectives important to the city. A holistic view requires the city to go beyond calculating measures mandated by fiscal rules of responsibility and discipline. These measures are designed for fiscal and financial control, which is but a small part of credit quality. A strict focus on compliance shortchanges the city's opportunity to strengthen its credit quality. The ability of a jurisdiction to understand its credit fundamentals, manage its fiscal base, and communicate these to citizens, other (levels of) governments, and capital markets is essential to leveraging SNG financing alternatives. Consider the case of Dakar in Box 6.1.

The task does not have to be daunting even if the precise algorithms by which the credit-rating agencies weigh the components of credit fundamentals are unknown. We argue that cities are hardly bystanders in glocalized financial systems and can become competent in running their fiscal governance responsibilities. Cities from any context, developed or developing, can apply these evaluation tools to move their own dials toward a longer term goal of credit quality improvement. While poorer jurisdictions in weaker institutional environments will continue to experience serious constraints, their concerted self-improvement efforts will position them for better access to resources, even if only from internal and donor sources. Cities that have robust economic bases and in stronger institutional environments will better position themselves to access financing from a variety of sources, including from capital markets.

Box 6.1 The Case of Dakar's Bond-Issuance Effort

The capital city of Senegal, Dakar, initiated efforts to expand financing options by undergoing a formal Public Expenditure and Financial Accountability (PEFA) review of its financial management system, which identified various deficiencies in planning and forecasting, and in dissemination of audit and evaluation information. After reforms to improve credit quality, Dakar sought external financing from loans. The constitutional framework of Senegal allows cities to borrow without central government guarantees, and Dakar's credit quality was sufficient for the French Development Agency to award €10 million in 2008, the West African Development Bank to lend the equivalent of US$17.5 million, and the Islamic Bank of Senegal to lend the equivalent of US$3.7 million. Despite challenges to revenue collection due to constraints imposed by the central government, Dakar's commitment to timely repayment of these loans primed it to seek municipal bonds in 2015, for which the city sought to gain better terms and lower costs than bank loans. In preparation of bond issuance, the city attained a US$500,000 grant in 2011 from the Bill & Melinda Gates Foundation to analyze the feasibility of launching a municipal bond. The country met many of the institutional preconditions: It was politically stable; had a stable macroeconomic environment; had both central government and private sector bond market infrastructure that it could potentially utilize; and, despite limited subnational revenue autonomy, the country allowed cities the right to borrow.

The city, too, demonstrated commitment to credit quality in its past performance in repaying external sources and in its strategy to address long-term urban planning. From 2011 to 2015, the city further improved its financial management systems; altered its approach to comprehensive planning, especially by involving the city council, various administrative and planning departments, civil society, business representatives, and religious leaders; and signaled its credit quality and commitment to influence investor's perceptions through roadshows and individual appeals. Dakar complied with the regulatory steps required by the Regional Council for Public Savings and Financial Markets (CREPMF).

Following a confidential rating by Moody's that further established benchmark goals regarding decision-making, budgetary planning, asset and debt management, and the predictability of revenues, Dakar received a BBB+ credit rating from the local agency, Bloomfield Credit Ratings. Even though the rating would allow Dakar to go to market without a guarantee, the city secured a 50 percent guarantee from the United States Agency for International Development. The impending bond issue of US$40 million levied a 6.6 percent interest rate and a maturity of seven years. The proceeds of the bond would have been used to create an affordable marketplace for the city's street vendors. It was denominated in small increments of approximately US$18 to encourage both retail and institutional investors. On the eve of the emission, institutional investors had pledged 72 percent. At the eleventh hour, the central government reversed its position of support—on the grounds of contingent liabilities on the state, the political affiliation of the market's developer, and the constitutional legality—and the bond issue was withdrawn from the market (Paice 2016; Gorelick 2018).

Policymakers must remember that no amount of borrowing can replace a solid fiscal base (Bahl and Bird, 2018). In particular, cities are well served to build budget and fiscal practices that accommodate capital-financing alternatives. Certainly national policies and fiscal institutions can enable or limit city efforts and fiscal autonomy as cities continue to operate at the discretion of higher level governments. However, access to SNG capital financing presents local jurisdictions an option where they, with national government and capital market commitments, can balance the concerns for financial prudence, reduce the need for national fiscal engagement, and increase financing alternatives to options that can be both efficient and effective.

This means that city policymakers must plan for longer term horizons in addition to meeting annual operating needs. When this happens, cities, along with national governments and financial sector firms, engage in mutually beneficial commitments for both short- and long-term projects. This is not about masters, whether public or private, that constrain the financing choices of cities. To the contrary, this is about SNG policymakers being able to leverage coproduction through a broader range of capital-financing options where credit contractibility exists, prudent fiscal policy dominates, and intergenerational equity requires it.

Conclusion

Cities throughout the world are deeply involved in the provision of crucial public goods and services. These pressures are expected to grow with rapid urbanization. Providing them with adequate alternatives to finance their infrastructure base remains a crucial fiscal governance task at central, regional, and local government levels. National mechanisms of information resolution and the tools for certifying and signaling underlying credit quality information shape access to capital financing for cities. At the city level, understanding and managing the core classes of underlying city credit fundamentals is of special importance and is the first step toward gaining secure access to capital financing. Using cities from around the world, which operate within diverse governance contexts, we highlight and showcase the critical credit quality fundamentals and discuss how implementation of such measures offers agency to city policymakers that work with financial sector firms.

7

Three Contexts of Information Resolution Reforms

With the importance of information resolution for subnational debt market development established, how do cities in three distinct contexts perform with respect to debt practices and outcomes? By taking a close look at three cases—Seoul, South Korea; Monterrey, Mexico; and Sofia, Bulgaria, this chapter aims to evaluate cities with distinct contexts against the book's key findings. All three countries underwent significant policy reforms that included improvements in their information resolution contexts. In addition, unlike several well-developed subnational government (SNG) capital markets, all three are relative newcomers to the scene. Specifically, this chapter explores the cities in their system- and local-information resolution environments to see how their debt practices and outcomes respond to improvements in contractibility (i.e., transparency, credit information disclosure, and regulatory quality) as well as city-level factors related to information density and credit quality, which are critical for capital financing (Moldogaziev et al. 2018; Sharma and Knight 2016; Hackworth 2007; Peng and Brucato 2004; Johnson and Kriz 2005).

Though Seoul has achieved its strongest credit quality assessments in recent years, it continues to rely heavily on public sector resources for its infrastructure financing projects. There remains significant underutilized capacity that Seoul would benefit from by unlocking the external market sources of capital financing. Monterrey is also a city with a strong underlying resource base. Yet, though the city is embedded in a country with a relatively reasonable experience of market-based subnational capital financing, it continues to rely primarily on loans, especially private loans. Finally, Bulgaria's domestic resources, both from public and private sectors, are limited. Unlike the other two cities, however, Sofia operates in a context with a very strong supranational presence. The city has access to significant resources from the European Union (EU) as part of targeted multi-country capital infrastructure development projects. The three cities, nevertheless, required critical improvements in information resolution to reduce their reliance on public loans and expand the menu of external funding sources. In Sofia's case, information resolution

Information Resolution and Subnational Capital Markets. Christine R. Martell, Tima T. Moldogaziev, and Salvador Espinosa, Oxford University Press. © Oxford University Press 2021. DOI: 10.1093/oso/9780190089337.003.0007

was also a prerequisite to access European funds in concert with subsidized co-financing infrastructure loans.

In the next section we develop and present a conceptual framework for assessing the policy changes pertaining to information resolution. We then briefly introduce the three cases and describe key features of their institutional contexts. After assessing the policy changes for the institutions and mechanisms of information resolution, the discussion then turns to the experiences of Seoul, Monterrey, and Sofia after such reforms were introduced. This is framed around a review of city access to capital finance, composition of city debt, and policy implications for future efforts in expanding borrowing alternatives.

Conceptual Framework

Figure 7.1 illustrates the conceptual framework guiding this chapter. The framework is anchored in the literature and empirical results documented in Chapter 4, which revealed the relationship between system-level transparency and depth of credit information and extent of financial disclosure with levels of subnational borrowing; Chapter 5, which showed how information resolution mechanisms shape the levels and composition of city debt; and Chapter 6, which further explored the information bases of credit quality and discussed how city policymakers may evaluate the informational content of own credit ratings over time or in comparison to other cities.

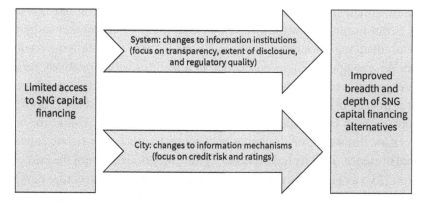

Figure 7.1 Conceptual framework for information resolution and policy process

The conceptual framework holds that the governance institutions under which SNGs operate, policies in the system that enhance information resolution institutions, and utilization of mechanisms of information certification and monitoring improve the breadth and depth of SNG capital-financing alternatives. Improvements to information resolution, through better contractibility and higher credit quality, will result in desirable outcomes: increased access to a range of financing options, including those from capital markets, contract structures and maturities commensurate with project purposes; potential benefits from lower borrowing costs; and better matching of debt with citizen values and policy priorities.

While the conceptual framework is simple, its application is not. Many policy choices can affect system credit contractibility and borrower credit quality, such that there is unlikely a one-to-one correspondence between a single policy and enhanced SNG access to and use of capital markets. The challenge is to examine policies through the lens of information resolution reform and to evaluate the relationship between those policies and borrowing outcomes. Three cases allow for exploratory testing of the nuances of how improvements in information resolution facilitate access to SNG capital markets.

Case Selection and Institutional Contexts

With the framework presented in mind, we analyze the specific cases from South Korea, Mexico, and Bulgaria. These countries present distinct histories of capital market and sociopolitical environments. Mexican cities operate in a federal system, while South Korea and Bulgaria are unitary countries. Despite their structural and historic differences, the three countries have all embarked on complex reforms to permit their local governments certain levels of administrative and fiscal autonomy. As governance reforms in all three countries brought about relatively more decentralized systems, they also included the need to diversify options for capital financing. Of the three countries, however, there remains a great degree of central government involvement in South Korea even today; Mexico is the most decentralized of the three countries, where states have significant clout over local governments; and Bulgaria continues its work on building relatively autonomous and capable local governments, albeit with significant oversight from the EU. Thus, the three cases present three distinct contexts of local-central (and local-supranational) government oversight arrangements.

Country Profiles

South Korea, which is now one of the most dynamic economies in Asia, went through a process of rapid industrialization after the 1953 Korean War. After the war, the country experienced periods of military dictatorship that led to the concentration of power in the central government. The country has since transitioned to a liberal democracy with a three-tier government structure that includes a central government, 16 regional governments (including Seoul Special Metropolitan District), and 232 local governments (Kook 2000). Governmental efforts continue to emphasize the reconstruction of the country's infrastructure commensurate with demands that advanced industrial democracies depend upon for their continued success, which requires substantial investment. A development of the capital market financing alternatives was inherently one of the last missing pieces to give local governments meaningful authority to complete their fiscal governance tasks.

Despite the centralist administrative organization of the country, and the strong presence and involvement of the central government in local affairs, subnational governments have progressively been allowed to seek capital market financing alternatives. This is partly a consequence of the decentralization efforts that have been taking place in the country since the mid-1980s. A critical turning point, however, occurred in 2006 when SNGs gained the ability to issue bonds for investment projects without central government approval, subject to certain debt limits and alignment with priorities established in legislation. Yet, the uptake of new capital-financing instruments remains slow, with the most common way to finance local government projects in the country coming from central government loans.

Mexico is a federation with 31 states and a federal district (where Mexico City, the country's capital, is located). The states further divide into 2,457 autonomous municipalities. Historically, the central government has played a significant role in decision-making and has controlled the most dynamic sources of tax revenue, leaving many states and municipalities as executors of centrally planned projects. This trend, however, has been progressively reversed, as decentralization efforts have been reshaping the role of SNGs in public service provision. Mexico has made efforts to increase the menu of instruments to finance strategic infrastructure projects. The need for alternative financing mechanisms was more noticeable after the signing of the North American Free Trade Agreement (NAFTA) with the United States and Canada in 1994, as this turned various regions into enterprising, export-oriented entities requiring substantial infrastructure improvements.

The Federal Governmental Accounting Act, passed by Congress in 2008, and the Fiscal Discipline of Federative Entities and Municipalities Act passed in 2016 (or the Fiscal Discipline Act) guide subnational practices in accounting, transparency, and disclosure. While the former relates to accounting standards, the latter includes a number of provisions to improve the accuracy, transparency, and disclosure of current accounts and both short- and long-term debt. Among the provisions, the Fiscal Discipline Act requires SNGs to report indebtedness details to the federal government (more specifically, to the Secretariat of Public Finance), including that of public-private partnerships, regardless of source of debt. The law also includes an alert system to monitor and signal excessive SNG indebtedness.

The third country included is Bulgaria, located in Eastern Europe and a member state of the EU. The country was formerly governed under a centralized, command-and-control planning system, but it has gone through significant institutional changes since the early 1990s after the collapse of the communist bloc. In particular, membership in the EU required significant structural changes to governance institutions, especially a realignment of central versus local government responsibilities, and subsequent changes in fiscal and financial responsibilities of levels of government in Bulgaria.

The current system includes a central government, 28 regional governments (including the nation's capital city, Sofia), and 273 local governments (excluding about 5,000 villages with little to no meaningful own economies of scale). The fiscal role of municipalities has increased significantly since the 1990s as a result of a gradual decentralization process. Yet, since the central government concentrates most of the revenue-raising responsibilities, there is a structural fiscal vertical imbalance that continues to make direct government subsidies and transfers necessary. At the same time, alternative external capital-financing sources available to Bulgaria are various EU initiatives on infrastructure revitalization, heavily targeted at transportation projects to better connect the economies of the various member states.

Financial Systems

South Korea's initial effort to build a robust financial system traces back to the late 1960s, with the enactment of the Capital Promotion Act. The most decisive reforms, however, were in response to a financial crisis that hit the Asian economies in 1997. The package of reforms introduced at that time aimed to address structural weaknesses in the financial system, restoration of investors' confidence, and the capitalization and reorganization of banking institutions

(Lee 2017). The priority of the central government after 1997 was on the development of a corporate bond market that, among other things, would capture a growing share of international financial flows. With this priority in mind, the central government passed legislation that included rules for a well-functioning competitive bid system, the disclosure of pertinent information in real time, and the design of a regulatory framework for debt securities that promoted transparency and added certainty to trading (Asian Development Bank 2018). Other measures that were particularly effective for the enhancement of market liquidity were the establishment of a reopening system, mandatory participation in an electronic exchange trading system, and the elimination of restrictions on foreign investment in stocks (Kang et al. 2006). Simultaneously, the country completed a series of reforms, which brought more fiscal autonomy to local governments and opened access to external sources of capital financing. SNG borrowing in the country continues to grow, especially in jurisdictions with consolidated city and county governments (Park 2013). However, significant room with respect to municipal securities trading platforms, bankruptcy solvency regimes, and monitoring infrastructure still remain (Li and Zili 2015).

Mexico's reform efforts in the last several decades have also included measures to foster the development of its capital market. Just like South Korea, some of the enacted structural reforms were a response to a financial crisis that, in this case, took place in 1994. Efforts to improve access opportunities to capital markets in the financial sector were part of a strategy to enhance the competitiveness of a progressively export-oriented economy with new clusters of regional development. Policymakers considered measures to expand the menu of financing opportunities for SNGs via capital markets. One of the challenges, however, was to ensure that this could be done without altering macroeconomic stability, and without creating incentives for fiscal indiscipline (Hernández-Trillo 2018; Hernandez-Trillo and Smith-Ramirez 2009). Subnational moral hazard behavior was, after all, a common problem in Mexico's federal system, given the historically strong degree of political centralization and the concentration of tax-collection responsibilities at the national level.

Bulgaria's financial sector reforms were motivated by its intention to join the EU. As Petranov and Miller (1999) explain, the macroeconomic performance of the country in the 1990s was among the weakest in Central and Eastern Europe, with low foreign investment, hyperinflationary pressures, and a financial crisis that hit the country's economy in 1996. Capital market reforms were an important component in the package of structural changes. Bulgaria introduced an extensive regulatory framework, which initially targeted private capital market development. These changes included measures such as the creation of institutions that would serve as pillars for the development of the capital market (e.g., Bulgarian Stock Exchange [BSE-Sofia], a central depository, and a state securities commission), but that also prepared the country to meet the provisions that the EU required from potential new members.

Bulgaria's reform process has taken into consideration that the EU fiscal governance model includes legislation that, on the one hand, attempts to preserve the autonomy of member countries but, on the other hand, seeks to maintain a level of homogeneity in fiscal and monetary decisions that ensures the long-term sustainability of the Union. The EU's Charter on Local Self-Government established that a local government is the cornerstone of a democratic regime and needs to be recognized in domestic legislation. For former communist countries like Bulgaria, this entailed a complete restructuring of its legal and administrative framework. As Drumeva (2001) explains, within the past governing system, public entities were legitimized "from above" and local self-government derived its authority from the state, resulting in local government schemes that were just replicas of what was envisioned for the central government. EU membership, therefore, has entailed reforms to increase the participation of municipalities in fiscal affairs and infrastructure provision.

Policy Reforms to Enhance Information Resolution

This section explores specific policy measures enacted in South Korea, Mexico, and Bulgaria to enhance factors directly associated with the improvement of information resolution—namely, the extent of disclosure, transparency of information, and regulatory quality—as well as policies aimed at improving access to mechanisms of information certification and monitoring.

Before the 1997 financial crisis, South Korea's SNG debt market was virtually nonexistent, but it has been rapidly developing ever since. While the most common way for SNGs is to borrow directly from the central government (via public loans for housing programs or regional development funds), the legal framework allows them to obtain private loans and issue municipal bonds, provided certain conditions are met. The Local Autonomy Act and the Local Finance Act are the main legal instruments that shape the fiscal relations between central and subnational governments.

The Local Finance Act constitutes the foundation of South Korea's intergovernmental fiscal system, as it prescribes the basic rules to finance local governments and ensure sound and transparent financial management. The Local Finance Act includes provisions that define the sharing of revenues and expenditures, how local subsidies are to be administered, provisions pertaining to local government budgets, general guidelines pertaining to debt management, and mandates with implications in terms of information resolution.

The Act, for example, requires SNGs to disclose the conditions surrounding the implementation of projects involving the issuance of municipal debt. These governments can borrow freely as long as key debt indicators are below what central authorities establish in a Local Bound Ceiling System (SNGWOFI 2019). When a potential issuer has debt indicators beyond acceptable levels, it must obtain central government approval. The central government also operates an information system with data about the management conditions and performance quality of local governments. This is designed to detect both administrative and fiscal problems at the municipal level as early as possible. There is also the Local Fiscal Crisis Alert System, which aims to prevent local government insolvency.

As recent studies document, South Korea has favorable conditions to further the development of its subnational debt markets since it has competitive financial and information intermediaries, and a well-developed legal and regulatory system (Smith et al. 2019). Reforms (especially after the 1997 financial crisis) have been profound, expanding in several domains. Several of these policy initiatives have improved the quality of information that governmental entities are required to report and disclose (Chun 2016). Improvements in the information environment included the adoption of international standards in public sector accounting, and financial reporting and auditing (IFAC 2019). The Korean Accounting Standards Board is in charge of issuing guidelines that borrowers seeking to issue debt must follow. As one would expect, this type of policy measure increases market participants' confidence, as the information that potential borrowers generate is more accurate, comparable, and standardized.

In the case of Mexico, the development of information resolution mechanisms has been a byproduct of a strategy to craft a regulatory system of subnational borrowing based on an explicit renunciation of using federal resources to bailout SNGs and the creation of a subnational debt framework that some consider as a hybrid between a rule-based and market-based system to foster fiscal discipline (Revilla 2013; Giugale et al. 2000).

With this framework, the central government sought to send a credible signal in the sense that no further bailouts would be granted to SNGs (something that, e.g., was deemed necessary as a result of financial crises in

1994 and 2008). To signal a credible commitment to such principle, the national government stopped playing the role of intermediary when servicing debt obligations. Up to that point, subnational borrowers could authorize the Ministry of Finance to take money directly from their revenue-sharing transfers to service their debts. The new regulatory framework terminated this possibility and encouraged a relatively more direct and transparent relationship between subnational borrowers and creditors.

As part of the reform package, Congress introduced the option that SNGs set up irrevocable trusts. These trusts established direct contractual obligations between borrowers and creditors that, among other things, identified the sources of collateral, the timeline for repayment, and the account where those financial resources would be deposited (Espinosa 2013; Espinosa and Martell 2015; Espinosa and Moreno 2014). With the establishment of these trust agreements, SNGs started engaging directly with lenders, which evidently made the improvement of the information environment a necessity. Although, given the high vertical imbalance in Mexico's intergovernmental revenue system, SNG borrowers often direct constitutionally guaranteed transfers to the trust as a form of debt repayment.

Efforts to enhance the information environment also included the enactment of the Federal Governmental Accounting Act in 2008. The Act established general criteria for the harmonization of accounting rules and procedures among public entities and among levels of government. Policymakers and legislators involved in its creation saw it as a necessary condition to ensure that the information contained in financial statements would be accurate, reliable, and comparable (both across governments and over the course of time). The Act includes numerous measures to structure Mexico's intergovernmental accounting system, including, for example, the establishment of specific information that public entities must include in their financial statements; specific accounting principles to be used in public accounts; the information to be used in the creation of revenue projections and budget plans; and, very importantly, mandates pertaining to the transparency, expected quality, and periodicity in which financial information needs to be disseminated. The Fiscal Discipline Act in 2016 augmented the standards. Among other measures, it requires SNGs to separately account for sources and uses of conditional and non-conditional transfers, so as to terminate any hidden cross-subsidizations.

In the case of Bulgaria, admittance to the EU in 2007 required widespread reforms to the country's macroeconomic and intergovernmental frameworks. The challenges for Bulgarian authorities were different from the cases of South Korea and Mexico, as they involved a simultaneous transition of most governance institutions and centrally planned economies to a system that would meet the EU membership criteria. Because top-down centralism had dominated, the development of basic local government capacities was paramount. As Stoilova (2004) explains, meeting the challenges of rapid decentralization called for the crafting of budget planning and management capabilities, the capacity to raise local taxes, and measures to facilitate access to an emerging domestic debt market.

The legislative reforms aimed at developing municipal debt markets included a new State Budget Act, Municipal Debt Act, Public Finance Act, Public Offering of Securities Act; as well as specific mandates, guidelines, and regulations from the Ministry of Finance; and internal regulations at the municipal level to effectively regulate debt financing (Kalcheva 2017). Of these reforms, the Public Finance Act includes explicit mandates aimed at improving the transparency, reliability, and dissemination of relevant municipal information. Such provisions, for example, establish how municipal budgets should be prepared, adopted, and implemented. The Act includes specific guidelines on municipal budget structure that the Ministry of Finance compiles and uses as input in planning the national budget. The Act also bestows this Ministry with the responsibility to define the procedure and timeline with which municipalities disclose information on their debt position, debt instruments, and indebtedness plans.

It is worthwhile mentioning that since Bulgaria is a member of the EU, it must fulfill obligations associated with such membership. One obligation directly affects the type of information that needs to be publicly available. Some of these requirements have been integrated into Bulgaria's national laws. For one example, the Public Finance Act mandates the de-consolidation of general government debt by central, regional, local, and public enterprise funds, and to disclose such information to the EU's statistical agency, Eurostat.

Bulgaria's reform efforts also included measures to strengthen municipal-borrowing capacity, which was an important signal that potential lenders expected, especially since many EU grants and development funds required borrowers to cover a percentage of their projects' costs. Despite these reform measures, as one would expect, not all local governments were in a position to access European funds (Tsonkova 2005). Bulgaria's EU membership, nevertheless, opened the possibility to access alternative financing mechanisms through cohesion funds and targeted programs for infrastructure development. Since the late 1980s, the EU budget includes funds aimed at accelerating economic development in relatively underdeveloped regions in the union. These policies created additional incentives to reform Bulgaria's institutional framework as government authorities saw an opportunity to attract much-needed financial resources to boost local infrastructure (re-)development (Paliova and Lybek 2014).

While Bulgarian municipalities are progressively becoming more autonomous, the central government still exerts an important role in the monitoring, analysis, and dissemination of information. This is a direct responsibility of the Local Government Financing Directorate (housed within the Ministry of Finance), which collects fiscal and financial information from all municipalities and places it in a centralized debt registry, freely available online. The accuracy of the generated information is of utmost importance, as it is the primary input in the preparation of consolidated municipal budget forecasts. More importantly, this registry gives a tool for national and local policymakers to assess and monitor SNG credit quality, debt levels by type of debt, as well as debt burdens within and between SNGs in the country.

The discussion so far shows that the central governments in the three countries participated actively in bringing about reforms that strengthened contractibility in their respective financial systems. This certainly enhanced information resolution institutions in each country and laid the foundations for SNG borrowing. This, plus adoption and improvements in accounting standards, facilitates the availability of information about important elements of a borrower's credit quality. In addition, the enacted policy measures in South Korea, Mexico, and Bulgaria have included actions aimed at improving the efficiency of the system by allowing private third parties to evaluate and monitor borrower credit quality. Financial sector firms began analyzing underlying credit qualities of SNGs and assessing the risk associated with the purchase of any financial instruments to be offered in the capital market. In particular, credit-rating agencies now play a critical role certifying and monitoring borrower information for cities in the three countries.

Global credit-rating firms evaluate credit qualities of SNGs in many countries, including the risks associated with their individual debt issues or special purpose vehicles. There are also domestic credit-rating agencies in South Korea, Mexico, and Bulgaria. In South Korea several domestic credit-rating firms evaluate local governments in the country (though some, e.g., Korea Ratings or Korea Investors Service, are subsidiaries of Fitch and Moody's, respectively). These agencies, especially those with global reach, have well-developed methodologies and indicators that potential investors can use to determine whether the financial strength of a borrower is solid enough to minimize the risk of insolvency and ensure timely repayment of SNGs' debt obligations. Figure 7.2 shows that Seoul's credit rating, reported by Standard & Poor's, experienced a three-notch improvement from A to AA from 2005 to 2016; Monterrey's credit rating from Moody's is stable at A1 (A+ when

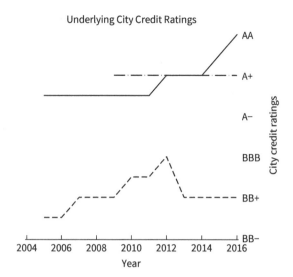

Figure 7.2 Credit ratings for three cities, trends in 2005–2016
Source: Line = Seoul, South Korea, ratings from Standard & Poor's; long dash dotted line = Monterrey, Mexico, ratings from Fitch; dashed line = Sofia, Bulgaria, ratings from Standard & Poor's.

compared to Fitch's and Standard & Poor's scales) and did not experience any change; while Sofia's credit rating from Standard & Poor's hovers just below the investment grade threshold, in most years at BB+ credit notch, during the same period of 2005 to 2016.

City Borrowing Breadth and Depth

Though the adopted SNG capital-financing reforms across South Korea, Mexico, and Bulgaria range a great deal, in concert they achieved significant improvements in the contexts of information resolution and tools of information certification and monitoring. Given its economic and political position, Seoul's metropolitan government is considered a special city, which results in a relatively elevated political role compared to other cities. Seoul is divided into 25 districts with varying levels of financial dependence on the city and the central government (of which Gangman district, e.g., receives the lowest share of its revenues from the central government, while for the district of Nowon, this share is among the highest) (Kim et al. 2012).

Almost all of Seoul's borrowing has been financed with public loans and bonds, with the latter fluctuating significantly from the inception of the bond issuing authority in 2006 to 2016. Seoul's bonded debt was used to finance housing (about 75 percent), a metropolitan subway (about 20 percent), and various other public purpose projects (remaining share). This debt has been evaluated by both domestic and global credit rating firms. Thus, the city has a certain level of experience working with financial intermediaries. At the same time, unlike in mature SNG markets, there is little capital market credit enhancement activity (e.g., letters of credit, bond insurance) observed for cities in South Korea. Most central government credit enhancement schemes appear to be around SNG infrastructure with significant national economic or symbolic value (i.e., Olympic and Paralympic games, national land planning and natural resource protection projects, or disaster risk and relocation measures). For local policymakers this means that, where possible, new debt is best served when aligned with national special projects that are eligible for public credit enhancements though co-financing or when supported by individual letters of credit from banks. Seoul is also utilizing the latest innovations in service financing. The most recent innovative financing activity of note by the city was the implementation of social impact bonds (SIBs) in 2016–2019 to finance education for children on welfare, an area attracting great attention from the city's public officials (Seoul Metropolitan Government 2016). This policy innovation unlocks a new way that external resources can be brought in to tackle one of the pressing social governance problems of the city and can transfer the risk to private actors if service performance measures fall short of expected levels.

The city of Monterrey has been accessing Mexican capital markets successfully for many years. As the third-largest metropolitan area in Mexico, with a dynamic and diversified economy, it sought to be at the forefront of capital planning and urban development projects in the country (Fitch 2016). Almost all the debt is tied to transportation, public utilities, and metropolitan transit purposes. In terms of types of debt, Monterrey has been moving into commercial bank loans more aggressively at the expense of development bank loans from Banobras (Mexico's development bank). One avenue that made this shift from public to commercial bank loans possible is the trust fund revenue arrangement (*fideicomiso*). Given an improving revenue base of the city in recent years and the expected growth in revenue sharing, the trust accounts are legal entities between the city and the investors that act as intercept vehicles for prompt debt servicing and repayment by channeling city revenues, often those from transfers, directly to the trust (Smith 2017).

In a way the trust fund intercepts act as special purpose credit enhancement vehicles, where future cashflows are securitized (Leigland and Mandri-Perrott 2008). Along with other traditional credit enhancement tools, trust fund intercepts guaranty stronger credit protections to investors and remove the expectation of a central government bailout from the SNG capital market. Monterrey rarely uses traditional debt securities, or bonds, which in the past have been issued on the Mexican Stock Market, however. With continued improvements to information resolution institutions in the country and strengthening of information certification and monitoring tools, such borrowing alternatives are a natural focus for Monterrey's future access to external resources.

A capital metropolitan area, generating more than a third of the nation's GDP, the city of Sofia is by far the most economically and politically important SNG in Bulgaria (City of Sofia 2003; Moraliyska 2018). Significant capital-financing projects, therefore, have been located in the city's 24 districts. Sofia's borrowing has largely been sourced with a combination of loans and grants from the EU and, like many capital projects in the country, any domestic borrowing from private bank loans was primarily utilized as a co-financing mechanism to attain grants from Europe and several other EU countries. The primary target of capital projects in the city seek to upgrade Sofia's infrastructure to a level commensurate with that in the advanced economies of the EU and to better link the city and the country to neighboring countries. Thus, projects in Sofia are predominantly to retrofit and bring energy efficiency to housing and public buildings, upgrade healthcare and education facilities, and improve public transportation. For example, updating and expanding the metro system in the city has received significant financing from European and domestic sources (Moraliyska 2018).

Bulgaria's domestic ability to offer credit enhancements to SNGs is weak, partly due to the sovereign' own credit rating that over the years has been borderline investment grade, and partly of the size of its financial markets. Despite its best efforts to improve its credit quality, policymakers in Sofia are unlikely to see a significant improvement in credit quality for its capital finance borrowing needs because its rating is constrained by the sovereign's. The city's efforts are still valuable, as they better position the city for credit enhancement by the EU. Co-guarantees from various EU sources is a significant credit enhancement option not available in South Korea or Mexico. SNGs in Bulgaria enjoy public sector, supranational tools of risk mitigation in the absence of traditional private sector debt insurance wraps or letters of credit (Raffer 2019). Consequently, when national or private sector credit enhancement mechanism are not available, city policymakers may want to seek supra- or trans-national co-guarantors, if and when available.

Overall, debt levels for capital financing have grown in all three cities from 2005 to 2016. As Panel a in Figure 7.3a shows, since 2010 Seoul and Monterrey have carried an average per capita debt level for infrastructure projects of over

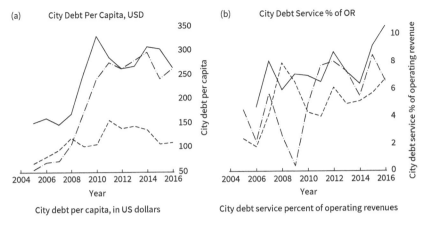

Figure 7.3 City debt per capita and city debt service percent of operating revenues, trends in 2005–2016 (Panels a and b)
Source: Line = Seoul, South Korea, ratings from Standard & Poor's; long dash dotted line = Monterrey, Mexico, ratings from Fitch; dashed line = Sofia, Bulgaria, ratings from Standard & Poor's.

USD270. Per capita borrowing in Sofia, meanwhile, fluctuated above USD125 during the same period. These levels of direct per capita city debt, however, are certainly much lower than the levels of debt for cities in the Canada or Japan, which we analyzed as part of a sample of cities in Chapter 5. Debt burdens are relatively low, as reflected in debt service levels in Seoul, Monterrey, and Sofia in Figure 7.3, Panel b. The average levels of debt service as a percentage of operating revenues during 2005–2016 for Sofia and Monterrey was around 5 percent and for Seoul a little below 8 percent. Note, however, that these measures do not account for other long-term liabilities, such as indirect debt, or liabilities of public funds, such as pension or social insurance plans.

Furthermore, central government support has always been an important source of capital financing for Seoul, but when it was insufficient, financing was available from commercial and foreign sources (Kim et al. 2012). Of the three cities, Seoul is also the only one to sporadically venture into debt securities. Its issuance of debt securities fluctuated sharply during 2005–2016, as seen in Panel a, Figure 7.4a. By 2016 most of the city's borrowing was through loans. Loans, however, in recent years were sourced from public sector sources rather than the private sector, as seen in Panel 7.4b. Despite its heavy reliance on public loans, Seoul is seeking to promote innovative forms of financing directly in service provision. Seoul's metropolitan government reports that it is the first city in Asia to adopt social impact financing. SIBs provide targeted external financing to social projects, both for operating and non-operating

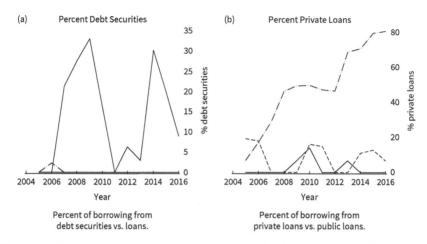

Figure 7.4 City debt percent from debt securities vs. city debt percent from loans; and city debt percent from private loans vs. city debt percent from public loans, trends in 2005–2016 (Panels a and b)

Source: Line = Seoul, South Korea, ratings from Standard & Poor's; long dash dotted line = Monterrey, Mexico, ratings from Fitch; dashed line = Sofia, Bulgaria, ratings from Standard & Poor's.

expenditures—in Seoul's case, the first SIB provided infrastructure and instructional support to foster children and their foster families. Launched in 2016, the USD9.4 million project was designed to care for children and offer support to families eligible for state welfare and was completed in 2019.[1] Given perceived signs of success, the second pilot project was launched in the autumn of 2020.

Monterrey borrows heavily from loans, with limited bond or debt securities activity. For loans, while in 2005 Monterrey sourced almost 80 percent of its borrowing from Mexico's public development bank, by 2015 the picture reversed in favor of private loans. Smith (2017) argues that commercial bank debt in Mexico, while more cost efficient than public development bank loans, is likely to be less cost efficient than trust fund debt or bonds issued on the Mexican Stock Market. The Fiscal Discipline Act, with its requirement that SNGs report all debt, may remove a structural incentive for Monterrey to prefer loans to bonds. Given that both system-level information resolution institutions and mechanisms of information certification and monitoring are strongly present in Mexico, capital markets could clearly be used more extensively. Still the movement away from public loans to private loans, while less

---

[1] Details of SIB are available on Seoul metropolitan government's website at http://english.seoul.go.kr/ seoul-implementing-sib-first-time-asia/ (last accessed on January 19, 2020).

efficient than debt securities, demonstrates Monterrey's access to a broader array of financing alternatives. Monterrey's credit quality is relatively weaker than Seoul's, however.

Sofia started accessing debt markets through short-term loans and debt securities between 1994 and 2003. These were primarily used to fill the holes in the city's operating budget. Significant borrowing for capital financing, though, has occurred since 2007. Harmonization of local government fiscal rules with the benchmarks of the European Union and the development funds that became available with membership in the European Union means that Sofia, and other local governments in Bulgaria, can enjoy capital-financing resources from outside of the country. Though the domestic financial sector in Bulgaria is relatively underdeveloped, it appears to be capable of offering some bank loans for co-financing purposes of EU funded projects (Raffer 2019). Unfortunately, Sofia's credit ratings are generally below, or borderline in some years, what is considered to be investment grade. Therefore, given the current weak fundamentals of credit quality, it is reasonable that debt securities are not a widely used borrowing option in its portfolio. Furthermore, even co-financing loans from private banks need the continued guarantees of the central government if Sofia's credit ratings remain below investment grade. Until the fundamentals that comprise the informational content of the city's credit quality improve, Sofia's options for financing, while broader than before the reforms, remain limited. In order to issue debt securities the city would need to continue using credit quality enhancements with tools such as guarantees from the central government and the co-financing mechanisms from the European Union.

Implications from Information Resolution Policy Reforms

From the case studies of three cities, the following conclusions emerge.

Seoul enjoys significant resources from the central government for its capital financing needs. The legislation to allow SNGs in South Korea to issue bonds is rather new, partially explaining why the city has only recently expanded to debt securities. However, with Seoul's strong credit quality and system-level credit information infrastructure, the legislation invites efficient borrowing options from the capital market. Seoul already began to utilize novel financing schemes, including innovations such as social impact financing that bring external resources to the city and address social policy needs. More sources of external financing exist for Seoul if policymakers were to seek resources for urban capital infrastructure independent of the central government's purse.

Monterrey appears to utilize private loans rather heavily, despite strong information resolution institutions and availability of global and domestic credit-rating firms for credit certification and monitoring. The current focus on commercial bank loans compared to public bank loans is still better as they offer credit enhancements through the city's trust fund intercepts and remove the bailout expectations from the SNG capital market. The city has the option for debt securities though, which would likely be more cost efficient and transparent than private bank loans, but until recently it faced regulatory and investor biases.

Finally, Sofia appears to have access to significant resources—despite having weak credit quality, which often slips into the non-investment grade range. The resources, however, are from the EU as it attempts to absorb Bulgaria into the common market through regional development and stabilization funds. Sofia borrows from domestic public and private sources primarily as a co-financing tool for the EU projects located in the city and the broader metropolitan area.

The three cities have alternatives at their disposal to seek greater access to capital market financing. Indeed, credit-rating firms have highlighted the strengths and weaknesses of each city that can enable or hinder such access. We summarize the strengths and weaknesses from Fitch and Standard & Poor's credit rating reports for these cities in Table 7.1.

Seoul's strong credit fundamentals received special attention. An assessment conducted by Standard & Poor's, for example, highlights the strength of local tax revenues and the soundness of fiscal management and budgetary performance (Standard & Poor's 2011, 2016). In this particular case, the credit agency also viewed the involvement of the central government as a positive factor, as it entailed close monitoring of Seoul's financial decisions.

The weaknesses identified by credit-rating firms give an idea of factors that subnational borrowers also need to take into consideration. Two factors seen as potentially concerning in the case of Seoul were related to its local tax structure and contingent liabilities. The city's tax structure that depends heavily on real estate transactions, whose revenues tend to align with the economic cycle, rather than on property taxation is seen as a weakness. Also, the city's decision to continue supporting mass-transportation projects using its general obligation pledge rather than the revenues from public transportation use (Seoul's underground metro-rail and metropolitan rapid transportation system) posed a significant contingent liability to the city. It is important to mention this particular concern because aspects of service provision can

Table 7.1 Perceived strengths and weaknesses in credit fundamentals: Seoul, South Korea; Monterrey, Mexico; and Sofia, Bulgaria

City	Strengths	Weaknesses
Seoul	• Strong and diversified economy as capital city of South Korea • Sound budgetary performance • Strong liquidity	• Large enterprise activities increase debt burden and contingent liabilities
Monterrey	• Payment guarantees from Mexico's Federal Development Bank • Expected growth in revenue sharing transfers • Strong reserve fund • Purchase of coverage for interest rates	• Repayment source control • Extraordinary considerations • Terms of the established coverage contracts • Change in base scenarios • Macroeconomic weaknesses • Cyclical stress exposure • Volatility in trends in revenue-sharing transfers, debt coverage ratio, and mean annual growth rate
Sofia	• Strategic position as Bulgaria's administrative, financial, and commercial center • Continuing strong operating budgetary performance • Improving revenue-side flexibility • Strong liquidity position	• Consolidated but uneven institutional framework • Significant expenditure pressures for maintenance and upgrade of aging infrastructure • A fast trend of increasing debt due to an ambitious capital investment program • Contingent liabilities related to the ownership of Municipal Bank and heating utility Toplofikacia

Sources: Credit reports for Sofia: Standard & Poor's (2011, 2016, and 2017); Seoul (Standard & Poor's 2012, 2016); and Monterrey (Fitch Ratings 2016).

be compartmentalized into specialized enterprise authorities for capital-financing pledges. While such organizational and repayment structures can have political costs, SNGs have relative autonomy to separate and link infrastructure financing sources to revenue streams that such investment is likely to generate.

Monterrey, as the third-largest metropolitan area in Mexico, has a dynamic and diversified economy. Overall, the city has always maintained good credit ratings, reflecting the strengths of its credit fundamentals. Fitch Ratings (2016), for example, considers the following factors as positive indicators of the city's credit quality: high percentage of locally generated revenues (as of 2015 the share was around 41 percent of total revenues), a notable tax collection efficiency, satisfactory levels of internal savings and investment, and economic and social welfare indicators above the national average. The perceived weaknesses in recent years were related to the existing level and volatility of indebtedness, debt sustainability, and the potential negative impact of increasing pension liabilities. Generally, key features that rating agencies ponder carefully when assessing subnational entities in Mexico are expected flows of revenue-sharing transfers and their dependence on guarantees from Banobras (as mentioned, the development bank of Mexico). Revenue-sharing transfers are the backbone of the finances of almost every local government in the country, and since these resources are distributed with no strings attached, credit-rating agencies see them as a very flexible and important source of debt repayment.

Developing local self-government institutions in Bulgaria required policymakers to redesign the entire institutional framework and reallocate rights and responsibilities among levels of government that under a socialist regime were seen largely as administrative units of the central government. The city of Sofia was among the first to take advantage of the opportunities that the new institutional framework permitted, acquiring loans from international institutions (World Bank, European Bank for Reconstruction and Development, Council of Europe Development Bank, among others), as well as issuing a bond for 50 million euros for urban infrastructure in 1999 (Markiewicz 2006).[2]

As Sofia became a more active consumer of private loans, the management of its credit rating fundamentals also gained relevance. As credit reports illustrate, credit-rating firms view Bulgaria's strategic position as a financial and commercial center in the Balkan region as advantageous. Sofia, as an economic and political center in the country, enjoys a strong liquidity position, improved budgetary flexibility, and the continued support from the EU. The remaining weaknesses are due to public sector corruption, limited predictability of the city's management and fiscal policy, and liabilities associated with Sofia's continued responsibilities to maintain and update aging public infrastructure (Standard & Poor's 2012, 2016).

SNGs interested in capital markets as an alternative for the financing of strategic projects gain useful insights from the experiences of the countries and cities studied in this chapter. In the three cases, changes aimed at making information about the borrowers' financial condition transparent and easily available have certainly had a positive impact on market perceptions. South Korea, Mexico, and Bulgaria faced different historical events and operate in contexts that other nations may not have. Countries seeking to improve subnational access to capital markets need to consider the particularities of their

---

[2] The debt issue was a 50 million euro bond offering a 9.75 percent interest rate, with a three-year maturity.

own governing structures, especially since national-level policy objectives signal the commitment to encourage (or discourage) SNG borrowing.

It is evident that Seoul, by achieving its strongest credit risk assessment in recent years, is ready for a more robust use of debt securities for its infrastructure financing projects. There remains significant underutilized capacity that Seoul would benefit from by unlocking the external market sources of capital financing. Monterrey is a city that enjoys a strong underlying resource base. Because of its strong credit quality, Monterrey is able to move away from public loans from the federal development bank. However, though the city is imbedded in the country with a relatively reasonable experience of market-based subnational capital financing, it continues to rely primarily on loans, especially commercial bank loans. Finally, Sofia's domestic resources, both from public and private sectors, are limited. Its credit risk is not always of investment grade quality as well. Unlike the other two countries, however, Sofia operates in a context with a very strong supranational presence. The city has access to significant resources from the EU as part of targeted multi-country capital infrastructure development projects. In Sofia's case, information resolution and reforms in accounting systems were a prerequisite to access European funds in concert with subsidized co-financing loans from domestic private banks. All three cities, nevertheless, required improvements in information resolution to broaden their range of financing alternatives, bringing a shift in financing from public loans to private loans and, in some cases, to bonds, increasingly supported by innovative credit enhancement arrangements and novel social-impact oriented financing alternatives.

8
Subnational Government Capital Financing

Lessons for Policy and Practice

This book advances the perspective that capital markets can be an important source of external financing for subnational governments (SNGs) across the globe as they face the dual contexts of decentralized governance and increased demand for infrastructure due to rapid urban growth. A key feature in expanding SNG access to capital that has been overlooked is the degree to which the credit system resolves information problems. A central assertion of this book is that successful SNG borrowing from capital markets goes hand in hand with information resolution institutions and mechanisms. Emphasizing information as a base of good policy is not novel (Caiden and Wildavsky 1974), and this book extends previous arguments to SNG borrowing. National governments, SNGs, and financial sector firms collectively have a role in promoting credit contractibility in the system and developing tools for information certification and monitoring. Building on an existing argument that national governments set the parameters for SNG borrowing through fiscal rules, in this book we argue that SNGs can make decisions about how they manage their fiscal governance task to move themselves from a reactive to a proactive stance. SNGs can and must become competent actors both with regards to top-down (national to local governments) and outside-in (financial sector firms to local governments) interactions and pressures. In other words, SNGs, especially cities, are not necessarily beholden to powerful (national government or financial sector) principals in that they now have substantial discretion to successfully manage their access to capital markets through information resolution mechanisms.

While there is still hesitancy about SNGs accessing capital markets, in a number of cases for good reason, many cities have demonstrated success in the markets and many more have the potential to do so (Pagano and Perry 2008; Bahl et al. 2013). There is a place for these SNG contenders to be capital market borrowers. The rapid development of the financial sector in many emerging economies provides local authorities with a number of financing

Information Resolution and Subnational Capital Markets. Christine R. Martell, Tima T. Moldogaziev, and Salvador Espinosa, Oxford University Press. © Oxford University Press 2021. DOI: 10.1093/oso/9780190089337.003.0008

alternatives (Freire 2014). Information resolution is critical for SNGs to become successful borrowers. At the national level this means maintaining systems that offer credit contractibility, be they for private or public sector use. This is beyond the fiscal rules that allow revenue and expenditure autonomy to SNGs, the authority and guidelines to borrow, regulatory reporting and dissemination requirements, and predictable default processes. A critical component is the national context that equips SNGs with institutions that support the transparency and depth of information provision, extent of disclosure, and regulatory quality.

While the importance of national institutions and contexts is undeniable, for many years, researchers and policymakers have focused primarily on intergovernmental institutions structured by national governments. In focusing on economic, financial and market, political, and legal institutions, previous research and policy direction gave insufficient attention to the institutions and mechanisms of information resolution with which SNGs around the globe must work. Policymakers must approach the appropriate use of capital markets with the tools that support and enhance agency at the local level.

Viewing SNG borrowing through the lens of agency puts a positive view on the role of finance in governance. Many studies look at the role of finance in governance as an adverse phenomenon. There can certainly be negative impacts, but those often come about because national and subnational policymakers misunderstand and misapply finance. SNG use of capital markets can, indeed, bring fiscal and equity disparities when unscrupulously used. Capital markets cannot and will not address social or redistributive policy concerns. The finance option in and of itself is not good or evil: it is simply a source of external capital finance for SNGs. To mitigate potential negative impacts, financial policy must be in concert with other policy domains, as policymakers need to balance multiple governance goals. Financial tasks can be arranged to support non-fiscal governance tasks, including those domains that seek an effective and equitable distribution of public goods and services.

Simultaneously, for local levels, especially cities, to fulfill their fundamental fiscal governance task, they must evaluate and maintain their underlying credit quality factors and to competently communicate information on underlying credit quality to markets. SNGs must be able to demonstrate their proficiency in fiscal policy and financial management to respond to the citizens' service and infrastructure needs, investment projects that are consonant with citizen preferences, plan for future capital needs and match them to internal and external resources. These building blocks of agency are critical for SNGs to use capital markets for their own gain, rather than let slip the benefits that the financial sector offers.

Underlying borrower credit ratings, an information-certification tool, offer governments means to evaluate and signal their credit quality. Moreover, the fundamentals of underlying credit quality provide information to city officials: through comparative analysis and benchmarking, city policymakers can gain insight into how to improve their creditworthiness. Even when the institutional contexts are not ideal for SNG borrowing, cities can take control over their fiscal domain by building their internal capacity to aid in understanding and resolving information problems. Information resolution mechanisms go hand in hand with a mindset of agency at the local level.

With this premise, and supported by the conclusions from previous chapters, this chapter presents local government policymakers with options for capital market access when both system credit contractibility and city underlying credit quality vary. Conditional on such variation, we offer a typology of financing alternatives, from which we derive recommendations on the use of credit enhancements to mitigate weaknesses in either system-level information resolution or city-level credit quality. The chapter further recommends policies that build contractibility and credit quality through information resolution mechanisms; and in doing so, addresses policy measures for national governments, SNGs, and international financial institutions. The chapter concludes with recommendations for future research.

Review of Key Empirical Findings

Through comparative quantitative and case analyses of countries and cities around the world, four overarching results emerge. The first key finding is that information resolution is critical to SNG borrowing and debt composition. The strength of SNG capital markets depends on the quality of the country's credit contractibility. Transparency and depth of credit information and extent of disclosure are associated with greater SNG debt levels. We deduce that the system's information resolution is, in its own right, an important institution alongside the other fundamental governance institutions. In fact, institutions of information resolution remain a significant predictor of SNG borrowing when other governance institutions are held constant. Moreover, of the four fundamental governance institutions, legal institutions emerge as a significant covariate of SNG borrowing, suggesting the need for policies that enhance the rule of law and tackle fiscal fraud, misappropriation, and waste in the public sector in order to stimulate SNG capital market activity.

A second key finding is that city debt levels are greater when SNGs obtain credit ratings and have stronger credit quality. The certification and communication of information, which is contained in the credit rating, are positively related with access to capital markets. Cities with greater administrative and fiscal autonomy and cities with strong credit quality fundamentals gain greater access to capital market borrowing. City credit ratings and the measures in the informational content of credit quality, a proxy for information signals, influence the levels and type of debt. This result holds even when controlling for the governance institutions in the context, including the institutions of information resolution. The message is clear: building local competence through information-resolving mechanisms has power beyond that afforded by national institutions. Cities with investment grade credit quality have relatively higher levels of borrowing, and cities with stronger credit quality have higher shares of debt from securities. Given these empirical results, the ability of a jurisdiction to understand its own credit fundamentals; manage its financial health; and communicate these to citizens, higher level governments, and credit markets is a key to access capital and widening SNG financing alternatives.

A third finding is that there is imperfect alignment between cities that are creditworthy and could benefit from debt securities and those that access debt securities but have weaker credit quality. A number of cities in the sample that do not use or underutilize a full range of financing options would be viable contenders to use debt securities. Large, primary cities use more capital market debt but, surprisingly, a lower share of debt securities. Conversely, a number of cities with poor credit quality have engaged in the issuance of debt securities more heavily. While the former cohort of cities would likely gain efficiencies by utilizing debt securities at lower borrowing costs by disseminating information about the strength of their underlying credit fundamentals, the latter group is likely paying higher interest costs for borrowing in the capital market or must incur costs required for credit enhancements. This is possibly an indication that need is a strong driver of access to capital markets, while the information of strong underlying city credit qualities is underleveraged in the management of external resources.

A fourth finding is that countries and cities demonstrate many paths to resolve information problems and to signal credit quality. The cases illustrate an array of policy choices made by three country-city pairs. Despite different backgrounds, motivations, and policy pathways, each of the cities had more financing options, both internal and external, after reforms to their information environments and availability of credit quality assessment and enhancement tools. The cases also show that information is necessary but not sufficient, for even when they demonstrate improvements to the information environment and broaden the range of alternative financing, they continue to rely on historically used internal financing sources. Nations that create information resolution institutions for the corporate market may benefit by extending them to the subnational market. Nations with strong information resolution institutions for SNGs may benefit from reviewing the policies that favor historically used, often with explicit or implicit bailout guarantees, financing sources. Cities, regardless of their credit quality, can appreciate that improvements will enhance their standing with a range of external financing alternatives.

In summary, the development of SNG capital financing options, conditional on fundamental institutions governing subnational borrowing, also depend in significant ways on information resolution institutions at the national level and the information resolution mechanisms that SNGs can utilize to assess, monitor, and communicate credit quality. Two dimensions of information resolution are important to realize the most efficient use of SNG capital markets: the system's information resolution institutions and the mechanisms for information resolution that SNGs could utilize to signal their creditworthiness. While national governments may control the parameters of access to capital markets (who, when, how, under what conditions) and may make arrangements for public and private options of information certification and monitoring, understanding how city credit quality matters and what information is contained in credit quality are equally significant. The most desirable conditions for SNG capital market access occur when both national and local policymakers understand the value of information resolution and utilize its benefits.

Typology of Capital-Financing Options

The result that information resolution institutions and information resolution mechanisms matter for SNG borrowing informs what capital financing options might best suit local governments with different underlying contexts and qualities. Figure 8.1 presents a typology of capital-financing options, which juxtaposes the quality of the system to resolve information problems, referred to as credit contractibility, against the city's underlying credit quality, which contains information about underlying city risk fundamentals.

The vertical dimension of the matrix indicates the degree of the system's credit contractibility, as measured by the nation's ability to overcome information problems with transparency, disclosure, and regulatory quality. The horizontal dimension indicates the strength of SNG's underlying credit quality, containing information on the jurisdiction's economic, fiscal, debt

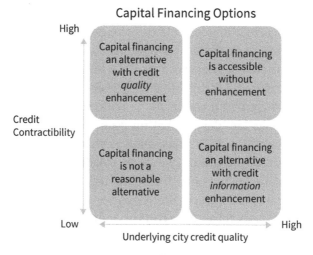

Figure 8.1 Capital financing options for SNGs: system credit contractibility vs. city credit quality

and financial, and governance fundamentals. Both credit contractibility and underlying credit quality range from low to high.

In cases where credit contractibility and credit quality are low, represented in the lower left quadrant of Figure 8.1, capital financing is not a reasonable alternative. For whatever reasons behind poor credit quality, SNGs in this category possess a low likelihood of debt servicing and repayment and the poor credit contractibility in the system would leave investors wary of executing transactions. The risk to investors would be too great, and enhancements to mitigate the risk would be inefficient and costly. These SNGs will most likely continue relying on publicly subsidized borrowing options and if engaged with private actors, engage only in relationship-based transactions where the cost of borrowing is not necessarily determined by underlying risks.

In the upper right quadrant reside SNGs where the national information resolution institutions are robust and where the informational components of their own credit quality is strong. These governments are well positioned to borrow from capital markets and will likely enjoy favorable borrowing costs. Moreover, since their underlying credit fundamentals are strong, they have the qualities to use capital markets without costly credit enhancements. These governments would have the freedom to pursue a broad range of capital market financial alternatives and to choose the financing instrument that best meets the nature of the investment, the source of repayment, and the terms of repayment.

SNGs that reside in the other two quadrants suffer imperfections to either their information resolution contexts or possess weak credit fundamentals that are reflected in their credit quality ratings. In cases where credit contractibility is high and borrower credit quality is low, represented in the upper left quadrant of Figure 8.1, capital financing is an alternative so long as the design and use of credit enhancements provide support for credit quality. Credit enhancements are "devices that mitigate or reduce the risks in debt transactions" (Freire 2014: 352). *Credit quality enhancements* can be achieved by protected payment pledges or intercepts; collateral deals; through debt-structuring decisions; credit pools; third-party letters of credit, insurance, or guarantees; or derivative contracts. SNGs may benefit from capital market access, but the benefits must absorb the costs of credit enhancement. See Box 8.1 for a summary and example of credit enhancements in Romania.

In cases where credit contractibility is low and borrower credit quality is high, represented in the lower right quadrant of Figure 8.1, capital financing of cities is an alternative so long as the design and use of information resolution mechanisms address the shortcomings in the system's information context. These are *information enhancements* that can be achieved through information intermediation or signaling. When system-level information resolution is weak, SNGs must seek contractibility on their own, using third-party mechanisms. In some contexts, such as the European Union, supranational public institutions and private sector firms can be of help by substituting for country-level weaknesses. In cross-border infrastructure projects, the strength of the partner with a relatively stronger level of contractibility may be leveraged. International public and quasi-public organizations may act as guarantors for SNGs with strong credit quality but from contexts with weak contractibility. Finally, legal contracts may seek to guarantee protections to investors to ensure that disclosure by the SNG does not fall short on material information. These alternative arrangements involve costs that are needed to plug the weaknesses in contractibility in the system, but they are critical to opening up external sources of financing for SNGs with otherwise strong underlying credit quality.

Thus, SNG options to use capital financing fall on a spectrum from none to full market access, depending on the degree of the system's credit contractibility and the borrower's underling credit quality. For cases between the ends of the spectrum, enhancements to either information or credit risk can support the use of capital financing by shoring up existing weaknesses. The application of this typology can help overcome the impediment to SNG capital markets that local financial markets do not offer good products to subnational borrowers (Freire 2014). A key implication of this typology is that the design

Box 8.1 Credit Enhancements: The Case of Romania

SNG borrowers can use credit enhancements to improve the attraction of their bond issues to investors (Pop and Georgescu 2016). Credit enhancements signal a borrower's commitment and help overcome the information asymmetries between lenders and borrowers, especially for jurisdictions that are new to the market, are infrequent borrowers, or are small. These mechanisms reduce the investor's credit risk and can be used to overcome shortcomings (but not gross deficits) in the borrowers' credit quality (Fabozzi et al. 2005; Petitt et al. 2015). Internal credit enhancements include overcollateralization, in which the borrower offers collateral greater than the value of the amount borrowed; reserve fund, such as a cash reserve, escrow account, or excess spread fund protected from the borrower's use; and debt subordination, where a junior tranche is subordinate to a senior tranche. External credit-enhancement mechanisms, provided by third parties, include stand-by letters of credit, guarantees, surety bonds, credit insurance, and bond pooling (Pop and Georgescu 2016).

Romanian municipal bonds issuance began in 2001, with 35 bonds listed by 2014. Regulations in Romania prohibit the use of national guarantees of local government debt, resulting in municipal governments offering a credit enhancement of revenue overcollateralization. Municipal bond declarations state that municipal borrowers will pledge all their collected revenues, which offers borrowers a low-cost means to self-enhance. As it turned out, information deficiencies about the risk-free rate and municipal revenue structures plagued the municipal market. Despite the overcollateralization, the country did not have clear procedures in place to handle defaults and credit bankruptcy proceedings. The lack of bankruptcy proceedings and administrative procedures requiring a commercial court order limited the value of the overcollateralization. When some Romanian municipalities failed to make their debt payments and investors remained unpaid, the markets responded with distrust, contaminating the Romanian bond market. Municipalities had not structured bonds with adequate credit enhancements, contributing to the underdevelopment of the municipal bond market between 2011 and 2014.

and use of enhancements should match the information weakness, be it the system's credit contractibility or the underlying bases of SNG's credit quality. With this distinction comes a choice between two types of enhancements: an enhancement of the system's contractibility versus an enhancement of the borrower's credit risk. This typology of necessary enhancements for SNG capital financing helps guide policy direction for national and SNGs, as well as financial sector firms.

Policy Recommendations

Taken as a whole, the analytical results uphold those of previous studies that governance institutions matter. Results also support the new argument advanced in this book that, regardless of key institutions and legal origins, policies that improve the information environment at the national level and credit quality certification and monitoring tools available to SNGs will improve their opportunities to access capital markets. Two forces appear at play: one has to do with the enabling factors of the information resolution context, or system's credit contractibility; the other has to do with the underlying informational content of credit quality. This section turns to recommendations in these areas.

Credit Contractibility via System-Level Information Resolution

Information resolution at the system level supports capital market financing. The national government can assist public (and private) capital market development by developing systems of information management, provision, and dissemination to build the credit environment. Efforts in these areas will increase the credit contractibility of the system and create the conditions for other levels of government to attend to their fiscal governance task.

Providing markets with reliable information about the credit environment requires the establishment of bankruptcy and insolvency rules for all types of borrowers and standards for self-regulatory organizations. These are necessary because insolvency rules can improve information to creditors by establishing clear default proceedings and give clarity to investors regarding investor rights and due process in default incidences. "Most of the developing countries implement ad hoc interventions, with no rules for managing the insolvency situation" (Freire 2014: 351). Without them, investors expect the national government to bailout defaulting subnational jurisdictions. Bailouts, however, are unfair and result in moral hazard behavior problems and cross-subsidies between jurisdictions. National governments often bailout the debt of defaulting jurisdictions by buying it in exchange for a loan due to the national government and/or fiscal reforms. These interventions can set back SNG access to capital markets by years or decades and are risky and costly for the national government. An alternative is to let the market allocate capital based on risk and price criteria.

For markets to reinforce fiscal discipline, the keys to success include clear procedures, as well as the transparency and dissemination of quality data. To achieve transparency and depth of credit information improvements requires enhancing data production and sharing by building platforms for information generation and provision. National governments can invest in systems that address access to, longevity of, and quality of government, industry, and self-regulatory organizational data. This includes increasing the visibility of positive and negative credit information; timely and relevant information about trading interest in prices, including post-trade price and volume, pre-trade price and volume, and the identity of market participants; and payment and settlement information of securities. Additionally, transparency should address the government's ability to manage its own data—to require management systems that control inconsistencies and hold the data producers accountable for quality data, including accounting and debt information. Efforts in this area would include adopting accounting standards, establishing rules for SNG data collection, and requiring SNG data dissemination. For SNGs in particular, data on fiscal health and financial condition is critical. In these instances, transparency refers predominantly to information flows to firms, investors, and other market actors. National governments can support co-production—along with SNGs, independent regulatory bodies, and the private sector—of city fiscal and governance information.

Credit contractibility also requires the disclosure of credit information. In addition to sharing credit, trade, and public finance data, disclosure should establish which actors should disclose what types of information at what stages of the debt-issuance process. That includes information that flows predominantly from borrowers to firms, lending entities, and market actors and might include information about financial, accounting, debt, and managerial practices so that investors can assess risk. Disclosure also refers to the dissemination of pricing information from various actors in the financial system, including financial service costs. Disclosure efforts can also extend to monitoring and evaluation, accurate data reporting, and self-certification. Emphasis on reducing the relative cost of information will also shift the balance between the costs of information and regulation, ultimately rendering regulatory compliance less costly.

Next, national governments can advance regulatory policies to control incentives and maintain the rule of law to facilitate capital market activity.

When left unchecked, borrower ill-discipline and disregard for the rule of law may result in the deterioration of credit contractibility, which in turn brings fewer options for capital financing and increased borrowing and issuance costs.

Information Mechanisms at the SNG Level

While fiscal rules governing SNG borrowing must always be considered from the perspective of how they affect credit contractibility, they must also be viewed through the lens of how they can enable or constrain borrower creditworthiness. National governments can evaluate how fiscal rules and arrangements encourage or hamper credit quality; and revise policies that currently inhibit SNG creditworthiness. A system that encourages SNGs to improve their credit quality may require changes to the distribution of revenues and resources. SNG borrowing authority is necessary for SNG capital market growth but is insufficient: SNG revenue-raising autonomy and authority are also necessary to increase borrower creditworthiness.

Furthermore, the national government's policy should be to help SNGs develop tools for self-evaluation of credit quality. To enhance information resolution, national governments may contribute to setting credit quality standards and processes for self-evaluation. Systematic analysis of SNG credit fundamentals, monitoring of such, and dissemination of the results, for individual jurisdictions and on a comparative basis, can add to the information environment yet also offer SNGs the means to evaluate their credit quality. As the costs of credit quality assessment depend on the time and effort it takes to evaluate credit risk, there is an interaction between SNG credit quality assessment and costs. Coordinated efforts to increase credit fundamentals data and dissemination of credit quality information will lower SNG issuance costs. Efforts that increase SNG credit quality will lower risk premiums and issuance costs and should be adopted (Freire 2014; Platz 2009).

Imbedded in the system-level information contexts and fiscal rules governing SNG borrowing, SNGs can make decisions to increase their agency. They can be active participants in leveraging financial markets by adopting policies to reduce information asymmetries among themselves and the national government, credit-rating agencies, citizens, and investors. Doing so requires a concerted effort by the jurisdiction to embrace a positive role of finance and to commit to strengthening agency. Government responsiveness to citizen values improves the chances of policy attaining desirable outcomes and achieving the fiscal governance task. A concern of critics of financialized governance is that debt financing has negative implications for equitable distribution of costs and benefits. Part of the SNG's governance task is to evaluate the values and preferences of the citizenry and to align urban plans and financial strategies with those values. Equity and distributional issues are as important as technical criteria for capital financing and need to be included in project selection and financing criteria. Having a breadth of capital financing alternatives allows SNGs the freedom to make financing decisions on the basis of their policy goals.

When it comes to capital finance, the mechanisms that SNGs utilize to assess the informational content of credit quality, disseminate this information to other parties, and monitor the credit fundamentals over time are critical. We are hardly the first to prescribe that SNGs must improve credit quality (see, e.g., Kaganova 2011; Freire and Petersen 2004; World Bank 2013). What is new is that we put a great part of responsibility on SNGs to commit to doing so; and by dissecting the credit fundamentals, we assess the discrete tools that local policymakers may employ to evaluate their city's credit quality fundamentals.

Policymakers, especially at the city level, can and must build technical competencies in evaluating their own credit risk factors over time and relative to comparable cities in the country, as well as to a set of peer cities in other countries. Jurisdictions should begin by taking inventory and evaluating their credit quality strengths and weaknesses. Even those jurisdictions that do not choose to undergo a formal credit evaluation from an independent party can conduct an analysis of their credit quality by using self-assessment tools (e.g., World Bank 2016; Eichler et al. 2012). All too often localities fail to access financing in concert with a capital improvement plan and land use practices (Freire 2014; World Bank 2013), exposing them to projections that they cannot realize and setting them up for failure to meet debt obligations. Whether self-evaluation leads to third-party credit ratings, or perhaps to an interim shadow credit rating, the information provided is useful for understanding credit risks, providing the SNG and investors with information needed to craft reasonable borrowing expectations.

Once a jurisdiction evaluates its credit quality, it can identify areas of improvement. The results of this study show that a city's economic base (population, GCP, and GCP per capita); fiscal base (operating expenditures and revenues, capital expenditures); existing debt burden (debt service and debt profile); and governance factors are salient for capital market access. Policymakers can learn about the core fundamentals of city creditworthiness and prioritize improvements in the areas that need support. Other areas of information resolution include details on revenue sources, including bases and rates, and databases thereof. For example, SNGs that have property or land-based taxes would want to manage and record land assets with transparent accounting methods and by defining objective land-valuation techniques upon which to base land leasing and pricing. SNGs can track performance over time to highlight improvements and guide additional policy changes.

Borrowers with better credit quality have benefits in the capital markets. SNGs can make their debt more attractive to investors by removing the need for credit enhancements. Lenders are more likely to favor borrowers that rely on their own creditworthiness over those that must operate on credit enhancements from other public or private sector actors. While lenders in weaker governance contexts may always prefer a sovereign guarantee, relying on such to backstop low credit quality poses bailout risks and muddles the risk-return connection. A focus on credit quality fundamentals allows SNGs to make choices about debt structure (levels, instruments, and maturity/payment structure), regardless of the source of debt, that align with realistic cash-flow projections. It is better to borrow less and borrow it well to establish a credit-worthy reputation, than to over-borrow and fail to make payments. Moreover, "organizing data so that the debt servicing and debt maturity profile can be readily determined is an important function of the debt management office" (Freire 2014: 359; Petersen and Crihfield 2000).

As with information resolution institutions at the system level, SNGs can also play a meaningful role in transparency and disclosure, especially when compensating for weak information contexts at the national level. Once a city understands its credit quality, it behooves itself to disseminate that information to reduce information asymmetries among key actors in the capital-financing process. Transparency and disclosure require the dissemination of results to departments, higher level governments, citizens, and the investment community. Mechanisms for reporting fiscal conditions abound, and it is up to the city to use them and convey its data, practices, and results. Examples include the annual budget, the capital budget, the capital improvement plan, the annual financial report, information on debt profile, and debt-issuance contracts and costs. Often national or subnational policies require SNGs to prepare reports and submit them for audit. Local policymakers can choose the level of information to convey and whether to leverage the audit as a communication tool. For example, when audits are not required, when the auditor's response is untimely, or when they are of poor quality, SNGs can choose to seek an audit from a competent third party.

Existing research shows that governance of economic development and planning is an important corollary for SNGs to use debt securities, and emphasizing credit quality requires information sharing and coordination with other levels of government, across departments, and within the jurisdiction's policy networks. Preconditions for effectively using external funds are for the borrower to align financing with a well-vetted capital improvement plan (CIP); to select projects that are sustainable in the long term and have a sufficient budget for operations and maintenance; and to provide timely and good financial reporting that signals strong financial health (Freire 2014). The latter emphasis on creditworthiness is critical, regardless of whether the financing instrument relies on implicit or explicit guarantees. Before seeking financial resources, SNGs should establish their credit quality by focusing on credit fundamentals. Moreover, long-term success requires coordination between financing and land-use planning and hazard risk, housing, infrastructure, and urban transport activities (World Bank 2013). "Putting financing first, without full consideration of the other dimensions, is a mistake because it often neglects the overriding need to coordinate infrastructure improvements (connecting) with policies (planning)" (World Bank 2013: 2). That is, the means of finance is secondary to the establishment of values, policy goals, and credit quality.

Whether borrowers solicit a third-party credit rating or simply self-evaluate their credit quality, they may benefit from the support of a like-minded community. Forming and/or joining consortia, networks, or member organizations (such as the United Cities and Local Governments) can provide support for SNGs by establishing comparative benchmarking tools and sharing practices to enhance credit quality. Such a community may eventually spawn self-regulatory mechanisms and credit quality standards. Ultimately, the SNG should exhibit credit quality improvements and be able to prepare for a formal credit quality analysis. The prospective borrower should come to own, embrace, and manage its fiscal and debt affairs, and the dissemination of its information. Collectively, these policy recommendations help decision-makers address their broader governance tasks. Knowing what constitutes the components of credit quality helps cities prioritize their scarce resources to better achieve their fiscal governance task.

Other Recommendations to Build SNG Capital Markets

The prescriptions for enhanced information resolution apply even in countries whose institutions and economies are less developed. While borrowing, especially from capital markets, may be in the distant future for many SNGs, efforts that build information will lay the groundwork for development success. The emphasis for these SNGs and countries will be on establishing the preconditions such as those ascribed in fiscal rules regarding SNG autonomy and authority. We recommend designing fiscal rules with an eye toward information resolution at the core.

For those SNGs that have more mature governance institutions but where ideal credit contractibility and creditworthiness are not fully present, policy actors can leverage markets with specialized interventions that encourage information resolution. National governments may choose to financially support SNGs in attaining private sector credit ratings and advising support. The initial costs to access capital markets may be quite high, especially for the first time a jurisdiction enters capital markets, as the "bond market implies costly and cumbersome hurdles for the aspiring local authority" (Freire 2014: 345). These costs include fees to the credit-rating agency, fees to the bank that underwrites the bonds and investor search costs, costs to market a bond issue, and costs to disseminate information. Support to first-time market borrowers to attain a private sector credit rating and a third-party financial advisor can reduce the barrier to enter markets by mitigating the transaction costs of information dissemination.

Investment development banks, municipal development funds, and subnational finance corporations or authorities are actors that can also help SNGs to access credit markets. Their goal should be to "help municipalities move gradually toward the local financial and capital markets to eventually gain direct access to funds" (Freire 2014: 362). As with national and subnational governments, their emphasis should be on information resolution. Often efforts focus on support for project preparation, loan application, and project implementation, though none of these activities explicitly focus on borrower credit quality fundamentals. Whatever function they perform, the root of their operations should focus on two elements: mitigating weaknesses in SNG information resolution and evaluation and monitoring of credit quality. Successful efforts include improving financial management, accounting and tax records, understanding land assets, and developing credit ratings and monitoring capacity. No amount of financial intermediation can substitute for a creditworthy local government, however (World Bank 2013). Policymakers have to be cognizant of the design of these institutions and be intentional about the incentive structures in the contracts. If the goal is to support SNGs as they build their credit quality and improve their agency, it is natural that those governments will eventually graduate to market access without the need for development assistance. As such, the need for international and domestic financial institutions should taper over the course of time, as more and more jurisdictions find solid financial footing on their own.

Market actors can leverage the distinction between system-level contractibility and local-level credit quality assessment mechanisms as they evaluate credit risk and design information resolution instruments and credit enhancements to mitigate the correct information problem. This means that in contexts with high contractibility, financial sector firms may create credit quality enhancement products for SNGs with weaker underlying credit quality. Conversely, in contexts with weaker credit contractibility, financial products may seek to offer information intermediation or enhancements that guard against poor regulations for SNGs with strong underlying credit quality.

In summary, regardless of the policy actor, efforts to improve SNG capital markets should contribute to improving credit contractibility and credit-worthiness. The national information resolution context matters, but SNGs also have a myriad of choices about how to evaluate their credit quality and enhance or signal credit risk. As credit contractibility and creditworthiness strengthen, financing options expand.

Concluding Thoughts and Avenues for Future Research

As SNGs, especially cities, are increasingly responsible for their activities—solid waste management, recycling, transportation, water and sanitation, recreation, healthcare facilities, energy, and greenhouse gas reduction—that require long-term infrastructure, they increasingly need a range of financing options to allow them to complete their governance tasks in an efficient, effective, and equitable manner. Financialized tools of governance, through the use of global resources at the local level through capital markets (Torrance 2008, 2009), are expected to remain viable financing options for SNGs. To leverage them, the critical objective is to overcome information problems resulting from national, intergovernmental, and local fiscal arrangements.

Decentralizing infrastructure finance should increase the SNG's incentive to manage risks, select projects based on local needs and preferences, and spend efficiently. "Because the political costs for these expenditures have been borne at the national level, towns and cities have not always had strong incentives to manage risks wisely, to spend money efficiently, or to do what is needed for continued creditworthiness. Cities are more accountable for their own development when the funds for that development are raised locally" (World Bank 2013: 71–72).

This book makes several theoretical and practical contributions. From a theoretical perspective, the book empirically tests and supports theories of information economics, demonstrating that information asymmetries can undermine the development of public sector capital markets. As in the private sector, the antidote to information problems is information resolution. We further show the need for information resolution mechanisms of underlying credit quality at the SNG level. Subnational capital markets will work better when these institutional and instrumental settings work in concert. When one part in the setting is weak, enhancement mechanisms, whether information or credit enhancements, can compensate for the weakness at a certain cost. The key is to match the type of enhancement approach to the type of shortcoming.

The recommendations articulated in this chapter derive from the results of the empirical analyses and case studies in previous chapters. They focus on building information resolution institutions, broadly referred to as credit contractibility in the system. Equally important is a position of this book that SNGs can, and must, be proactive participants who seek out both internal and external capital-financing resources. No amount of vertical institutional development replaces the need to understand one's own credit quality strengths and weaknesses. In particular, this book exposes the informational fundamentals of credit quality from which SNGs can learn. The key lesson is that city policymakers are capable of building capacity to assess their credit quality and take actions that can mitigate the impact of weaker institutional dimensions. However, capital market access is not an end in itself. The decision to borrow, whether from internal or external resources, needs to ensure that financing allows borrowers to obtain their policy objectives. To evaluate this, SNGs must connect with their citizens' values and priorities, and connect public financial management with policy choices, actions, and results (New York University 2020; Johnson et al. 2014).

The limited scope of our research leaves us thirsty for more knowledge. A number of recommendations for future research regarding credit quality, fiscal and financial instruments, credit enhancements, borrowing costs, citizen's role and preferences, and geographies emerge.

As we promote an active role for SNGs in establishing their own credit quality, we recommend the evaluation of qualities of cities that have consistently maintained fiscal discipline in the face of challenging circumstances. Many countries rely on strong regulatory controls to manage national and subnational debt to reduce the risk of insolvency (World Bank 2013). Fiscal rules are regulatory stopgap measures that could be replaced, or at least reinforced, with market discipline. The goal, though, is to encourage SNGs to self-monitor and disclose key information. Many borrowers in countries with nascent SNG capital markets operate under fiscal rules obliged by national legislation. Some jurisdictions find every reason to violate those fiscal rules, and others uphold them or resort to even more stringent standards. What can we learn from the latter group about their credit risk fundamentals to move beyond fiscal responsibility rules? Can SNG credit quality assessments and focus on credit risk fundamentals obviate the need for nationally determined fiscal standards? Would it be more efficient for convention to move beyond a blanket one-size-fits-all debt rule to nuanced assessment of SNG borrowing capacity? What can we learn from some well-performing cities that have effectively moved from regulatory control and market control to self-control?

We recommend to further study systematic evaluation of enhancement tools based on the enhancement typology introduced here. Specifically, it would be valuable to explore the impacts of different types of credit enhancements on both borrowers' behavior and on capital market development in varying institutional contexts. We speculate that only when enhancement tools match the information shortcoming will they fully advance subnational capital markets. In other cases, they may help only the higher quality jurisdictions access capital financing but may segment the market and retard such access to jurisdictions with weaker underlying credit quality (Espinosa and Martell 2015).

More comparative data are needed on the costs of borrowing. Subsidized finance by the public sector has bedeviled the growth of capital markets. What reasonable city official would want to borrow for a higher cost from capital markets when it could borrow at a steep discount from public sources? This reality stunts the efficient use of capital, even though the policy objective of bringing financing to jurisdictions that cannot access it otherwise is noble. The trick is to alter the use of subsidies away from political project investment and toward information-revealing investments. However, there is a dearth of comparative data and analysis about the relative financing costs to SNG borrowers (Bahl et al. 2013). For cities across the globe, there is a need for the systematic evaluation of cost of capital-financing alternatives; of different debt instrument design features, including enhancements; and of issuance costs.

The research shows the importance of SNG governance as a fundamental dimension of credit quality, but little comparative research to date has connected the citizen to SNG debt finance. Yet, there are multiple entry points for citizens to be part of the debt finance process, ranging from value and preference revelation; to project selection and design; to preference on debt and fee structure; to feedback and monitoring; to investing and/or having a fiduciary role (Martell 2010; Freire 2014).[1] Citizen engagement has benefits for both democracy and project effectiveness (willingness to pay, ability to fund

---

[1] At least two cities—Denver, Colorado, and Johannesburg, South Africa—have issued bonds directly to citizens. Denver issued small-denomination mini-bonds on five occasions (Ely and Martell 2016), and Johannesburg issued retail bonds, known as *Jozibonds*: "About Jozi Bonds," Joburg, https://www.joburg.org.za/work_/Pages/Work%20in%20Joburg/Investor%20Relations/Table%20links/About-Jozi-bonds.aspx, Accessed December 19, 2019.

operations and maintenance, support of selection), equity, and efficiency. Tools such as hearings, surveys, referenda, and online tools for financial transparency can elicit citizen preferences and willingness to pay to increase project effectiveness.[2]

Bringing in citizens' voices increases efficiency by aligning investment with citizen preferences. Investors demand comprehensive feasibility studies that detail the project's financial analysis, assumptions, sensitivity analysis, and revenue- collection strategy. It is important to bring in the citizen's voice at the time of pre-selection or no later than feasibility studies: "It is vital to involve the customers in a timely way and to reach agreement on feasible and afford- able tariffs at [the feasibility study] stage" (Freire 2014: 329). The connection between citizens and SNG debt is ripe for future research, namely, to address the specific question: How does citizen participation affect the efficiency, eq- uity, and effectiveness of debt outcomes?

The theoretical and practical underpinnings explored in this book are likely to apply to a range of SNG-borrowing geographies. Moving for- ward, researchers should consider them as they assess broader geograph- ical configurations, including metropolitan and cross-border financing arrangements. It is our hope that the contributions of this book will spur the competency of national and subnational policymakers to fulfill their govern- ance tasks. The contributions herein only scratch the surface of capital market financing arrangements, and future extensions must continue to refine our understanding of a broad spectrum of SNG financing options from a compar- ative perspective.

---

[2] See, for example, Balancing Act, a product cities can purchase to assist in transparency, accountability, and citizen participation, www.abalancingact.com.

References

Ahmad, Ehtisham, Maria Albino-War, and Raju Singh. 2005. *Subnational Public Financial Management: Institutions and Macroeconomic Considerations*. Washington, D.C.: International Monetary Fund. WP/05/108.

Ahmad, Ehtisham, Dan Dowling, Denise Chan, Sarah Colenbrander, and Nick Godfrey. 2019. *Scaling Up Investment for Sustainable Urban Infrastructure: A Guide to National and Subnational Reform*. Coalition for Urban Transitions. London and Washington, DC.

Akerlof, George A. 1970. "The Market for 'Lemons': Qualitative Uncertainty and the Market Mechanism." *Quarterly Journal of Economics* 84(3): 488–500.

Aldasaro, Iñaki, and Mike Seiferling. 2014. *Vertical Fiscal Imbalances and the Accumulation of Government Debt*. Washington, D.C.: International Monetary Fund. WP/14/209.

Alesina, Alberto, Gerald D. Cohen, and Nouriel Roubini. 1993. "Electoral Business Cycle in Industrial Democracies." *European Journal of Political Economy* 9(1): 1–23.

Alm, James. 2015. "Financing Urban Infrastructure: Knows, Unknowns, and a Way Forward." *Journal of Economic Surveys* 29(2): 230–62.

Ammar, Salwa, William Duncombe, Yilin Hou, Bernard Jump, and Ronald Wright. 2001. "Using Fuzzy Rule-Based Systems to Evaluate Overall Financial Performance of Governments: An Enhancement to the Bond Rating Process." *Public Budgeting and Finance* 21(4): 91–110.

Andersen, Asger Lau, David Dreyer Lassen, Lasse Holbøll, and Westh Nielson. 2010. "The Impact of Fiscal Governance on Bond Markets: Evidence from Late Budgets and State Government Borrowing Costs." Department of Economics, University of Copenhagen.

Andrews, Matt. 2010. "Good Government Means Different Things in Different Countries." *Governance* 23(1): 7–35.

Anguelov, Dimitar, Helga Leitner, and Eric Sheppard. 2018. "Engineering the Financialization of Urban Entrepreneurialism: The JESSICA Urban Development Initiative in the European Union." *International Journal of Urban and Regional Research* 42(2): 573–93.

Arndt, Christiane, and Charles P. Oman. 2006. *Governance Indicators for Development*. No. 33. Paris: OECD Publishing.

Arena, Matteo P. 2011. "The Corporate Choice Between Public Debt, Bank Loans, Traditional Private Debt Placements, and 144A Debt Issue." *Review of Quantitative Finance and Accounting* 36: 391–416.

Ashton, Philip, Marc Doussard, and Rachel Weber. 2016. "Reconstituting the State: City Powers and Exposures in Chicago's Infrastructure Leases." *Urban Studies* 53(7): 1384–400.

Asian Development Bank. 2018. *ASEAN+3 Bond Market Guide: Republic of Korea*. Manila, Philippines.

Attinasi, Maria Grazia, and Alberto Brugnoli. 2001. *Financial Instruments for Urban Development Support*. Bocconi, Milan: EGEA.

Awadzi, Elsie Addo. 2015. *Designing Legal Frameworks for Public Debt Management*. Washington, D.C.: International Monetary Fund. WP/15/147.

Bae, Kee-Hong, and Vidhan K. Goyal. 2009. "Creditor Rights, Enforcement, and Bank Loans." *Journal of Finance* 64(2): 823–60.

Bahl, Roy, and Richard M. Bird. 2018. *Fiscal Decentralization and Local Finance in Developing Countries, Development from Below*. Northampton, MA: Edward Elgar.

Bahl, Roy, and Johannes F. Linn. 2014. *Governing and Financing Cities in the Developing World.* Cambridge, MA: Lincoln Institute of Land Policy.

Bahl, Roy, Johannes F. Linn, and Deborah L. Wetzel. 2013. *Financing Metropolitan Governments in Developing Countries.* Cambridge, MA: Lincoln Institute of Land Policy.

Bahl, Roy, and Jorge Martinez-Vazquez. 2008. "The Property Tax in Developing Countries: Current Practice and Prospects." In Roy Bahl, Jorge Martinez-Vazquez, and Joan Youngman, eds., *Making the Property Tax Work: Experiences in Developing and Transitional Countries*, ch. 1, 3–16. Cambridge, MA: Lincoln Institute of Land Policy.

Bamber, Linda Smith, and Youngsoon Susan Cheon. 1998. "Discretionary Management Earnings Forecast Disclosures: Antecedents and Outcomes Associated with Forecast Venue and Forecast Specificity Choices." *Journal of Accounting Research* 36(2): 167–90.

Bayliss, Kate. 2014. "The financialisation of water in England and Wales." School of Oriental and African Studies, London.

Benton, Allyson Lucinda, and Heidi Jane M. Smith. 2017. "The Impact of Parties and Elections on Municipal Debt Policy in Mexico." *Governance: An International Journal of Policy, Administration, and Institutions* 30(4): 621–39.

Berlin, Mitchell, and Jan Loeys. 1988. "Bond Covenants and Delegated Monitoring." *Journal of Finance* 43: 397–412.

Berlin, Mitchell, and Loretta J. Mester. 1992. "Debt Covenants and Renegotiation." *Journal of Financial Intermediation* 2: 95–133.

Bertelli, Anthony M. 2012. *The Political Economy of Public Sector Governance.* New York: Cambridge University Press.

Bertomeu, Jeremy, and Iván Marinovic. 2016. "A Theory of Hard and Soft Information." *The Accounting Review* 91(1): 1–20.

Bharath, Sreedhar T., Paolo Pasquariello, and Guojun Wu. 2009. "Does Asymmetric Information Drive Capital Structure Decisions?" *Review of Financial Studies* 22(8): 3211–33.

Bird, Richard M., and Michael Smart. 2002. "Intergovernmental Fiscal Transfers: International Lessons for Developing Countries." *World Development* 30(6): 899–912.

Blackwell, David W., and David S. Kidwell. 1988. "An Investigation of Cost Differences Between Public Sales and Private Placements of Debt." *Journal of Financial Economics* 22: 253–78.

Blackwell, David W., and Drew B. Winters. 1997. "Banking Relationships and the Effect of Monitoring on Loan Pricing." *Journal of Financial Research* 29(2): 275–89.

Blais, Andre, Donald Blake, and Stephane Dion. 1993. "Do Parties Make a Difference? Parties and the Size of Government in Liberal Democracies." *American Journal of Political Science* 37(1): 40–62.

Blanco, Andrés G., Vicente Fretes Cibils, and Andrés F. Muñoz. 2016. *Expandiendo el uso de la valorización del suelo: La captura de plusvalías en América Latina y el Caribe.* Washington, D.C.: Banco Interamericano de Desarrollo.

Bland, Robert L. 1985. "The Interest Cost Savings from Experience in the Municipal Bond Market." *Public Administration Review* 45(1): 233–37.

Block, Steven A., and Paul M. Vaaler. 2004. "The Price of Democracy: Sovereign Risk Ratings, Bond Spreads and Political Business Cycles in Developing Countries." *Journal of International Money and Finance* 23(6): 917–946.

Bongaerts, Dion, KJ Martijn Cremers, and William N. Goetzmann. 2012. "Tiebreaker: Certification and Multiple Credit Ratings." *The Journal of Finance* 67(1): 113–152.

Bonilla, Marcia, and Isabelle Zapparoli. 2017. *The Challenge of Financing Urban Infrastructure for Sustainable Cities.* Washington, D.C.: Inter-American Development Bank.

Borrelli, Stephen A., and Terry J. Royed. 1995. "Government Strength and Budget Deficits in Advanced Democracies." *European Journal of Political Research* 28(2): 225–60.

Botosan, Christine A. 1997. "Disclosure Level and the Cost of Equity Capital." *The Accounting Review* 72(3): 323–49.

Braswell, Ronald C., E. Joe Nosari, and DeWitt L. Sumners. 1983. "A Comparison of the True Interest Costs of Competitive and Negotiated Underwritings in the Municipal Bond Market: Note." *Journal of Money, Credit and Banking* 15(10): 102–6.

Butler, Alexander W., Larry Fauver, and Sandra Mortal. 2009. "Corruption, Municipal Connections, and Municipal Finance." *Review of Financial Studies* 22(7): 2873–905.

Büyükkarabacak, Berrak, and Neven Valev. 2012. "Credit Information Sharing and Banking Crises: An Empirical Investigation." *Journal of Macroeconomics* 34(3): 788–800.

Caiden, Naomi, and Aaron Wildavsky. 1974. *Planning and Budgeting in Poor Countries.* New York: John Wiley & Sons.

Campos, Nauro F., and Jeffrey B. Nugent. 1999. "Development Performance and the Institutions of Governance: Evidence from East Asia and Latin America." *World Development* 27(3): 439–52.

Cantillo, Miguel, and Julian Wright. 2000. "How Do Firms Choose Their Lenders? An Empirical Investigation." *The Review of Financial Studies* 13(1): 155–89.

Cantor, Richard. 2004. "An Introduction to Recent Research on Credit Ratings." *Journal of Banking and Finance* 28(1–2): 2565–73.

Cantor, Richard, and Frank Packer. 1996. "Sovereign Risk Assessment and Agency Credit Ratings." *European Financial Management* 2(2): 247–256.

Canuto, Otaviano, and Lili Liu. 2010. *Subnational Debt Finance and the Global Crisis.* Washington, D.C.: World Bank.

Canuto, Otaviano, and Lili Liu. 2013. *Until Debt Do Us Part, Subnational Debt, Insolvency, and Markets.* Washington D.C.: World Bank.

Carey, M., S. Prowse, J. Rhea, and G. Udell. 1993. "The Economics of the Private Placement Markets: A New Look." *Financial Markets, Institutions, and Instrument* 2: 1–66.

Chemmanur, Thomas J., and Paolo Fulghieri. 1994. "Reputation, Renegotiation, and the Choice Between Bank Loans and Publicly Traded Debt." *Review of Financial Studies* 7: 475–506.

Christophers, Brett. 2015. "The limits to financialization." *Dialogues in human geography* 5, no. 2: 183–200.

Chun, Kyung-Hoon. 2016. "Investor Protection in Korean Capital Market Through Disclosures and Litigation." *Journal of Korean Law* 16: 193–231.

City of Sofia. 2003. *Sofia City Strategy*, n.d., https://openknowledge.worldbank.org/handle/10986/16712 (last accessed October 1, 2019).

Committee on the Global Financial System. 2019. "Establishing Viable Capital Markets." CGFS Papers No 62. Bank for International Settlements.

da Cruz, Nuno F., Philipp Rode, and Michael McQuarrie. 2019. "New Urban Governance: A Review of Current Themes and Future Priorities." *Journal of Urban Affairs* 41(1): 1–19.

de Mello Jr., Luiz R. 2001. "Fiscal Decentralization and Borrowing Costs: The Case of Local Governments." *Public Finance Review* 29(2): 108–38.

de Mello, Jr., Luiz R. 2005. "Globalization and Fiscal Federalism: Does Openness Constrain Subnational Budget Imbalances?" *Public Budgeting and Finance* 25(1): 1–14.

de Mello Jr., Liuz R., and Matias Barenstein. 2001. *Fiscal Decentralization and Governance: A Cross-Country Analysis.* Washington, D.C.: International Monetary Fund. WP/01/71.

Depken, Craig A., and Courtney L. LaFountain. 2006. "Fiscal Consequences of Public Corruption: Empirical Evidence from State Bond Ratings." *Public Choice* 126(1/2): 75–85.

Deshkar, Sameer, and Vinayak Adane. 2016. "Community Resilience Approach for Prioritizing Infrastructure Development in Urban Areas." In *Urban Disasters and Resilience in Asia*, ed. Rajib Shaw, Atta-ur-Rahman, Akhilesh Surjan, and Gulan Ara Parvin, ch. 16, 245–267. Amsterdam: Elsevier.

Dhaliwal, Dan S., Inder K. Khurana, and Raynolde Pereira. 2011. "Firm Disclosure Policy and the Choice Between Private and Public Debt." *Contemporary Accounting Research* 28(1): 293–330.

Diamond, Douglas W. 1984. "Financial Intermediation and Delegated Monitoring." *Review of Economic Studies* 51: 393–414.

Diamond, Douglas W. 1991. "Monitoring and Reputation: The Choice Between Bank Loans and Directly Placed Debt." *Journal of Political Economy* 99: 688–721.

Diamond, Douglas W., and Robert E. Verrecchia. 1991. "Disclosure, Liquidity, and the Cost of Capital." *Journal of Finance* 46(4): 1325–59.

Djankov, Simeon, Caralee McLiesh, and Andrei Shleifer. 2007. "Private Credit in 129 Countries." *Journal of Financial Economics* 84(2): 299–329.

Djankov, Simeon, Oliver Hart, Caralee McLiesh, and Andrei Shleifer. 2008. "Debt Enforcement Around the World." *Journal of Political Economy* 116(6): 1105–49.

Downing, Chris, and Frank Zhang. 2004. "Trading Activity and Price Volatility in the Municipal Bond Market." *Journal of Finance* 59(2): 899–931.

Drumeva, E. 2001. "Local Government in Bulgaria." In *Stabilization of Local Governments*, ed. E. Kandeva, 141–79. Budapest: LGI Books.

Easterwood, John C., and Palani-Rajan Kadapakkam. 1991. "The Role of Private and Public Debt in Corporate Capital Structure." *Financial Management* 20(3): 49–57.

Ederington, Louis, Jess B. Yawitz, and Brian E. Roberts. 1987. "The Informational Content of Bond Ratings." *The Journal of Financial Research* 10(3): 211–26.

Eichler, Jörn Philip, Alexander Wegener, and Ute Zimmermann. 2012. "Financing Local Infrastructure—Linking Local Governments and Financial Markets." Deutsche Gesellschaft für Internationale Zusammenarbeit (GIZ), Frankfurt, Germany.

Eklund, Johan E., and Sameeksha Desai. 2014. "Ownership and Allocation of Capital: Evidence from 44 Countries." *Journal of Institutional and Theoretical Economics* 170(3): 427–52.

Ely, Todd L., and Christine R. Martell. 2016. "Costs of Raising (Social) Capital Through Mini-Bonds." *Municipal Finance Journal* 37(3): 23–44.

Espinosa, Salvador. 2013. "Subnational Bond Market Development: What Drives the Yield Spreads of Mexican Cebures?" *Latin American Policy* 4(2): 306–19.

Espinosa, Salvador, and Christine R. Martell. 2015. "Building Bond Repayment Capacity in Developing Countries: A Study on Property Tax Collections and Debt Affordability in Mexico." *International Journal of Public Administration* 38(3): 227–36.

Espinosa, Salvador, and J. O. Moreno. 2014. "Regional Development and Cross-Border Infrastructure Finance: Comparing the Yield-Spread Determinants of Mexican and U.S. Sub-Sovereign Government Bonds." *Journal of Structured Finance* 20(1): 64–75.

Estache, Antonio. 2010. *Infrastructure Finance in Developing Countries: An Overview*. EIB Papers, ISSN 0257–7755, 15(2): 60–88, http://hdl.handle.net/10419/45371.

Fabozzi, F. J., A. B. Sanders, D. Yuen, and C. Ramsey. 2005. "Nonagency CMOs." In *The Handbook of Fixed Income Securities*, ed., F. J. Fabozzi, 7th ed., 579–88. New York: McGraw-Hill.

Faguet, Jean-Paul. 2008. "Decentralisation's Effects on Public Investment: Evidence and Policy Lessons from Bolivia and Colombia." *Journal of Development Studies* 44(8): 1100–21.

Farvacque-Vitkovic, Catherine, and Mihaly Kopany. 2013. *Municipal Finance, a Handbook for Local Governments*. Washington, D.C.: World Bank.

Farvacque-Vitkovic, Catherine, and Mihaly Kopani. 2019. *Better Cities Better World: A Handbook on Local Governments Self-Assessments*. Wahsington, D.C.: International Bank for Reconstruction and Development/World Bank.

Fitch. 2015. *Global-NonUS: Interpreting the Financial Ratios in Local and Regional Government Rating Reports*. New York: Fitch Ratings.

Fitch Ratings. 2016. *Reporte de Calificación: Municipio de Monterrey, Nuevo León*. Finanzas Públicas. México.

Fitzpatrick, Jody, Malcolm Goggin, Tanya Heikkila, Donald Klinger, Jacob Machado, and Christine Martell. 2011. "A New Look at Comparative Public Administration: Trends in Research and an Agenda for the Future." *Public Administration Review* 71(6): 821–30.

Freire, Mila, and John Petersen. 2004. *Subnational Capital Markets in Developing Countries.* Washington D.C.: World Bank and Oxford University Press.

Freire, Maria E. 2013. "Subnational Finance Outside the United States: Recent Developments." *Municipal Finance Journal* 34(1): 95–112.

Freire, Maria Emilia. 2014. "Managing External Resources." In *Municipal Finances: A Handbook for Local Governments*, ed. Catherine Farvacque-Vitkovic and Mihaly Kopanya, 325–378. Washington D.C.: World Bank.

Gamkhar, Shama, and Mona Koerner. 2002. "Capital Financing of Schools: A Comparison of Lease Purchase Revenue Bonds and General Obligation Bonds." *Public Budgeting & Finance* 22(2): 21–39.

Giannetti, Caterina, and Nicola Jentzsch. "Credit Reporting, Financial Intermediation and Identification Systems: International Evidence." *Journal of International Money and Finance* 33 (2013): 60–80.

Gill, Stephen. 1995. "Globalisation, Market Civilisation, and the Disciplinary Neoliberalism." *Millennium: Journal of International Studies* 24(3): 399–423.

Giugale, Marcelo, Adam Korobow, and Steven Webb. 2000. *A New Model for Market-Based Regulation of Subnational Borrowing.* Washington, D.C.: World Bank. WP2370.

Gogovana Saminikov, Marija, Elena Veselinova, Ilija Gruevski, Risto Fotov, and Risto Binovski. 2017. "Municipal Bonds in Developing Countries: Case Study: Municipality of Stip, Republic of Macedonia." *Management Dynamics in the Knowledge Economy* 5(2): 155–74.

Gorelick, Jeremy. 2018. "Supporting the Future of Municipal Bonds in Sub-Saharan Africa: The Centrality of Enabling Environments and Regulatory Frameworks." *Environment & Urbanization* 30(1): 103–22.

Granof, Michael H. 1984. "Tax Exempt Leasing: A Framework for Analysis." *Public Administration Review* 44 (May/June): 232–40.

Greenwood, Jeremy, and Bruce D. Smith. 1997. "Financial Markets in Development, and the Development of Financial Markets." *Journal of Economic Dynamics and Control* 21: 145–81.

Green, Richard C., Burton Hollifield, and Norman Schürhoff. 2007. "Financial Intermediation and the Costs of Trading in An Opaque Market." *The Review of Financial Studies* 20(2): 275–314.

Green, Richard C., Dan Li, and Norman Schurhoff. 2010. "Price Discovery in Illiquid Markets: Do Financial Asset Prices Rise Faster Than They Fall?" *Journal of Finance* 65(5): 1669–1702.

Greer, Robert A., and Dwight V. Denison. 2016. "Determinants of Debt Concentration at the State Level." *Public Budgeting & Finance* 36(4): 111–30.

Greer, R. A., T. T. Moldogaziev, and T. A. Scott. 2018. "Polycentric Governance and the Impact of Special Districts on Fiscal Common Pools." *International Journal of the Commons* 12(2): 108–36.

Grindle, Merilee S. 2004. "Good Enough Governance: Poverty Reduction and Reform in Developing Countries." *Governance: An International Journal of Policy, Administration, and Institutions* 17(4): 525–48.

Grossman, Sanford J., and Oliver D. Hart. 1983. "An Analysis of the Principal-Agent Problem." *Econometrica* 51(1): 7–46.

Grossman, Sanford J., and Joseph E. Stiglitz. 1980. "On the Impossibility of Informationally Efficient Markets." *American Economic Review* 70(3): 393–408.

GuarantCo. 2019. *Study of Bangladesh Bond Market*, April, https://guarantco.com/gco/wp-content/uploads/2019/Documents/news/Study-of-Bangladesh-Bond-Market.pdf.

Guzman, Tatyana, and Temirlan Moldogaziev. 2012. "Which Bonds Are More Expensive? The Cost Differentials by Debt Issue Purpose and the Method of Sale: An Empirical Analysis." *Public Budgeting & Finance* 32(3): 79–101.

Hackworth, Jason. 2007. *The Neoliberal City: Governance, Ideology, and Development in American Urbanism*. Ithaca: Cornell University Press.

Halbert, Ludovic, and Katia Attuyer. 2016. "Introduction: The Financialisation of Urban Production: Conditions, Mediations and Transformations." *Urban Affairs* 53(7): 1347–61.

Hanusch, Marek, and Paul M. Vaaler. 2013. "Credit Rating Agencies and Elections in Emerging Democracies: Guardians of Fiscal Discipline?." *Economics Letters* 119(3): 251–254.

Harbers, Imke. 2015. "Taxation and the Unequal Reach of the State: Mapping State Capacity in Ecuador." *Governance: An International Journal of Policy, Administration, and Institutions* 28(3): 373–91.

Harris, Lawrence E. and Michael S. Piwowar. 2006. "Secondary Trading Costs in the Municipal Bond Market." *Journal of Finance* 61(3): 1361–97.

Harris, Milton, and Artur Raviv. 1990. "Capital Structure and the Informational Role of Debt." *The Journal of Finance* XLV(2): 321–49.

Heinkel, Robert. 1982. "A Theory of Capital Structure Relevance under Imperfect Information." *The Journal of Finance* 37(5): 1141–49.

Hernández-Trillo, F. 2018. When lack of accountability allows observing unobservables: moral hazard in sub-national government credit markets in Mexico. *Applied Economic Letters* 25(5): 326–30.

Hernandez-Trillo, F., and R. Smith-Ramirez. 2009. "Credit Ratings in the Presence of Bailout: The Case of Mexican Subnational Government Debt." *Economia* 10(1): 45–79.

Hewson, M., and T. Sinclair, eds. 1999. *Approaches to Global Governance Theory*, Albany: State University of New York Press.

Hildreth, W. Bartley. 1993. State and Local Governments as Borrowers: Strategic Choices and the Capital Market. *Public Administration Review* 53(1): 41–9.

Hildreth, W. Bartley, and Gerald J. Miller. 2002. "Debt and the Local Economy: Problems in Benchmarking Local Government Debt Affordability." *Public Budgeting & Finance* 22(4): 99–113.

Hildreth, W. Bartley, and C. Kurt Zorn. 2005. "The Evolution of the State and Local Government Municipal Debt Market over the Past Quarter Century." *Public Budgeting and Finance* 25(4S): 127–53.

IFAC. 2019. Korea. International Federation of Accountants, n.d., https://www.ifac.org/about-ifac/membership/country/korea (last accessed January 17, 2020).

IMF. 2019. Fiscal Decentralization Dataset. https://data.imf.org/?sk=1C28EBFB-62B3-4B0C-AED3-048EEEBB684F. Washington, D.C.: International Monetary Fund. (last accessed August 23, 2019).

Ingram, Gregory K., Zhi Liu, and Karin L. Brandt. 2013. "Metropolitan Infrastructure and Capital Finance." In *Financing Metropolitan Governments in Developing Countries*, ed. Roy W. Bahl, Johannes F. Linn, and Deborah L. Wetzel, 339–366. Cambridge, MA: Lincoln Institute of Land Policy.

Inman, Robert P. 2003. "Transfers and Bailouts: Enforcing Local Fiscal Discipline with Lessons from U.S. Federalism." In *Fiscal Decentralization and the Challenge of Hard Budget Constraints*, ed. Jonathan A. Rodden, Gunnar S. Eskeland, and Jennie Litvack, 35–84. Cambridge, MA: MIT Press.

Ivonchyk, Mikhail, and Tima T. Moldogaziev. 2021. "Is There A Global Convergence of Management Foci in City Credit Quality Assessments? A Computational Analysis Approach." *Urban Geography*: 1–25.

Jaffee, Dwight M. 1972. "A Theory and Test of Credit Rationing: Further Notes." *American Economic Review* 62(3): 484–88.

Jaffee, Dwight M., and Franco Modigliani. 1969. "A Theory and Test of Credit Rationing." *American Economic Review* 59(5): 850–72.

Jalan, Joytsna, and Martin Vavallion. 2002. "Geographic Poverty Traps? A Micro Model of Consumption Growth in China." *Journal of Applied Econometrics* 17(4): 329–46.

Jensen, M. C., and W. H. Meckling. 1976. "Theory of the Firm: Managerial Behavior, Agency Costs and Ownership Structure." *Journal of Financial Economics* 3: 305–60.

Jimenez, Benedict S. 2011. "Management Quality and State Bond Ratings: Exploring the Links Between Public Management and Fiscal Outcomes." *International Journal of Public Administration* 34(12): 783–99.

Joehnk, Michael D., and David S. Kidwell. 1980. "A Look at Competitive and Negotiated Underwriting Costs in the Municipal Bond Market." *Public Administration Review* 40(3): 222–25.

Johnson, Craig L. 1995. "Managing Financial Resources to Meet Environmental Infrastructure Needs: The Case of State Revolving Funds." *Public Productivity & Management Review* 18(3): 263–75.

Johnson, Craig L., and Kenneth A. Kriz. 2005. "Fiscal Institutions, Credit Ratings, and Borrowing Costs." *Public Budgeting and Finance* 25(1): 84–103.

Johnson, Craig L., Martin J. Luby, and Tima T. Moldogaziev. 2014. *State and Local Financial Instruments: Policy Changes and Management.* Cheltenham, UK: Edward Elgar.

Kaganova, Olga. 2011. "Guidebook on Capital Investment Planning for Local Governments." Urban Development Series Knowledge Papers, No. 13, World Bank, Washington, D.C.

Kalcheva, D. 2017. "Access to Debt Financing: Opportunities for Improvement of the Investment Capacity of Bulgarian Municipalities for the Period 2003–2015." *Economic Alternatives* (3): 390–404.

Kale, Jayant R., and Costanza Meneghetti. 2011. "The Choice Between Public and Private Debt: A Survey." *IIMB Management Review* 23: 5–14.

Kaminsky, Graciela, Richard Lyons, and Sergio Schmukler. 2001. *Mutual Fund Investment in Emerging Markets: An Overview.* Washington, D.C.: World Bank.

Kang, K., G. Kim, and C. Rhee. 2006. "Developing the Government Bond Market in South Korea: History, Challenges, and Implications for Asian Countries." *Asian Economic Papers* 4(2): 91–113.

Kaufman, Daniel, Aart Kraay, and Massimo Mastruzzi. 2007. *The Worldwide Governance Indicators Project: Answering the Critics.* Washington, D.C.: World Bank.

Kaufman, Daniel, Aart Kraay, and Massimo Mastruzzi. 2010. "Response to 'What Do the Worldwide Governance Indicators Measure?'" *European Journal of Development Research* 22(1): 55–58.

Kehew, Robert, Tomoko Matsukawa, and John Petersen. 2005. *Local Financing for Sub-Sovereign Infrastructure in Developing Countries: Case Studies of Innovative Domestic Credit Enhancement Entities and Techniques.* Washington, D.C.: World Bank.

Kersting, Norbert, Janice Caulfield, R. Andrew Nickson, Dele Olowu, and Hellmut Wollmann. 2009. *Local Governance Reform in Global Perspective.* Wiesbaden: VS Verlag für Sozialwissenschaften.

Kidwell, David S., and Robert J. Rogowski. 1983. "Bond Banks: A State Assistance Program That Helps Reduce New Issue Borrowing Costs." *Public Administration Review* 43(2): 108–13.

Kim, H., et al. 2012. *Korea's Development Experience Modularization: Urban Railway Development Policy in Korea.* Korea Transport Institute (KOTI).

Kioko, Sharon N., and Pengju Zhang. 2019. "Impact of Tax and Expenditure Limits on Local Government Use of Tax-Supported Debt." *Public Finance Review* 47(2): 409–32.

Kisgen, Darren J. 2006. "Credit Ratings and Capital Structure." *The Journal of Finance* 61(3): 1035–1072.

Kook, J. H. 2000. "Intergovernmental Fiscal Relationship and Transfers in Korea." *Hitotsubashi Journal of Economics* 41: 137–51.

Kreps, David M. 1990. *A Course in Microeconomic Theory*. Princeton, NJ: Princeton University Press.

Krishnaswami, Sudha, Paul A. Spindt, and Venkat Subramaniam. 1999. "Information Asymmetry, Monitoring, and the Placement Structure of Corporate Debt." *Journal of Financial Economics* 51: 407–34.

Kwan, Simon H., and Willard T. Carleton. 2010. "Financial Contracting and the Choice Between Private Placement and Publicly Offered Bonds." *Journal of Money, Credit and Banking* 42(5): 907–29.

Laeven, Luc. 2014. *The Development of Local Capital Markets: Rationale and Challenges*. Washington, D.C.: International Monetary Fund.

Lang, M., and R. Lundholm. 1996. "Corporate Disclosure Policy and Analyst Behavior." *The Accounting Review* 71(4): 467–92.

Lawrence, Geoffrey. 2015 "Defending Financialization." *Dialogues in Human Geography* 5(2): 201–205.

La Porta, Rafael, Florencio Lopez-de-Silanes, and Andrei Shleifer. 2008. "The Economic Consequences of Legal Origins." *Journal of Economic Literature* 46(2): 285–332.

La Porta, Rafael, Florencio Lopez-de-Silanes, and Andrei Shleifer. 2013. "Law and Finance After a Decade of Research." In *Corporate Finance*, vol. 2A of *Handbook of the Economics of Finance*, ed. George M. Constantinides, Milton Harris, and Rene M. Stulz, 425–91. Amsterdam: Elsevier.

La Porta, Rafael, Florencio Lopez-de-Silanes, Andrei Shleifer, and Robert W. Vishny. 1997. "Legal Determinants of External Finance." *The Journal of Finance* 52(3): 1131–50.

La Porta, Rafael, Florencio Lopez-de-Silanes, Andrei Shleifer, and Robert W. Vishny. 1998. "Law and Finance." *The Journal of Political Economy* 106(6): 1113–55.

Leaven, Luc. 2014. The Development of Local Capital Markets: Rationale and Challenges. IMF Working Paper, WP/14/234.

Lee, Jong-Wha. 2017. "Twenty Years After the Financial Crisis in the Republic of Korea." ADBI Working Paper Series No. 790. Asian Development Bank, Tokyo, Japan.

Leigland, James. 1997. "Accelerating Municipal Bond Market Development in Emerging Economies: An Assessment of Strategies and Progress." *Public Budgeting and Finance* 17(2): 57–79.

Leigland, James, and Rosalind H. Thomas. 1999. "Municipal Bonds as Alternatives to PPPs: Facilitating Direct Municipal Access to Private Capital." *Development Southern Africa* 16(4): 729–50.

Leigland, James, and Cledan Mandri-Perrott. 2008. *Enhancing the Creditworthiness of Municipal Bonds: Innovations from Mexico*. Washington, D.C.: The World Bank.

Leland, Hayne E., and David H. Pyle. 1977. "Informational Asymmetries, Financial Structure, and Financial Intermediation." *Journal of Finance* 32(2): 371–87.

Lewis, Blaine D. 2003. "Local Government Borrowing and Repayment in Indonesia: Does Fiscal Capacity Matter." *World Development* 31(6): 1047–63.

Li, Lin, and Zhang Zili. 2015. "The Administration of Municipal Debt Experience from South Korea." *Securities Market Herald*: 11–20.

Liberti, José María, and Mitchell A. Petersen. 2017. "Information: Hard and Soft." Working Paper. Northwestern University, August, http://www.kellogg.northwestern.edu/faculty/petersen/htm/papers/hard%20and%20soft%20information.pdf.

Liu, Cheol, Tima T. Moldogaziev, and John L. Mikesell. 2017. "Corruption and the Growth of Public Debt." *Public Administration Review* 77(5): 681–90.

Liu, Gao, and Rui Sun. 2016. "Economic Openness and Subnational Borrowing." *Public Budgeting and Finance* 36(2): 45–69.

Liu, Lili, and Juan Pradelli. 2012. "Financing Infrastructure and Monitoring Fiscal Risks at the Subnational Level." Policy Research Working Paper WPS6069. World Bank Group, Washington, D.C.

Liu, Lili, and Kim Song Tan. 2009. "Subnational Credit Ratings: A Comparative Review." Policy Research Working Papers No. 5013. World Bank, Washington, D.C.

Loviscek, Anthony L., and Frederick D. Crowley. 1988. "Analyzing Changes in Municipal Bond Ratings: A Different Perspective." *Urban Studies* 25(2): 124–32.

Loviscek, Anthony L., and Frederick D. Crowley. 1990. "What Is in a Municipal Bond Rating?" *Financial Review* 25(1): 25–53.

Majuder, Rajarshi. 2012. "Removing Poverty and Inequality in India: The Role of Infrastructure." MRPA Paper No. 40941, Munich Personal RePEc Archive, http://mpraub.uni-muenchen. de/40941/.

Markiewicz, M. 2006. "Country Report: Local Government Borrowing in Bulgaria. The Future of Local Government Finance: Case Studies for Romania, Bulgaria and Macedonia." Center for Economic Analyses-CEA, Skopje, Macedonia.

Marlowe, Justin. 2010. "GASB 34's Information Relevance: Evidence from New Issue Local Government Debt," April 14, https://ssrn.com/abstract=1589343 or http://dx.doi.org/10.2139/ssrn.1589343.

Martell, Christine R. 2010. "Citizen Investors: Financing Subnational Governments in Developing Countries." In *Urban Infrastructure and Governance,* ed. G. Ramesh, 263–82. Abingdon, UK: Taylor and Francis.

Martell, Christine R. 2016. "Enhancing Access to Capital Financing for Sustainable Urban Infrastructure: A Review of the Literature." Economic and Sector Work, Manuscript. Inter-American Development Bank, Washington D.C.

Martell, Christine R., and George M. Guess. 2006. "Development of Local Government Debt Financing Markets: Application of a Market-Based Framework." *Public Budgeting and Finance* 26(1): 88–119.

Martell, Christine R., Sharon N. Kioko, and Tima Moldogaziev. 2013. "Impact of Unfunded Pension Obligations on Credit Quality of State Governments." *Public Budgeting and Finance* 33(3): 24–54.

Mehl, Arnaud, and Julien Reynaud. 2010. "Risky Public Domestic Debt Composition in Emerging Economies." *Journal of International Money and Finance* 29: 1–18.

Melnik, Arie L., and Steven E. Plaut. 1995. "Disclosure Costs, Regulation, and the Expansion of the Private-Placement Market." *Journal of Accounting, Auditing, & Finance* 10(1): 23–39.

Merton, Robert C. 1995. "A Functional Perspective of Financial Intermediation." *Financial Management* 24(2): 23–41.

Moldogaziev, Tima T., Salvador Espinosa, and Christine R. Martell. 2018. "Fiscal Governance, Information Capacity, and Subnational Capital Finance." *Public Finance Review* 46(6): 974–1001.

Moldogaziev, Tima T., Robert A. Greer, and Jekyung Lee. 2019. "Private Placements and the Cost of Borrowing in the Municipal Debt Market." *Public Budgeting & Finance* 39(3): 44–74.

Moldogaziev, Tima T., and Tatyana Guzman. 2015. "Economic Crises, Economic Structure, and State Credit Quality Through-the-Cycle." *Public Budgeting and Finance* 35(4): 42–67.

Moody's. 2013. *Rating Methodology. Regional and Local Governments.* New York: Moody's Investors Service.

Moody's. 2014. *Rating Methodology: US Local Government General Obligation Debt.* New York: Moody's Investors Service.

Moraliyska, Monika. 2018. "The EU Cohesion Policy's Impact on Regional Economic Development: The Case of Bulgaria." *Journal of Economic and Social Studies* 7(1): 5–23.

Morrissey, Oliver, and Manop Udomkerdmongkol. 2012. "Governance, Private Investment and Foreign Direct Investment in Developing Countries." *World Development* 40(3): 437–45.

New York University. 2020. *Advice, Money, Results: Rethinking International Support for Managing Public Finance.* Report by an International Working Group, New York University, Robert F. Wagner Graduate School of Public Service, New York.

Noel, Michel. 2000. *Building Subnational Debt Markets in Developing and Transition Economies.* Washington, D.C.: World Bank. WP2339.

North, Douglas, Daron Acemoglu, Francis Fukuyama, and Dani Rodrik. 2008. *Governance, Growth, and Development Decision-Making.* Washington, D.C.: International Bank for Reconstruction and Development/World Bank.

Oates, Wallace. 2005. "Towards a Second-Generation Theory of Fiscal Federalism." *International Tax and Public Finance* 12(4): 349–73.

Oates, Wallace E. 1972. *Fiscal Federalism.* New York: Harcourt Brace Jovanovich.

O'Brien, R. 1992. *Global Financial Integration: The End of Geography.* London: Pinter Publishers.

OECD/UCLG. 2016. *Subnational Governments Around the World: Structure and Finance.* Paris: Organisation for Economic Co-operation and Development.

OECD/UNCL. 2016. *Subnational Governments Around the World: Structure and Finance.* Paris: Organisation for Economic Co-operation and Development.

OECD/UNCL. 2019. *World Observatory on Subnational Government Finance and Investment— Key Findings.* Paris: Organisation for Economic Co-operation and Development.

OJOTEU. 2013. *Official Journal of the European Union (OJOTEU).* L 174, June 26, 2013. Available in multiple languages at http://eur-lex.europa.eu/legal-content/EN/ALL/?uri=OJ%3AL%3A2013%3A17%3ATOC.

Pacewicz, Josh. 2016. "The city as a fiscal derivative: Financialization, urban development, and the politics of earmarking." *City & Community* 15, no. 3: 264–288.

Padovani, Emanuele, Luca Rescigno, and Jacopo Ceccatelli. 2018. "Municipal Bond Debt and Sustainability in a Non-Mature Financial Market: The Case of Italy." *Sustainability* 10: 3249. DOI: 10.3390/su10093249.

Pagano, Michael A., and Christopher W. Hoene. 2018. "City Budgets in an Era of Increased Uncertainty." Brookings Metropolitan Policy Program, Washington, D.C.

Pagano, Michael A., and David Perry. 2004. "Financing Infrastructure in the 21st Century City." *Public Works Management & Policy* 13(1): 22–38.

Paice, Edward. 2016. "Dakar's Municipal Bond Issue: A Tale of Two Cities." Briefing Note 1603. Africa Research Institute, London.

Paliova, Iana, and Tonny Lybek. 2014. "Bulgaria's EU Funds Absorption: Maximizing the Potential!" IMF Working Paper No. 14/21. International Monetary Fund, Washington, D.C.

Palumbo, George, and Mark P. Zaporowski. 2012. "Determinants of Municipal Bond Ratings for General-Purpose Governments: An Empirical Analysis." *Public Budgeting and Finance* 32(2): 86–102.

Park, Ji-Hyung. 2013. "Local Government Reform: Is It Effective on Debt Burdens?" *Public Finance and Management* 13(3): 195–214.

Peng, Jun, and Peter F. Brucato. 2004. "An Empirical Analysis of Market and Institutional Mechanisms for Alleviating Information Asymmetry in the Municipal Bond Market." *Journal of Economics and Finance* 28(2): 226–38.

Petersen, John, with John B. Crihfield. 2000. "Linkages Between Local Governments and Financial Markets: A Tool Kit to Developing Sub-Sovereign Credit Markets in Emerging Economies." Urban and Local Government Working Paper. World Bank, Washington D.C.

Peterson, George E. 2002. "Banks or Bonds? Building a Municipal Credit Market." The Urban Institute, Washington, D.C.

Peterson, M. A., and R. G. Rajan. 1997. "Trade Credit: Theories and Evidence." *The Review of Financial Studies* 10: 661–91.

Peterson, Paul. 1995. "Who Should Do What? Divided Responsibility in the Federal System." *Brookings Review* 13: 6–11.

Petitt, B. S., J. E. Pinto, and W. L. Pirie. 2015. *Fixed Income Analysis*. 3rd ed. CFA Institute Investment Series. Hoboken, NJ: John Wiley & Sons.

Pop, Cornelia, and Maria-Andrada Georgescu. 2016. "Credit Enhancements and the Romanian Municipal Bond Market." *Transylvanian Review of Administrative Sciences* 48: 104–23.

Petranov, Stefan, and Jeffrey Miller. 1999. "Bulgaria's Capital Markets in the Context of EU Accession: A Status Report." Center for the Study of Democracy, Washington, D.C./Sofia.

Pierre, Jon. 2005. "Comparative Urban Governance: Uncovering Complex Causalities." *Urban Affairs Review* 40(4): 446–62. DOI: 10.1177/1078087404273442.

Pike, Andy, and Jane Pollard. 2010. "Economic Geographies of Financialization." *Economic Geography* 86(1): 29–51.

Pinna, Massimo. 2015. "An Empirical Analysis of the Municipal Bond Market in Italy: Sovereign Risk and Sub-Sovereign Levels of Government." *Public Budgeting & Finance* 35: 68–94.

Platz, Daniel. 2009. "Infrastructure Finance in Developing Countries—The Potential of Sub-Sovereign Bonds." Working Paper No. 76. Department of Economic and Social Affairs, United Nations, New York.

Plotkin, Sidney. 1987. *Keep Out: The Struggle for Land Use Control*. Berkeley: University of California Press.

Public-Private Infrastructure Advisory Facility (PPIAF). 2013. "The Importance of Domestic Municipal Bond Market Development: Characteristics of Sub-National Infrastructure Financing." Creditworthiness Brief, December, Washington D.C.

Prud'homme, Rémy. 1995. "The Dangers of Decentralization." *World Bank Research Observer* 10(2): 201–20.

Raffer, Christian. 2019. "Local Public Finance: Bulgaria." *Local Public Finance in Europe*, ed. Rene Geissler et al., chap. 7. Bertelsmann Stiftung and Hertie School of Governance.

Rajan, R. G. 1992. "Insiders and Outsiders: The Choice Between Informed and Arm's-Length Debt." *Journal of Finance* 67(4): 1367–400.

Rajan R. G., and L. Zingales. 1995. "What Do We Know About Capital Structure? Some Evidence from International Data." *The Journal of Finance* 50: 1421–60.

Rajan, Raghuram G., and Luigi Zingales. 1998. "Which Capitalism? Lessons from the East Asian Crisis." *Journal of Applied Corporate Finance* 11(3): 40–48.

Ramakrishnan, Ram T. S., and Anjan Thakor. 1984. "Information Reliability and a Theory of Financial Intermediation." *Review of Economic Studies* 51: 415–32.

Rauh, Joshua D., and Amir Sufi. 2010. "Capital Structure and Debt Structure." *The Review of Financial Studies* 23(12): 4242–80.

Reck, Jackeline, and Earl Wilson. 2006. "Information Transparency and Pricing in the Municipal Bond Secondary Market." *Journal of Accounting and Public Policy* 25(1): 1–31.

Reid, Gary J. 1990. "Minimizing Municipal Debt Issuance Costs: Lessons from Empirical Research." *State & Local Government Review* 22(2): 64–72.

Revilla, Ernesto. 2013. "Subnational Debt Management in Mexico: A Tale of Two Crises." In *Until Debt Do Us Apart: Subnational Debt, Insolvency, and Markets*, ed. O. Canuto and L. Liu, 145–176. Washington, D.C: International Bank of Reconstruction and Development/World Bank.

Robbins, Mark D., and Bill Simonsen. 2007. "Competition and Selection in Municipal Bond Sales: Evidence from Missouri." *Public Budgeting & Finance* 27(2): 88–103.

Robbins, Mark D., and Bill Simonsen. 2010. "The Quality and Relevance of Municipal Bond Disclosure: What Bond Analysts Think." *Municipal Finance Journal* 31(1): 1–20.

Robbins, Mark D., and Bill Simonsen. 2013. "Municipal Bond New Issue Transaction Costs." *Public Budgeting & Finance* 33(1): 1–24.

Rodden, Jonathan A., Gunnar S. Eskeland, and Jennie Litvack. 2003. *Fiscal Decentralization and the Challenge of Hard Budget Constraints*. Cambridge, MA: MIT Press.

Rolnik, Raquel. 2013. "Late neoliberalism: the financialization of homeownership and housing rights." *International journal of urban and regional research* 37, no. 3: 1058–1066.

Rosenman, Emily. 2019. "Capital and conscience: poverty management and the financialization of good intentions in the San Francisco Bay Area." *Urban Geography* 40, no. 8: 1124–1147.

Ross, Stephen A. 1977. "The Determination of Financial Structure: The Incentive Signalling Approach." *The Bell Journal of Economics* 40: 23–40.

Roubini, Nouriel, Jeffrey Sachs, Seppo Honkapohja, and Daniel Cohen. 1989. "Government Spending and Budget Deficits in the Industrial Countries." *Economic Policy* 4(8): 100–32.

Sáez, Lawrence. 2016. "The Political Budget Cycle and Subnational Debt Expenditures in Federations: Panel Data Evidence from India." *Governance: An International Journal of Policy, Administration, and Institutions* 29(1): 47–65.

Sassen, Saskia. 1996. *Losing Control? Sovereignty in the Age of Globalization*. New York: Columbia University Press.

Sawyer, Malcolm. 2014. "Financial development, financialisation and economic growth." *Financialization, Economy, Society and Sustainable Development*.

Sbragia, Alberta M. 1996. *Debt Wish: Entrepreneurial Cities, U.S. Federalism, and Economic Development*. Pittsburgh: University of Pittsburgh Press.

Schneider, Aaron. 2006. "Responding to Fiscal Stress: Fiscal Institutions and Fiscal Adjustment in Four Brazilian States." *Journal of Development Studies* 42(3): 402–25.

Schroeder, Larry. 2003. "Municipal Powers and Functions: the Assignment Question." In *Restructuring Local Government Finance in Developing Countries: Lessons from South Africa*, ed. Roy Bahl and Paul Smoke, 23–70. Northampton, MA: Edward Elgar.

Seitz, Helmut. 2000. "Fiscal Policy, Deficits and Politics of Subnational Governments: The Case of the German Länder." *Public Choice* 102(3–4): 183–218.

Sellers, Jefferey M., and Anders Lindstrom. 2007. "Decentralization, Local Government, and the Welfare State." *Governance: An International Journal of Policy, Administration, and Institutions* 20(4): 609–32.

Sengupta, Partha. 1998. "Corporate Disclosure Quality and the Cost of Debt." *The Accounting Review* 73(4): 459–74.

Seoul Metropolitan Government (SMG). 2016. "Seoul Implementing SIB for the First Time in Asia," n.d., http://english.seoul.go.kr/seoul-implementing-sib-first-time-asia/ (last accessed December 16, 2019).

Sharma, Rajiv, and Eric Knight. 2016. "The Role of Information Density in Infrastructure Investment." *Growth and Change* 47(4): 520–34.

Simonsen, William, and Mark D. Robbins. 1996. "Does It Make Any Difference Anymore? Competitive Versus Negotiated Municipal Bond Issuance." *Public Administration Review* 56(1): 57–64.

Simonsen, Bill, Mark D. Robbins, and Lee Helgerson. 2001. "The Influence of Jurisdiction Size and Sale Type on Municipal Bond Interest Rates: An Empirical Analysis." *Public Administration Review* 61(6): 709–17.

Sinclair, Timothy J. 1994a. "Between State and Market: Hegemony and Institutions of Collective Action Under Conditions of International Capital Mobility." *Policy Sciences* 27: 447–66.

Sinclair, Timothy J. 1994b. "Passing Judgement: Credit Rating Processes as Regulatory Mechanisms of Governance in the Emerging World Order." *Review of International Political Economy* 1(1): 133–59.

Sinclair, Timothy J. 2005. *The New Masters of Capital: American Bond Rating Agencies and the Politics of Creditworthines*. Ithaca: Cornell University Press.

Smith, Heidi Jane. 2017. "Increasing Decision Making Capacities of Local Governments: Mexico's Quest for Economic Growth," September 28, https://www.cepal.org/sites/default/files/events/files/smith_1.pdf.

Smith, Neil. 1990. *Uneven Development: Nature, Capital, and the Production of Space.* Oxford: Blackwell.

SNGWOFI. 2019. "World Observatory on Subnational Government Finance and Investment: Korea," n.d., http://www.sng-wofi.org/ (last accessed December 16, 2019).

Spence, Michael. 1974. "Competitive and Optimal Responses to Signals: An Analysis of Efficiency and Distribution." *Journal of Economic Theory* 7(3): 296–332.

Schroeder, Larry. 2003. "Municipal Powers and Functions: The Assignment Question," in Bahl, R., and P. Smoke, eds. *Restructuring Local Government Finance in Developing Countries: Lessons from South Africa.* Cheltenham, UK: Edward Elgar.

Standard & Poor's. 2010. *Methodology for Rating International Local and Regional Governments.* September 20.

Standard & Poor's. 2011. *Ratings Direct: Seoul Metropolitan Government.* July 6.

Standard & Poor's. 2013. *U.S. Local Governments General Obligation Ratings: Methodology and Assumptions.* New York: Standard and Poor's.

Standard & Poor's. 2014. *Methodology for Rating non-U.S. Local and Regional Governments.* New York: Standard and Poor's.

Stiglitz, Joseph E. 1977a. "Monopoly, Non-Linear Pricing and Imperfect Information: The Insurance Market." *Review of Economic Studies* 44(3): 407–30.

Stiglitz, Joseph E. 1977b. "Symposium on Economics of Information: Introduction." *Review of Economic Studies* 44(3): 389–91.

Stiglitz, Joseph E., and Andrew Weiss. 1981. "Credit Rationing in Markets with Imperfect Information." *American Economic Review* 71(3): 393–410.

Tanzi, Vito. 1995. "Basic Issues of Decentralization and Tax Assignment." In *Reforming China's Public Finances*, ed. E. Ahmad et al., 164–177. Washington, D.C.: International Monetary Fund.

Tanzi, Vito. 1996. "Fiscal Federalism and Decentralization: A Review of Some Efficiency and Macroeconomic Aspects." Annual World Bank Conference on Development Economics. International Bank for Reconstruction and Development/World Bank, Washington, D.C.

Tendler, Judith. 1997. *Good Government in the Tropic.* Baltimore: Johns Hopkins University Press.

Ter-Minassian, Teresa. 1997. "Decentralizing Government." *Finance and Development* 34(3): 36–39.

Thakor, Anjan V. 1991. "Game Theory in Finance." *Financial Management* 20 (Spring): 71–94.

Thomas, Melissa A. 2010. "What Do the Worldwide Governance Indicators Measure?" *The European Journal of Development Research* 22(1): 31–54.

Torrance, Morag. 2008. "Forging Glocal Governance? Urban Infrastructures as Networked Financial Products." *International Journal of Urban and Regional Research* 32(1): 1–21.

Torrance, Morag. 2009. "Reconceptualizing Urban Governance Through a New Paradigm for Urban Infrastructure Networks." *Journal of Economic Geography* 9(6): 805–22.

Tsonkova, Vanya. 2005. *The Municipal Bonds Market in Bulgaria or Route to European Union Accession.* "Vassil Levski" National Military University, Bulgaria, n.d., http://www.actrus.ro/reviste/4_2005/a6.pdf (last accessed December 1, 2019).

United Nations. 2018. *The World's Cities in 2018—Data Booklet* (ST/ESA/ SER.A/417). Department of Economic and Social Affairs, Population Division.

United Nations. 2019. Sustainable Development Goals Indicators Database. (https://unstats.un.org/sdgs/indicators/database/).

Webb, Steven. 2004. *Laws of Fiscal Responsibility for Subnational Discipline: The Latin American Experience.* Washington, D.C.: World Bank. WP3309.

Weber, Rachel. 2010. "Selling City Futurdes: The Financialization of Urban Redevelopment Policy." *Economic Geography* 86(3): 251–74,

Weingast, Barry R. 2014. "Second Generation Fiscal Federalism: Political Aspects of Decentralization and Economic Development." *World Development* 53: 14–25.

White, Lawrence J. 2010. "The Credit Rating Agencies." *Journal of Economic Perspectives* 24(2): 211–26.

Wildasin, David A. 1997. "Externalities and Bailouts: Hard and Soft Budget Constraints in Intergovernmental Fiscal Relations." Development Research Group, Policy Research Working Paper No. 1843. World Bank, Washington, D.C.

Wildasin, David A. 2010. *Fiscal Aspects of Evolving Federations.* Cambridge: Cambridge University Press.

Williamson, Stephen D. 1986. "Costly Monitoring, Financial Intermediation, and Equilibrium Credit Rationing." *Journal of Monetary Economics* 18: 159–79.

World Bank (WB). 2007. *Developing the Domestic Government Debt Market: From Diagnostics to Reform Implementation.* Washington, D.C.: World Bank.

World Bank. 2013. *Planning, Connecting & Financing Cities—Now.* Washington D.C.: World Bank.

World Bank. 2016. *Subnational Debt Management Performance Assessment (DeMPA) Methodology.* Washington D.C.: Economic Policy and Debt Department, World Bank.

World Bank. 2018. Data. https://data.worldbank.org/indicator/sp.urb.totl.in.zs.

World Bank (WB) and International Monetary Fund (IMF). 2001. *Developing Government Bond Markets: A Handbook.* Washington, D.C.: World Bank/International Monetary Fund.

Yosha, O. 1995. "Information Disclosure Costs and the Choice of Financing Source." *Journal of Financial Intermediation* 4(1): 3–20.

Zandi, Mark, and Nicholas S. Perna. 1994. "Regional Economics: Its Influence on Municipal Credit Risk." In *The Handbook of Municipal Bonds*, ed. Susan C. Heide et al., 465–474. Chicago: Probus.

Zorn, C. Kurt, and Shah Towfighi. 1986. "Not All Bond Banks Are Created Equal." *Public Budgeting & Finance* 6(3): 57–69.

Index

For the benefit of digital users, indexed terms that span two pages (e.g., 52–53) may, on occasion, appear on only one of those pages.

Tables, figures and boxes are indicated by *t*, *f* and *b* following the page number